Twentieth Century
Lefton China and Collectibles
A Numbered Price Guide for Collectors

Karen Barton

Schiffer Publishing Ltd

4880 Lower Valley Road, Atglen, PA 19310 USA

The information contained in this book has been collected from the Internet, antique stores, and my own personal collection. I can guarantee the accuracy of the information that came from my private collection, as well as the information I gathered from Lefton pieces in the antique stores I visited. The information gathered from the Internet, however, is only as accurate as the information posted. I have tried to guarantee the accuracy of this information by listing only Lefton pieces that had pictures of Lefton identification marks. If there was any question as to the number, I e-mailed the owner of the piece. Whenever possible I used my Lefton books to double-check the accuracy of this information. Neither the author nor the publisher assumes responsibility for any inaccuracies or losses that might be incurred as a result of consulting this guide.

"Lefton China" is a registered trademark of the Geo. Zoltan Lefton Company. Although some background information for this book was obtained from materials published by the Geo. Zoltan Lefton Company, the Geo. Zoltan Lefton Company did not authorize this book nor specifically furnish or approve any of the information contained herein. This book is derived from the author's independent research.

Copyright © 2001 by Karen Barton
Library of Congress Card Number: 00-111903

Designed by John P. Cheek
Type set in ZapfHumanist Dm BT/Humanist 521 BT

ISBN: 0-7643-1332-0
Printed in China
1 2 3 4

Published by Schiffer Publishing Ltd.
4880 Lower Valley Road
Atglen, PA 19310
Phone: (610) 593-1777; Fax: (610) 593-2002
E-mail: Schifferbk@aol.com
Please visit our web site catalog at
www.schifferbooks.com
We are always looking for people to write books on new and related subjects. If you have an idea for a book, please contact us at the above address.

This book may be purchased from the publisher.
Include $3.95 for shipping.
Please try your bookstore first.
You may write for a free catalog.

In Europe, Schiffer books are distributed by
Bushwood Books
6 Marksbury Avenue
Kew Gardens
Surrey TW9 4JF England
Phone: 44 (0) 20 8392 8585
Fax: 44 (0) 20 8392 9876
E-mail: Bushwd@aol.com
Free postage in the UK. Europe: air mail at cost.

Dedication

This book is dedicated:

To my husband and friend John Barton, who gave up hunting and fishing weekends and vacations to drive our RV thousands of miles over five states so I could gather pieces and information for this book. Who didn't say a word when he had to go back to retrieve the reference books I had left at the last antique store . . . twice. Who never complained about the money I spent. And who made this book possible for publication by retaking photographs of every piece pictured in this book (when I was told that the 500 photographs I had submitted for publication weren't acceptable) and by converting my years worth of work done on a spreadsheet (which I learned was an unacceptable format for the typesetting program) into Microsoft Word. Thank goodness I married a Systems Architect!

And to my mother Donna Krause, who started it all by buying me my first Lefton piece!

#4741. 4 1/2" egg box with applied flowers. $23.00.

#3183. Cup and saucer, *To My Mother*. $15.00.

Acknowledgments and Thanks

4" boy and girl with flower baskets, pair. $50.00.

I would like to thank all the sellers who listed their Lefton pieces on the Internet. A special thanks goes to those sellers who made the price guide section of this book possible by not only supplying detailed descriptions and photographs of their Lefton pieces, but also added a photograph of the Lefton identification marks so these pieces could be authenticated.

I would like to again thank those antique dealers who willingly opened up their display cases so that I could record the numbers on their Lefton pieces, and who pointed out any Lefton pieces they thought I might have missed. Their help and input on what they would like to see in a book on Lefton was greatly appreciated.

A heartfelt thanks goes to Lauri Neisus who willingly shared information about her Lefton collection. The information I received from her on her Sweet Violets set, as well as the copies she sent me of her brochures on Americana, Fruit Basket (Tutti Fruit), and Berry Harvest provided the hard to find information needed to complete listings for those highly collectible sets.

And I would like to thank Mr. J.P. Rodriznik of the Geo. Zoltan Lefton Company who gave me permission to use the information posted on the company's web page. This valuable information was used to add to my section on Lefton history and Lefton's Collections.

My deepest thanks and appreciation go to my husband John and our son Brian. They put up with my long hours on the computer, tolerated a dirty house, clothes, and dishes, and ate fast food without complaint those many times when I lost track of time and forgot all about dinner. I love you both very much . . . you too Scott!

Contents

Introduction

I started collecting Lefton and writing this book the way I started doing the majority of things I've done in my life . . . totally by accident and definitely unplanned.

It all began when my mother came for a week's visit. Being an antique lover, she wanted to check out the antique stores in our area. Although I had been an antique lover like her for almost twenty years, (strictly furniture and unbreakables), for various reasons I had gradually gotten away from antiques and had pretty much lost all interest in them at the time of her visit. Spending the next week in antique stores was not something I was looking forward to. However, hit the antique stores we did and as I accompanied my mother down the isles of our first store, I found myself becoming intrigued with the different styles and manufacturers of china.

Having recently scaled down to a smaller home, I had no intention of buying anything. In one of the last showcases we looked at, however, was a piece that caught my eye. It was a 4" egg shaped box with a pink bow and applied flowers that was unusual, tiny, and inexpensive . . . so I decided I'd get it. Holding it in my hand I continued down the isle, and another piece caught my eye. This one looked like a gift box wrapped with ribbon and had a flower as the bow. It too was unusual, tiny, and inexpensive, so I decided to get it also. Later that evening when I examined them more closely, I discovered that they were both Lefton pieces.

Needless to say, by the end of that week I was hooked on Lefton, and less than three months later I was the proud owner of over three hundred pieces!

A couple of weeks after I began my Lefton shopping spree, I discovered that one of the stores had books on Lefton China, so I bought them. Every evening I would spend hours looking at these books and studying the pictures. I carried them with me on my shopping trips to verify a piece was indeed Lefton, and that I was paying a reasonable price for it.

Gradually I found myself less often picking up a piece to see if it was a Lefton, and more often having my eyes

Miniature pink sugar and creamer with violet pattern. $40.00.

stop as I recognized a piece from the books, or one that had the characteristics that only Lefton pieces have. Also, I found myself using my books less often for identification, but merely as a price guide.

Living in Minnesota, I found it more convenient in the winter months to shop for Lefton on the Internet. I also had the added convenience of being able to quickly access the computer records I kept on Lefton pieces. Any time a piece came up on the Internet that wasn't in my books, I entered it into my spreadsheet. Surfing the Internet made me aware that Lefton also made several lines of "collectibles," such as Roadside U.S.A., Colonial Village, Christopher, and Historic American Lighthouses, just to name a few. None of them were listed in the books I had so I began entering those into my files also.

Having access to the thousands of pieces of Lefton that are auctioned off every week on the Internet, it took less than a year to acquire over 7600 different pieces of Lefton in my file. Shortly into the project, however, I realized that it would take someone years to research and catalog it all, and even then I wondered if it could be done. The amount of Lefton pieces on the secondary market seems endless, and Lefton keeps making more. Loving a challenge and having a lot of free time on my hands, I kept entering different pieces just to see how many I could find. The result is this book.

6 1/2" padlock bank, made in Italy. $28.00.

Author's Note

I have tried to write this book so that it will be easy for the beginner to use as well as for the advanced Lefton collector. I have included a section showing one example each of over one hundred different patterns that Lefton used on their pieces. Once you know a pattern is one used by Lefton, you will recognize other Lefton pieces with the same pattern.

Although the pictures in the pattern section will help you recognize some Lefton pieces, they don't provide examples of the various styles, sizes, shapes, and finishes that Lefton used on so many of their other pieces. For this reason, I decided to include a section in the book that contains photos of pieces from my own Lefton collection. (All photos in this book are from my personal collection.) Although I don't collect pieces from every category listed in the price guide section, I believe you will find enough variety to help you get to know the characteristics that make Lefton so outstanding.

Unique to this book—in contrast to other books on Lefton—is my section on Lefton's collectibles line. Until I got connected to the Internet, I thought Lefton only made china! It has been fun discovering the variety of collectibles Lefton made and continues to produce even now. To help you learn more about this side of Lefton, I have written a short description of about twenty of Lefton's collections and included a photograph of one piece from each collection. You will find these items also listed in the price guide section.

I have not come close to showing pictures of all the different Lefton pieces that were made—nor has this been my intent. First of all, I'm convinced that's an impossible task; second of all, other authors have already published picture books on Lefton. My goal in writing this book was to get as much information about Lefton pieces as possible into one source. I am hoping that Lefton collectors as well as dealers will find this book a helpful and convenient addition to the other Lefton books that are already published.

There are so many more beautiful and unusual Lefton pieces I would like to have been able to include in this book. Unfortunately, Lefton didn't number many of their pieces, and since this is a numbered price guide, I was not able to include them in this book. What a challenging opportunity they would make for a new book on Lefton!

#04419. Pin cushion girl with thimble holder. $25.00

Lefton China Made In Japan. 1946-1953.

© Geo. Z. Lefton. 1950-1957.

Lefton's Japan. 1948-1953.

Lefton China Hand Painted. 1949-1964.

"L" above crown. 1953-1975.

Lefton China Hand Painted Reg. U.S. Pat. Off. 1949-1964.

Lefton China Hand Painted. 1955+

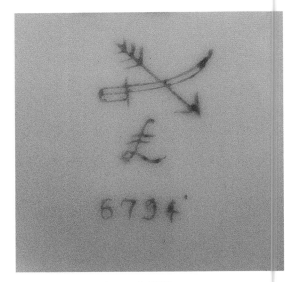

Crossed arrow and sword. 1971+

Lefton China Hand Painted Reg. U.S. Pat. Off. 1955+

Lefton China Made In England.

"L" below crown. 1968+.

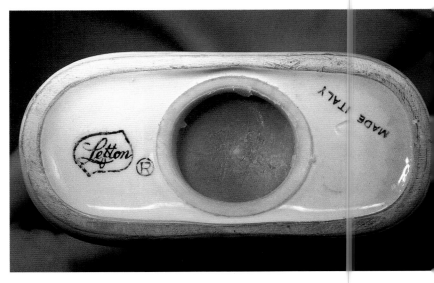

Made in Italy.

ESD mark. Canadian Lefton had the Lefton logo or paper label plus the ESD mark.

Lefton Trade Mark Exclusives. 1960-1983.

Lefton's Exclusive Japan. 1946-1953.

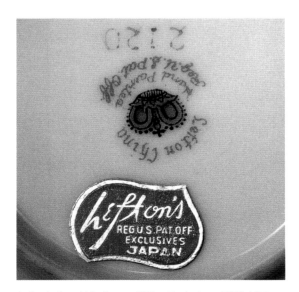

Lefton's Reg. U.S. Patent Office Exclusives 1953-1971.

Lefton ® Trade Mark Exclusives Japan. 1962-1990.

Lefton's Collections

Do you remember the fun it was collecting things as a child? Whether it was baseball cards, stamps, coins, or butterflies the thrill was finding those special pieces to add to your collection. As adults we still like to collect things, so in addition to their other pieces Lefton has created a series of "collections." Below is a brief description about some of Lefton's collections and photos of representative pieces from each one.

AMERICAN BEAUTY FLORALS

Lefton has been making flower figurines for over fifty years. Using the finest porcelain, master craftsmen have captured the incredible details of real flowers by adding one petal at a time. The result is a bloom that is different from any other one created. These flowers are so lifelike, the only thing missing is the fragrance.

#13092. 5" red rose, American Beauty Floral. $22.00.

AMERICAN DECOYS

For years people have been collecting hunting decoys. For many collectors, however, the number of pieces they were able to add to their collection was limited to the space available to put these life size decoys. In 1983, designer Tomoyuki Toda teamed up with Lefton and solved this problem by recreating these beautiful decoys into exact miniature replicas of the life size ones. Whether grouped together or scattered throughout the house, you will have no problem finding the perfect spot for ALL the birds in Lefton's "American Decoy" collection.

#04022. *Loon*, American Decoys. $25.00.

CHILD WITHIN, THE

This collection was designed by Maggie Garvin to help us rediscover the child within each of us. Skilled hands have individually crafted each part of every charming subject and it is not unusual to find an artisan's fingerprint embossed in

#11634. *Rudy the Reindeer*, The Child Within. $10.00.

the sculptured clay these figurines are made of. Inspired by her own children's imagination, Maggie has created seventeen of these delightful figurines. They are Whiskers the Rabbit, Elsie the Cow, Peanut the Elephant, Frosty the Polar Bear, Sweetie the Strawberries, Vinny the Grapes, Pinky the Watermelons, Mac the Apples, Tweety the Baby Bird, Buttercup the Butterfly, Budd the Frog, Flora the Rose Bouquet, Buzz the Bumble Bee, Sunshine the Sunflower, Snowflake the Snowman, Chrissy the Christmas Tree, and Rudy the Reindeer.

THE CHRISTOPHER COLLECTION

The Christopher Collection was introduced in 1982. Later, as part of this collection, Lefton introduced the Bethlehem Collection and Heavenly Hobos. It is one of the largest collections Lefton made and includes not only figurines, but also bells, picture frames, wedding cake toppers, and musicals, just to name a few. Each piece possesses the same high quality, fine detail, and captivating imagination that you've come to expect from Lefton.

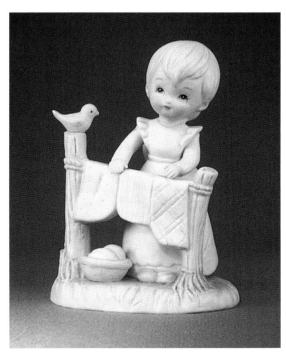

#03979. 4 1/2" Girl Doing Laundry "*Lord Bless Our Work*," Christopher Collection. $22.00.

COLONIAL VILLAGE

This is one of Lefton's largest and more popular collections. It made its debut in 1986 with twelve buildings and only a small number of accessories. The enthusiasm it received from retailers and customers resulted in Lefton researchers, designers, sculptors, and ceramists redoubling

their efforts to develop new additions for the collection. Each new item had to stand alone as well as enhance the whole collection. This high standard is what distinguishes the Colonial Village collection from other similar collections. As new pieces have been added over the years, the collection has grown significantly in size. Today there are over seventy structures as well as hundreds of ceramic citizens, animals, antique vehicles, accessories, and scenic materials. The popularity of this collection has resulted in its own catalogue, club, and newsletter.

#01324. *O'Doul's Ice House*, Colonial Village. $42.00.

COUNTRY HIGHJINKS

This collection captures the amusing antics of a variety of whimsical barnyard animals. Intricately sculptured out of resin, these highly detailed pieces express all the mischievous merriment their name implies. These pieces were introduced into the Lefton series of collectibles in 1994. Although small in size, they are sure to bring a big smile as they remind us of all those mischievous antics performed by the special animals we share our home and lives with.

#01549. Lamb and hen on hay wagon, Country Highjinks. $15.00.

GARY PATTERSON COLLECTION

For over thirty years, Gary Patterson has been making us laugh with his hilarious images of the ups and downs of everyday life. Whether your pastimes are work or play related, the figurines he has created for this Lefton collection are sure to show you different views of life. Made of resin and mounted on a wooden base, each titled piece reminds us of the ever-present, funny side to daily experiences.

#11751. *"Sports Fan,"* Gary Patterson Collection. $40.00.

GREAT AMERICAN CAROUSEL

No carnival would be complete without a carousel. Delighting riders of all ages, these majestic animals seem to come alive as they go up and down and around to the delightful music played on the carousel pipe organ. Tobin

#08624. 12" *American Spirit/Heartland*, Great American Carousel. $125.00.

Fraley has recreated the splendor of the carousel with his figurines from Lefton's Great American Carousel Collection. Each carousel animal is either based upon an actual existing figure or is sculptured in the style of one of the great carousel companies. This collection contains a variety of figurines in many different sizes. Some move up and down, and some play popular songs of the era. No matter which figurine you choose for your collection, these beautifully detailed figurines will recall an age of wonder and innocence.

GOOD NEWS BEARS

The Good News Bears Collection is made exclusively for G.Z. Lefton Co. and designed by Amy J. Wulfing. This warm and whimsical series of young bear figurines will enchant the faithful and send a loving message by gift-giving. About the collection Amy writes, "The 'Good News' is God's word. He touches our everyday life. The Good News Bears are a joyful reminder of God's love for us. He is always by our side. May God's grace and peace be with you."

#11032. 3 1/2" *"You are precious in his sight,"* Good News Bears. $15.00.

HISTORIC AMERICAN LIGHTHOUSES

Since the collection's 1992 inception, Lefton designers have worked closely with the Historic American Lighthouse Foundation to ensure the authenticity of each of their replicas. In an effort to help preserve these remarkable real-life beacons as part of our nation's colorful heritage for future generations, Lefton has pledged a percentage of each Historic American Lighthouse sale for the invaluable work of saving as many beacons as possible. This collection consists of lighthouses, illuminated lighthouses, teapots, magnets, plates, trinket boxes and ornaments. Introduced in 2000 were lighthouse lamps, cookie jars, and candles.

#12232. *Assateague, Virginia*, Historic American Lighthouses. $25.00.

HONEY BEARS

Introduced in 1983, the Honey Bears collection is another creation of artist/designer Marika Berman. These cute little bear people are made of porcelain bisque and each one comes with its own wooden display base. Whether young or old, any age Lefton collector will find these whimsical creatures a delightful addition to their Lefton collection.

#03588. Teacher with pupil, Honey Bears. $15.00.

LI'L COUNTRY FOLK

The Li'l Country Folk Collection was designed by Debbie Bell Jarratt exclusively for G.Z. Lefton Co. Debbie has been designing American collectibles for over a quarter of a century. Each figure in the Li'l Country Folk Collection is lovingly created and adorned with Debbie's signature butterfly. This important collection is a testament to her divinely inspired talent and imagination.

10497. *Count Thy Blessings*, Li'l Country Folk. $22.00.

MARIKA'S ORIGINALS

Marika Berman is the designer of "Marika's Originals" and also of many cute holiday and houseware novelty pieces that Lefton produced. She started freelancing for Lefton in 1954 at a time when they were too small to employ a full

#7537. Boy pushing dog in wheelbarrow, Marika's Originals. $30.00.

time artist. She was the full time house staff designer from 1963 until 1990. In addition to being known as "Marika," she was frequently given another name and sex as well, such as Christopher, Sebastian or Bryan Woods in the case of the earlier Colonial Village items. Lefton is still using the Logo that she designed for that collection.

NEST EGG COLLECTION

Although Lefton has been making bird figurines since its early beginnings, the idea took flight to start a collection of specific birds. They called it the Nest Egg Collection. Birds have always been a favorite gift and collectible for years—for any season or for any reason. Attention to detail with affordable pricing make this collection attractive to all collectors.

#03993. 4 3/4" Canary, Nest Egg Collection. $25.00.

ROADSIDE U.S.A.— BILLBOARDS

As Americans took to the open road, outdoor billboards became the most effective means of advertising. Created in 1994, "Billboards of Yesteryear" represents the finest examples of advertising art spanning the years from 1914 to the mid 1950s. Artist/Designer David Stravitz has searched out and meticulously re-created these billboards in the same authentic style and color as the originals, giving the artist the opportunity to preserve and present the billboard as an authentic American art form.

ROADSIDE U.S.A.—CLASSIC CINEMAS

The local movie house was the most popular attraction in every town and city along Roadside U.S.A. The miniature movie theaters in Lefton's Classic Cinema series not only depict the unusual architecture, lights, and magnificent posters of these theatres, but highlight some of the top award winning movies of all time. Each one is a music box that plays a song relating to or the theme song of these famous classical movies.

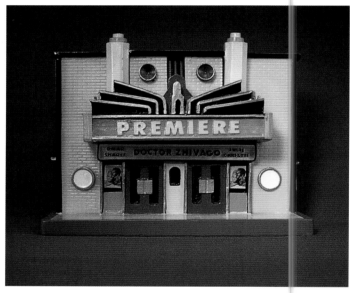

#10529. Classic Cinema, *Premiere Theatre*, Roadside U.S.A. Plays "Lara's Theme." $20.00.

ROADSIDE U.S.A.—GREAT AMERICAN DINERS

Diners are a uniquely American phenomenon. Characterized by their long counters and booths, they were the independent forerunners of today's fast food franchises.

#01608. Billboard *"Work for Victory,"* Roadside U.S.A. $15.00.

#01179. Great American Diners, *Market Diner*, Roadside U.S.A. $38.00.

Black Chintz
#1934. Cream and sugar. $80.00.

Blue Paisley
#2338. 7 1/4" plate. $18.00.

Bluebird
#282. Salt and pepper shakers. $50.00.

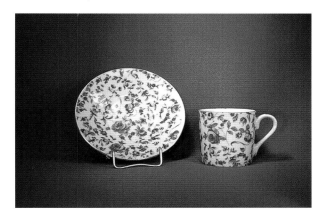

Blue Rose Chintz
#2120. Demitasse cup and saucer. $25.00.

Blue Country Charm
#4614. Jam jar. $20.00.

Bossie the Cow
#6513. Mug. $15.00.

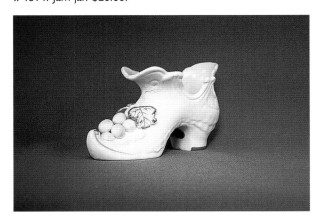

Blue Grapes (Applied)
#2453. 4" bisque shoe. $18.00.

Brown Heritage Floral
#613. 2 3/4" salt and pepper shakers. $30.00.

27

Brown Heritage Fruit
#20130. Snack set. $35.00.

Christy
#443. Leaf shaped nappy dish. $18.00.

Cabbage Cutie
#2126. Salt and Pepper shakers. $45.00.

Cosmos
#1084. Footed candy dish. $55.00.

Celery Line
#6744. 6" planter. $15.00.

Cotillion, Blue
#3192. Sugar and creamer. $35.00.

Christmas Cardinal
#1206. Napkin holder. $20.00.

Cotillion, Pink
#3187. Sugar and creamer. $35.00.

Crimson Rose
#674. 7 1/2" plate. $27.00.

Cuddles
#149. Sugar and creamer. $55.00.

Dainty Miss
#322. Sugar and creamer. $80.00.

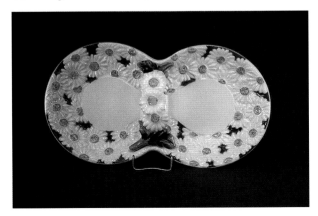

Daisytime
#492. Two compartment dish. $36.00.

Dancing Leaves
#7278. 8 1/2" compote. $24.00.

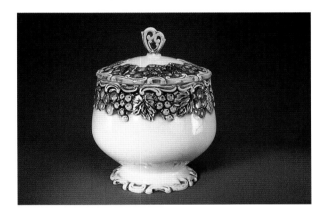

Della Robbia
#1742. Cookie jar. $70.00.

Eastern Star
#3788. Salt and pepper shakers. $10.00.

Elegant Rose
#2048. Egg cup. $35.00

Elegant White
#071. 3 1/2" wheelbarrow planter. $15.00.

Floral Bouquet (yellow)
#674. Mug. $8.00.

Festival
#2630. 3 1/2" coaster. $6.50.

Floral Chintz
#2120. Demitasse cup and saucer. $50.00.

Fiesta
#5349. Mug. $10.00.

Floral Mood
#428. 4" bell. $16.00.

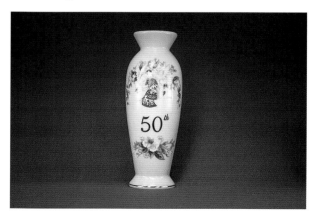

Fiftieth Anniversary
#1102. 6 1/2" bud vase. $15.00

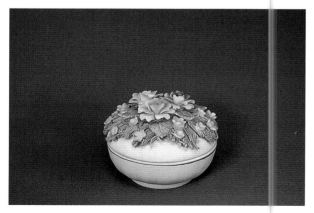

Flower Garden
#2443. 2 1/2" round box. $32.00.

Forget-Me-Not (Applied Floral)
#270. 6" pink vase. $55.00.

Fruit Delight
#3133. Jam jar. $18.00.

Forget-Me-Not (Blue Floral)
#4189. 5 1/4" pitcher and bowl. $40.00.

Fruit Fantasia
#6727. Jam jar. $28.00.

French Rose
#3263. Stacking jars. $32.00.

Fruits of Italy
#1212. Tidbit tray (top plate not shown). $45.00.

Fruit Basket (Tutti Fruit)
#1680. Jam jar. $38.00.

Garden Daisy
#1561. 4 1/2" planter. $18.00.

Golden Tree
#1880. Sugar and creamer. $40.00.

Golden Wheat
#20595. Sugar and creamer. $28.00.

Grape
#2664. Sugar and creamer. $28.00.

Green Heritage Floral
#1153. Two tiered tidbit tray. $65.00.

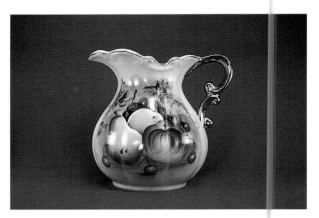

Green Heritage Fruit
#6279. 6" Pitcher (bowl not shown). $33.00.

Green Orchard
#4130. Cookie jar. $58.00.

Harvest Pansy
#7977. Pitcher and bowl. $28.00.

Heavenly Rose
#2758. Cup and saucer. $45.00.

Heirloom Elegance
Salt and pepper shakers. $38.00.

Hot Poppy
#4597. 4 1/2" basket. $15.00.

Holly Garland
#2040. Egg cup. $38.00.

Lilacs and Rhinestones
#137. 7" vase. $55.00.

Holly with Touches of Candy Cane Red
#033. Candle holder, divided handle. $25.00.

Lilac Chintz
#1344. Cigarette or toothpick holder. $18.00.

Honey Bee (Bee Line)
#1288. Salt and pepper shakers. $28.00.

Luscious Lilac
#2950. 4" vase. $30.00.

Magnolia
#2518. Coffee pot. $145.00.

Moss Rose
#922. Salt and pepper shakers. $22.00.

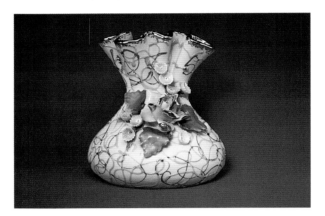

Mardi Gras
#50439. 6" vase. $75.00.

Mr. Toodles
#3290. Jam jar with spoon. $55.00.

Miss Priss
#1511. Salt and pepper shakers. $39.00.

Mushroom Forest
#6356. Mug. $12.00.

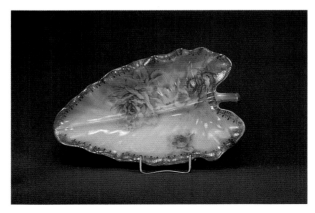

Misty Rose
#5517. 7" nappy dish. $28.00.

Only a Rose
#415. 4" planter. $38.00.

Paisley Fantasia
#6734. Sugar bowl. $32.00.

Pear N Apple, Green
#3761. Canister, four in complete set. $95.00

Pear N Apple, Gold
#4131. Canisters, four in complete set. $95.00.

Pear and Apple, White
#4262. Bone dish. $18.00.

Petite Fleurs
#6433. 6" leaf shaped nappy. $18.00.

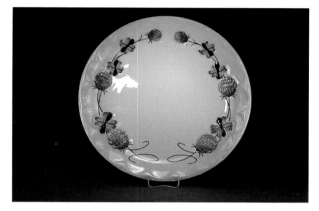

Pink Clover
#2483. 10" dinner plate. $22.00.

Pink Daisy
#5161. Chip-n-dip. $48.00.

Poinsettia
#4390. Salt and pepper. $23.00.

Renaissance
#3564. 3" candle holders. $18.00.

Rose and Violet Chintz
#7245. Miniature sugar bowl. $20.00.

Rose Chintz
#912. Sugar and creamer. $65.00.

Rose Heirloom
#1378. Demitasse cup and saucer. $28.00.

Rustic Daisy
#3858. Jam jar. $22.00.

Spring Bouquet
#4829. Sugar and creamer. $40.00.

Summertime
#261. Snack set. $30.00.

Sweet Violets
#2847. Two compartment dish. $32.00.

Symphony in Fruit
#1018. Two compartment divided dish. $28.00.

Tree with Presents
#1064. 8 1/4" Plate. $15.00.

Thumbelina
#1697. Jam jar. $65.00.

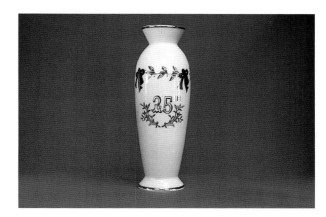

Twenty-Fifth Anniversary
#8049. 7" Vase. $9.00.

Tisket A Tasket
#7297. Butter dish. $28.00.

Vineyard
#3029. Sugar and Creamer. $30.00.

To A Wild Rose
#2602. 7 1/4" nappy dish. $20.00.

Violets
#2300. Cup and saucer. $40.00.

Violets
Cup and saucer. $32.00.

Violet Chintz
#794. Mini sugar and creamer. $55.00.

Violet Heirloom
#1378. Demitasse cup and saucer. $35.00.

Wheat Poppy
#1378. Cookie jar. $42.00.

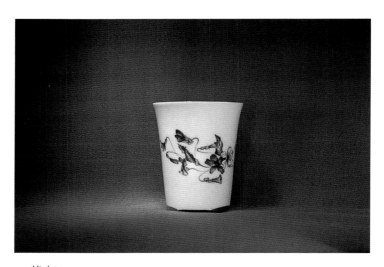

Violets
#052. 4" tumbler with violets. $25.00.

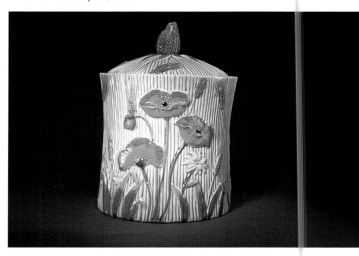

#953. 7" angel in tree, pair. $185.00.

#955. 5" lyre vase, pair. $140.00.

#962. 5 1/2" leaf dish with applied roses and sponge gold accents. $55.00.

#770. 6" vase, girl climbing tree with birds, pair. $110.00.

Angels

#002. Kissing angels, pair. $45.00.

#130. Angel of the month. $50.00.

#149. 3 1/2" music angels, each. $28.00.

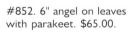

#489. 4" angel of the month. $38.00.

#852. 6" angel on leaves with parakeet. $65.00.

#1755. Soap dish, Majestic Gold. $15.00.

#6121. Soap dish with tumbler holder. $32.00.

Bells

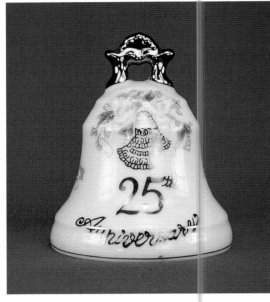

#151. 4" bisque bell with floral branch handle. $18.00.

#1041. 2 3/4" bell with applied flowers. $18.00.

#2118. 3 1/4" *25th Anniversary* bell. $12.00.

Birds

#142A. 4" parrot. $38.00.

#142B. 4" parrot. $38.00.

#440. 6" open winged robin on driftwood. $35.00.

#217. 7 1/2" crane. $50.00.

#464. 4 1/2" hummingbird. $35.00.

#465. 5 1/2"
hummingbird.
$55.00.

#467. 5 1/2"
hummingbirds.
$60.00.

#467. 5" Baltimore
oriole with baby.
$55.00.

#467. 5" robin with baby. $60.00.

#1001. 7" robin, Antique Ivory. $28.00.

#864. 5" robin on base with nest. $28.00.

#1271. 7" bluebird
on branch. $45.00.

#1184. 5" painted bunting. $22.00.

#1282. 7" robin
on branch. $45.00.

#1284. 7" cardinal on branch. $45.00.

#1531. 5" crane. $35.00.

#1528. 5 1/2" long tailed roosters, pair. $85.00.

#1706. 7" capped chickadee. $100.00.

#3414. 5" snow goose, limited edition. $45.00.

#3505. 5" canary with fledglings. $55.00.

#4206. 5" woodpecker. $18.00.

#4206. 5" red breasted grosbeak. $18.00.

Boxes

#872. Box with gold ribbon. $18.00.

#1055. Lady with cake. $30.00.

#2486. Pin box with pansies. $18.00.

#1681. Box with yellow ribbon and flower. $15.00.

#2771. Butterfly box. $20.00.

#3433. Pin box with birds. $15.00.

#4341. 5" square bisque candy dish with applied flowers. $32.00.

#5090. Pin box with owls. $13.00.

#4419. Chick hatching from egg. $15.00.

#07391. 3" box, black background with pink roses. $12.00.

#2723. Signed Geo. Z. Lefton floral cup and saucer. $55.00.

Geo. Z. Lefton signature on #2722 below.

#2722. Signed Geo. Z. Lefton fruit cup and saucer. $55.00.

#2320. Cup of the month, February Violet. $30.00.

#2829. Cup of the month, May Lily of the Valley. $20.00.

#20327. Floral cup and saucer, ribbed. $45.00.

#438. Pink cup and saucer with roses. $22.00.

#20583. Cup and saucer, turquoise with rose. $40.00.

#20583. Cup and saucer, green with gold angel. $40.00.

Dishes and Decorative Pieces

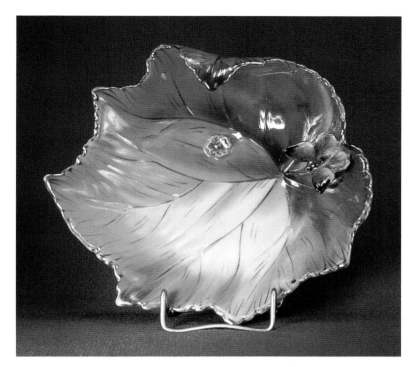

#001. 5 1/2" leaf dish with applied butterfly and flower. $32.00.

#486. 6 1/2" rose bowl. $35.00.

#723. Console set, white with pink roses. $75.00.

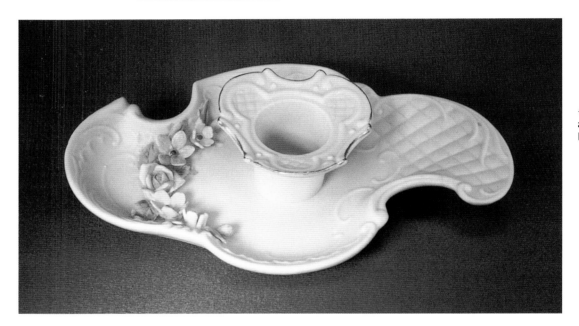

#902. Candle holder with applied flowers, Antique Ivory. $20.00.

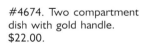

#4674. Two compartment dish with gold handle. $22.00.

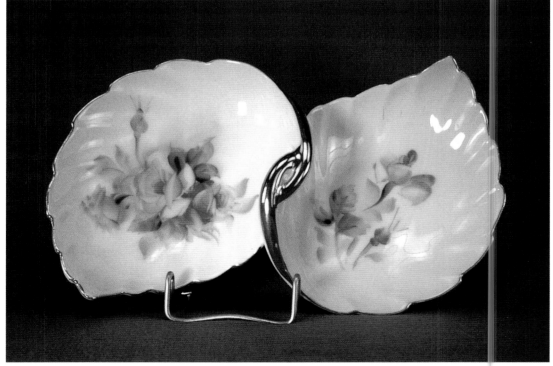

#681. 5 1/2" leaf dish with hand painted flowers. $25.00.

#744. Leaf dish with hand painted flowers. $28.00.

#4814. 4" latticed heart shaped dish, French Rose. $22.00.

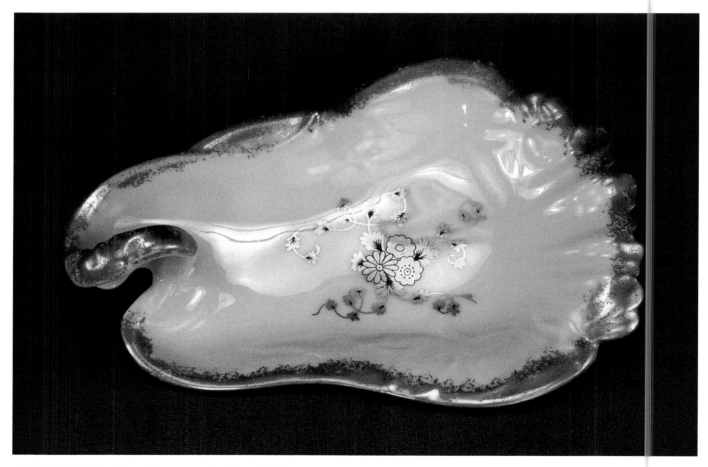

#5763. 7 1/2" dish with gold pattern and edging. $20.00.

#20334. Decorative dish, 1 of 3 in set. $20.00.

#20334. Decorative dish, 3 of 3 in set. $20.00.

#20334. Decorative dish, 2 of 3 in set. $20.00.

Figurines

#326. *Little Adorables* figurine, limited edition of 720. $50.00.

#345. 8" Colonial man. $80.00.

#326. *Little Adorables* figurine, limited edition of 720. $50.00.

#2431. 6 1/2" woman
in flower stall. $95.00.

#3045. 7" Colonial couple,
Norman and Elaine. $145.00.

#3058A. Girl at well. $40.00.

#3697. 5" Gay Nineties figurine with umbrella. $85.00.

#3058B. Girl picking apples. $40.00.

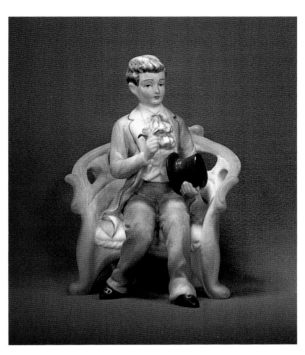

#3825. Man on chair holding hat. $55.00.

#5088. 6 1/4" kitchen scene with man and woman. $105.00.

#5688. 6 3/4" Typist. $75.00.

81

#5756. Old couple in park playing cards. $85.00.

#5701. Two old ladies whispering. $105.00.

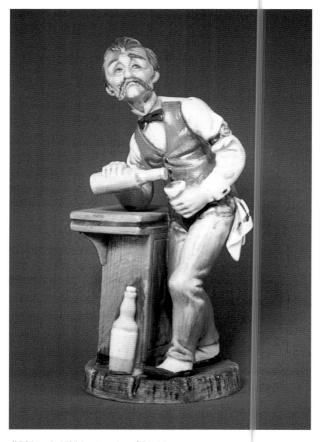

#5806. 8 1/2" bartender. $55.00.

#7227. 4" Flower girl of the month, each. $40.00.

#10008. 5" Orientals with rhinestones, pair. $90.00.

#8948. Girl with matching doll. $65.00.

Jam Jars

Stacked grapefruit jam jar. $18.00.

#2334. Blue Paisley jam jar. $50.00.

#1958. Della Robbia jam jar. $18.00.

#2661. Grape jam jar. $28.00.

#1465. Plymouth Rock Rooster planter. $35.00.

#1809. White urn with handles. $18.00.

#2772. Valentine boy and girl with hearts. $28.00.

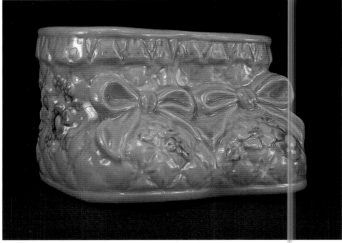

#2964. Luscious Lilac pitcher with applied flowers. $28.00.

#04870. Baby bootie planter. $15.00.

#50515. Ponytail girl with dog. $30.00.

Plates

#305. 8" Berry Harvest plate. $28.00.

#2141. Blue Paisley lemon plate. $28.00.

#977. 9 1/4" Americana dinner plate. $33.00.

#2864. 6 1/2" Sweet Violets plate. $28.00.

#3455. 9" French Rose plate. $23.00.

#5724. Misty Rose lemon plate. $32.00.

#4589. Spring Bouquet lunch plate. $10.00.

#7043. Yellow Tulip cake plate. $38.00.

Salt & Pepper Shakers

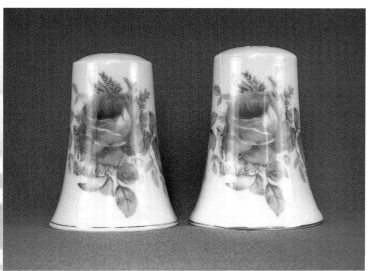

#676. Elegant Rose. $22.00.

#1657. Fruit Basket (Tutti Fruit). $28.00.

#676. Violets. $25.00.

#2346. Blue Paisley. $28.00.

#1227. Hand painted Violets. $18.00.

#3032. Vineyard. $18.00.

Smoking Items

Duck Ashtray. $18.00.

#286. Cigarette holder, pink with Lily of the Valley. $35.00.

#140. 5" swan ashtray, pink with Lily of the Valley. $28.00.

#934. Elegant Rose stacking leaf ashtrays. $42.00.

Teapots and Coffee Pots

#3122. Coffee/chocolate pot,
Floral Design. $165.00.

#07543. Lavender Rose teapot,
musical "*Tea For Two*." $75.00.

#2663. Grape teapot. $65.00.

#3191. Blue Cotillion coffee pot. $85.00.

#4829. Elegant Rose teapot, ribbed. $55.00.

#5691. Misty Rose teapot. $145.00.

Tidbit Trays and Compotes

Elegant Rose tidbit tray. $25.00.

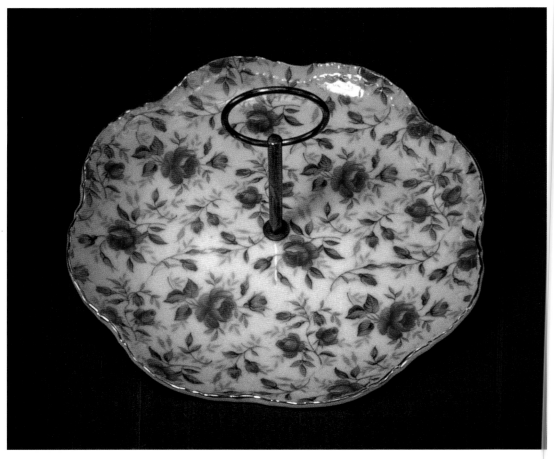

#671. Rose Chintz tidbit tray. $28.00.

#70443. Mardi Gras pitcher vase. $75.00.

#70541. 6 3/4" two handled vase, pink with rhinestones. $40.00.

#2188. 4 1/2" vase, applied blue grapes. $25.00.

Wall Hangings

#508. Heart shaped plate, "*To Mother.*" $22.00.

#516. Square plate with fruit.. $20.00.

#711. Reticulated plate with cherries, gold trim. $23.00.

#2816. 8 1/4" plate, light blue with white roses. $28.00.

#6927. Scalloped edge
plate with fruit. $30.00.

#6932. 4" plate with
flowers. $12.00.

#60409. 6" plate with grapes. $28.00.

#60593. 8" reticulated plate with roses. $28.00.

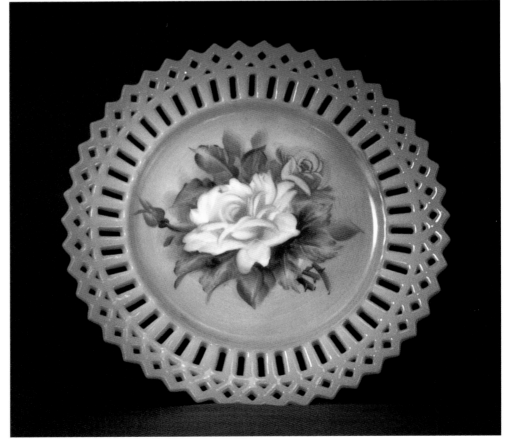

Bibliography

DeLozier, Loretta. *Collector's Encyclopedia of Lefton China*. Paducah, Kentucky: Collector's Books, Schroeder Publishing Co., Inc., 1995.

DeLozier, Loretta. *Collector's Encyclopedia of Lefton China, Book II*. Paducah, Kentucky: Collector's Books, Schroeder Publishing Co., Inc., 1997.

DeLozier, Loretta. *Collector's Encyclopedia of Lefton China, Book III*. Paducah, Kentucky: Collector's Books, Schroeder Publishing Co., Inc., 1999.

DeLozier, Loretta. *Lefton China Price Guide*. Paducah, Kentucky: Collector's Books, Schroeder Publishing Co., Inc., 1999.

McCarthy, Ruth. *Lefton China*. Atglen, Pennsylvania: Schiffer Publishing Ltd., 1998.

Price Guide

RARE AND UNUSUAL ITEMS

196	6" Basket w/Sponge Gold and Pink Roses	$75
321	7" Sled, White w/Sponge Gold and Pink Roses	$115
436	5" Cherub Holding Bowl with Hands and Feet	$140
544	4 1/2" Angel w/Animals	$50
591	Double Vase w/Two Angels Playing Instruments	$275
672	7 1/2" Wht Cornucopia Bisque Vases w/Roses, Pair	$100
742	6 1/2" Vase, Bisque w/Bird & Musical Angel, Pair	$250
770	Vase, Girl Climbing Tree to See Birds in Nest	$95
774	6 1/4" Cornucopia Vases, Pastel Green Bisque w/Roses	$110
810	9 1/4" Cart w/Two Angels in Pastel Bisque	$275
825	6" Shell Bowl w/Angel, Grey-Green w/Pearl Luster	$118
837	7" Bowl, Grey-Green w/Cherubs & Roses, Pearl Luster	$160
861	7" Cart w/Cherub, Bisque	$225
862	Boat Shaped Bowl w/Two Cherubs & Applied Roses	$175
931	4" Cross w/Angel Praying, Pastel Bisque	$55
940	6 1/2" Well Planter w/Birds, Pastel Grey-Green Bisque	$70
942	8" Bowl w/Small Boy on Rim, Grey-Green Bisque	$185
951	3 1/2" Angel on Tree w/Flowers & Nest, Grey-Green	$55
952	5" Angel on Tree w/Flowers & Nest, Grey-Green, Pair	$145
953	7" Angel on Tree w/Flowers & Nest, Grey-Green, Pair	$185
955	5" White Lyre Vases w/Pink Roses & Gold Accents, Pair	$140
959	8 1/2" Bowl, Shell Shaped w/Angel	$195
961	6" Leaf Dish Decorated in Sponge Gold w/Pink Roses	$55
962	5 1/2" Leaf Dish w/Roses & Sponge Gold Accents	$55
964	5 1/2" Basket, Pastel Bisque w/Cherubs	$120

AMERICAN BEAUTY COLLECTION/FLOWERS

00423	5 1/2" American Beauty Rose, 4 Assorted	$24
00424	5" American Beauty Rose, 4 Assorted	$22
00425	7" American Beauty Double Dogwood, Each	$26
00426	5 1/2" American Beauty Lily, 3 Assorted	$35
00429	4" American Beauty Carnation, 3 Assorted	$21
00619	5 1/2" American Beauty Pink Rose	$25
00621	3 1/2" American Beauty Pink Rose	$15
00622	3 1/2" American Beauty Pink Rose	$17
00623	5 1/2" American Beauty Pink Rose	$32
00624	5 1/2" American Beauty Pink Rose	$40
00693	5 1/2" American Beauty Coral Rose	$32
00792	7" American Beauty Pink Rose	$60
00796	5 1/2" American Beauty Red Rose	$40
00800	3 1/2" American Beauty Red Rose	$15
00802	14" American Beauty Red Rose with Stem	$20
00803	6" American Beauty Iris	$40
00804	4" American Beauty Magnolia	$24
01038	4" American Beauty Tea Rose	$17
01040	5 1/2" American Beauty Tea Rose	$32
01041	5 1/2" American Beauty Tea Rose	$40
01273	5 1/2" American Beauty Pink Rose, Musical "Für Elise"	$30
01274	5 1/2" American Beauty Coral Rose, Musical "Für Elise"	$30
01275	5 1/2" American Beauty Tea Rose, Musical "Für Elise"	$30
01276	4 1/2" American Beauty Pink Magnolia, Musical "Für Elise"	$30
01284	14" American Beauty Pink Rose With Stem	$20
01288	4 1/2" American Beauty White Magnolia, Musical "Für Elise"	$30
01385	5 1/2" American Beauty Red Rose, Musical "Für Elise"	$30
01422	5 1/2" American Beauty Pink Lily	$35
01483	5" American Beauty Tea Rose	$19

01484	5" American Beauty Red Rose	$19
01486	5" American Beauty Pink Rose	$19
01488	5" American Beauty White Rose	$19
01489	3 1/2" American Beauty White Dogwood	$15
01493	5" American Beauty Lily	$27
01494	5" American Beauty Pink Lily	$27
01496	5" American Beauty Red Rose	$36
01497	5" American Beauty Pink Rose	$36
01498	5" American Beauty Tea Rose	$36
01499	6" American Beauty White Orchid	$36
01501	7" American Beauty Lily w/Hummingbird	$75
01502	6" American Beauty Hibiscus w/Hummingbird	$70
01503	8 1/2" American Beauty Iris	$75
01504	9 1/2" American Beauty Lady Slipper	$70
2722B	4 1/2" Apple Blossom	$28
04991	4 1/2" Yellow Rose - 1985	$25
06723	4" American Beauty Iris	$12
06724	4" American Beauty Orchid	$12
07760	4" American Beauty Double White Dogwood	$12
07966	5 3/4" American Beauty Magnolia	$22
10127	3 1/2" American Beauty Dogwood w/Butterfly	$13
10138	5 1/2" American Beauty Rose, 4 Assorted	$25
10670	7 1/2" American Beauty Double Rose, 2 Assorted	$35
10671	7 1/2" American Beauty White Peony	$35
10672	7 1/2" American Beauty Pink Peony	$35
10673	3 1/2" Snow Rose	$40
10675	4 1/2" American Beauty Violet	$26
10676	5 1/2" American Beauty Rose, 3 Assorted	$36
10701	3 1/2" American Beauty Rose, 4 Assorted	$15
10756	6" American Beauty Pink Rose, "Waltz of the Flowers"	$40
10915	6" American Beauty Calla Lily	$23
10916	7" American Beauty Rose, 3 Assorted	$33
10917	10 1/2" American Beauty Iris	$75
10918	10 1/2" American Beauty Double Iris	$75
10919	10 1/2" American Beauty Iris	$75
10920	7" American Beauty Magnolia	$26
10921	4" American Beauty Pansy, 2 Assorted	$12
11320	4" American Beauty Pansy, 3 Assorted	$13
11325	4" American Beauty Pansy, Musical "Für Elise," 3 Assorted	$18
11330	3 1/2" American Beauty Rose, Musical "Für Elise," 3 Assorted	$18
11731	5" Double Rose, 3 Assorted	$30
11733	5 1/2" Hyacinth	$33
11735	6 1/2" Triple Rose, 3 Assorted	$33
11899	3" American Beauty Triple Pansy	$28
11900	3 1/2" Pink Rose Floral Message Pot "With Love"	$15
11901	3 1/4" Red Rose Floral Message Pot "With Love"	$15
11902	3" American Beauty Triple Sweet Pea	$15
11903	3 1/4" White Rose Floral Message Pot "With Love"	$15
11905	2 3/4" American Beauty Triple Violet	$18
11906	6 1/4" Double Anthurium	$26
11908	5" Pink and White Dogwood	$29
11909	6" White and Pink Magnolia	$35
11911	6 1/4" Tiger Lily	$35
11913	7 1/2" Morning Glory, 2 Assorted	$40
11915	9 1/2" Red Roses	$95
11916	9 1/2" Pink Roses	$95
11918	9 1/2" Pink Iris	$95
11919	9 3/4" Purple Iris	$95
11923	6" Double Hibiscus	$40

AMERICAN BEAUTY COLLECTION/FLOWERS (cont'd)

11925	5" White Double Narcissus	$28
11926	4 1/2" American Beauty Double Pansy	$30
11932	8 1/2" White Calla Lily	$95
11933	8 1/2" Pink Calla Lily	$95
11934	4 1/2" Millennium Rose	$45
12396	6" American Beauty Double Tulip	$25
13092	5" American Beauty Double Rose	$22
13093	5 1/2" American Beauty Single Rose	$20
13105	4" American Beauty Single Pansy	$20
13107	5" American Beauty Double Pansy	$20
13108	4" American Beauty Magnolia	$18
13110	6" American Beauty Triple Orchid	$40

AMERICANA

160	8" Celery Dish	$55
162	15" Wooden Spoon	$28
164	15" Serving Bowl	$70
927	9" Three Compartment Dish	$75
936	Cup and Saucer	$35
937	Three Compartment Dish	$55
938	Two Compartment Dish	$60
939	9 1/4" Plate w/Plastic Handle	$50
940	Compote	$75
942	One Tier Tidbit Tray	$32
942	Two Tier Tidbit Tray	$95
943	Cookie Jar	$120
944	5" Candy Box	$65
945	Spice Jars, Each	$25
946	Canister Set, 4 Piece Set	$125
947	Plate	$35
948	7 1/2" x 4 3/4" Console Dish	$95
949	Candle Holders, Pair	$80
950	8 3/4" Oil and Vinegar, Pair	$65
951	6 1/2" Pitcher & Bowl Wall Pocket, Pair	$40
952	Teapot	$115
953	Sugar and Creamer	$60
955	Salt and Pepper	$25
956	Jam Jar, Plate and Spoon	$32
957	Snack Set	$35
958	Butter Dish	$65
959	4" Pitcher and Bowl	$55
960	Egg Cup	$35
961	Spoon Rest w/Salt Shaker	$65
962	Gravy Boat	$65
963	6 3/4" Plate	$30
965	Platter	$55
966	7" Bowl	$35
967	Bowl	$40
968	6 1/4" Match Box	$50
969	Salt Box	$45
970	Bowl	$42
972	15 1/4" Three Compartment Dish	$85
973	Plate	$30
974	6 3/4" Plate	$30
976	10 1/2" Plate	$35
977	9 1/4" Plate	$33
978	9 1/2" Casserole, Americana	$95
979	Salad Bowl, Fork and Spoon	$85
980	12" Cake Plate w/Server	$65
1243	7"x11" Divided Dish	$40
1244	Platter	$38
1980	7 1/2" Plate	$18
2015	6" Pitcher	$45
3243	Teapot	$55
6960	ESD Three Compartment Dish, "Regal Rose"	$45
6961	ESD Two Compartment Dish, "Regal Rose"	$42
6963	ESD Handled Plate, "Regal Rose"	$45
6965	ESD Salt and Pepper, "Regal Rose"	$20
6971	ESD Cookie Jar, "Regal Rose"	$95
6973	ESD Jam Jar, Plate and Spoon, "Regal Rose"	$40
6974	ESD Salt and Pepper, "Regal Rose"	$20
21145	ESD Cup and Saucer, "Regal Rose"	$28
21148	ESD 9 1/4" Dinner Plates, "Regal Rose"	$23

ANGELS

002	4 3/4" Kissing Angels, Pair	$45
00055	4" Angel w/Mandolin and Song Sheet	$15
098	4" Happy Birthday Girl w/Holder for Candle	$25
099	4" Happy Birthday Girl or Boy with Cake	$25
110	4 3/4" Flower Girls, Each	$18
130	4" Angel Bride	$35
130	4" Angel of the Month	$50
132	"Easter Angel" Holding Three Decorated Eggs	$35
149	3 1/2" Musical Girl Playing Instruments, Each	$28
00180	3 1/2" Angel on Half Moon	$12
255	4" Day of the Week Working Girls	$35
280	Angel of the Month w/Stones	$30
311	4" Angel of the Month	$38
00370	4" Angel Playing Harp - 1991	$15
489	4" Angel of the Month, Each	$38
556	5 1/2" Boy Angel of the Month, Each	$35
574	4" Day of the Week Angel, Each	$22
723	4" Angel w/Lambs	$28
746	4" Angel w/Choir Book	$15
766	4" Musical Girl and Boy, Pair	$60
00780	3 3/4" Angel Holding Flower, Blue & White, Pair	$15
808	4" Angels, Detailed w/Gold Wings, Each	$45
809	4" Angel of the Month	$28
830	4 1/2" Angel w/Flower Basket, Pair	$75
852	6" Angel Playing Instrument on Leaf w/Bird	$65
00901	6" Pair of Angel Wall Hangings, Sevilla - 1993	$40
00907	2 1/2" Guardian Angel	$10
985	5" Flower Girl of the Month, Each	$45
987	6" Angel w/Bird Bath	$42
1052	4 1/2" Little Bo Peep Angel	$35
1055	Angel and Devil, Each	$55
1192	4" Angel of the Month - 1998	$20
1223	Boy and Girl Angels Kissing on Bench	$35
1258	3 1/2" Christmas Angel Playing Harp	$15
1259	3 1/2" Christmas Angel Playing Cello	$15
1301	3 1/2" Musical Angels, Set of 3	$24
1323	4" Angel of the Month w/Flower, Each	$15
1369	4" Angel	$15
01397	6 3/4" Guardian Angel	$32
01398	6" Guardian Angel	$30
01399	5 1/2" Angel Waterball "Angels We Have Heard"	$26
1411	4" Angel of the Month, Each	$32
1415	4 1/4" Angel Bust, Pair	$80
1478	4 1/2" Angel with Pearl Luster	$18
01551	2 1/2" Guardian Angel	$10
01552	2 1/2" Guardian Angel	$10
01580	5 1/2" Angel, 3 Assorted	$15
01582	6 3/4" Angel, 3 Assorted	$20
01584	4" Praying Boy and Girl Angels, Pair - 1994	$20
01585	4 1/4" Angel, 4 Assorted	$6
10586	4 1/4" Angel, 3 Assorted	$7
1699	3 1/4" Angel in Flower Playing Instrument, Each	$50
1929	4" Angel Playing the Accordion	$18
1952	4 1/2" Boy Angel of the Month, Each	$25
1987	3" Angel of the Month, Each - 1957	$40
02079	3 1/2" Kissing Angels, Pair	$18
2082	5 1/2" Angel, w/Applied Roses	$32
2231	7 1/2" Guardian Angel w/Girl	$45
2293	4" Barefoot Angel Playing Instrument, Each	$12
2323	4 3/4" Angel in Bisque	$35
2343	6" Angel Holding Scroll, Bisque	$25
2473	4 1/2" Angel Wearing Cape w/Harp	$15
2543	4" Christmas Angel w/Musical Instrument, Pair	$25
2600	3 1/4" Angel of the Month	$25
2774	Valentine Angel	$18

2950	Angel Leaning Against Treehouse, Hummel Like	$18
2951	Kneeling Angel Holding a Lamb	$18
03225	Angel of the Month, Each - 1983	$15
03444	3" Barefoot Angel w/Ponytail and Flower - 1983	$10
3332	Angel of the Month, Each	$30
3639	6" Angel, Musical Birthday	$75
03675	3" Angel of the Month	$15
03823	3" Kneeling Angel w/Harp - 1983	$10
4152	4 1/2" Standing on Flowers	$18
4336	4 1/2" Angel of the Month, Each	$28
4565	4 1/4" Kneeling Boy and Girl Angels, Pair	$30
4799	Girl Angels in Red & White - Marika's Originals	$28
4836	4" Angel Holding a Bell	$25
04883	3 1/2" Angel of the Month, Each - 1985	$20
4992	Angel Playing Accordion	$23
05019	4 1/2" Angel Holding Harp	$23
05317	6 3/4" Guardian Angel	$35
05420	4" Angel, 4 Assorted	$8
05425	5" Gloria Angel	$18
05742	6" Angel w/Harp - 1986	$30
6224	5" Birthday Girl w/Stone	$25
06328	3 1/2" Angels Playing Instruments, 3 Assorted	$6
06365	3" Angel w/Lamb	$18
6394	4" Angel Playing Banjo	$15
6640	Zodiac Angel	$38
6777	3 1/2" Kissing Angels, Pair	$15
06800	4" Angel of the Month, Each - 1988	$15
6883	3 1/4" x 4" Day of the Week Angel in Frame, Each	$38
6949	5" Day of the Week Angel in Round Frame, Each	$38
6985	Musical Birthday Angel Plays "Happy Birthday"	$45
06995	7 1/2" Musical Guardian Angel "Amazing Grace"	$45
7074	Christmas Angels Singing, 3 Piece Set	$30
7177	6" Musical Angel of the Month	$35
7228	4" Angel with Holly Playing Violin	$15
7335	4" Dark Skinned Angel w/Flower and Rhinestone	$18
07701	4" Boy and Girl Angels, Pair - 1990	$20
07975	4 1/2" Praying Angels, 2 Assorted	$10
07988	3" Angels Playing Instruments, 4 in Set - 1991	$15
8088	4" Angel w/Basket	$28
8192	4" Musician, Porcelain w/Gold Trim	$38
8265	Angel Walking Dog	$15
8269	5" Kissing Angel	$32
8273	4" Bride Angel	$35
8281	4" Day of the Week Angel, Each	$45
8650	4" Zodiac Angel, Each	$45
8701	4 1/2" Angels Standing on Base w/Flowers, Each	$65
10077	5" Lace Angel	$75
10302	3 3/4" Angel Playing Instrument	$35
10703	Guardian Angel w/Two Children	$35
10748	6" Angel	$33
10810	6 1/4" Angel, Celestial Cherubs by Jeffrey	$30
10811	6" Angel, Celestial Cherubs by Jeffrey	$30
10812	6" Angel, Celestial Cherubs by Jeffrey	$30
10813	4 1/2" Angel w/Waterball, Celestial Cherubs by Jeffrey	$28
10814	4" Angel w/Waterball, Celestial Cherubs by Jeffrey	$28
10815	4" Angel, Celestial Cherubs by Jeffrey	$22
10816	4 1/4" Angel, Celestial Cherubs by Jeffrey	$20
10817	5 1/4" Celestial Cherubs by Jeffrey, "You Light Up My Life"	$33
10818	4 1/2" Celestial Cherubs by Jeffrey, "Wind Beneath My Wings"	$37
10819	Angel Waterball, 3 Assorted	$9
10861	5 3/4" Musical Angels, Set of 3 - 1996	$30
10881	7 1/2" Angels Divine Collection "Millennial Angel"	$25
10882	7 1/2" Angels Divine Collection, "Celestial Song"	$25
10883	7 1/2" Angels Divine Collection, "Gabriel Divine Protector"	$25
10884	7 1/2" Angels Divine Collection "Heralding Angel"	$25
10885	7 1/2" Angels Divine Collection "Seraphonic Angel"	$25
10886	7 1/2" Angels Divine Collection, "Angel of Prosperity"	$25
10887	7" Angels Divine Collection, Wall Plaque	$27
10888	7" Angels Divine Collection, Wall Plaque	$27
10889	8 1/2" Angels Divine Collection Musical, "Amazing Grace"	$25
10890	8 1/2" Angels Divine Collection Musical, "Canon in D"	$25
10891	8 1/2" Angels Divine Collection Musical, "Amazing Grace"	$25

10892	5 1/2" Angels Divine Collection Waterball, "Amazing Grace"	$28
10893	5 1/2" Angels Divine Collection Waterball, "Canon in D"	$28
10894	5 1/2" Angels Divine Collection Waterball, "Amazing Grace"	$28
10948	3" Musical Angels, 6 Assorted	$10
11114	4 1/4" Angels, 3 Assorted	$7
11875	9" Guardian Angel w/Two Children - 1998	$32
11880	6 1/2" Guardian Angel w/Two Children - 1998	$23
11881	6 1/2" Guardian Angel w/Two Children - 1998	$28
11924	4" Angel of the Month, Each - 1998	$12

ANIMALS

00052	3" Koala Bear and Bird	$12
053	5" Horse	$36
064	White or Pink Poodle Sitting Up	$30
065	7 1/4" Standing Horse	$75
066	Horse	$60
094	Cat	$32
00115	3" Koala Bears Dressed as Cowboys, 3 Piece Set	$30
00125	Girl Kitty w/Mouse in Shopping Bag	$14
131	6 1/2" Bear	$48
132	5 1/2" Otter	$36
00154	Sitting Unicorn w/Shamrocks - 1987	$15
157	5" Poodles, White w/Lilacs	$45
164	Little White Poodle w/Collar	$12
168	3 1/2" Cat	$18
169	4" Beagle Puppy	$28
193	3" Pink Mouse w/Rhinestone Eyes	$32
240	Monkeys Playing Instruments, 3 Assorted	$35
257	Patriotic Mouse	$18
00303	2 1/2" Girl Bunnies Wearing Dresses, Each	$12
00312	Dog Skiing	$17
00324	3 1/2" Cat in Dress and Hat	$15
00325	Puppy w/Gun and Duck	$15
351	8 1/4" Bobcat and Raccoon	$125
352	9 1/2" Fox and Hare	$125
370	4 1/2" Girl Frog Brushing Her Hair	$12
371	4 1/2" Boy Frog Smoking a Pipe	$12
00412	4 1/2" Dog, Each	$20
00413	5" Dog, Each	$20
00422	3 1/4" Irish Pigs, Set of 3	$28
437	4" Lamb	$20
445	6 1/2" Bull	$35
446	6 1/2" Long Holstein Cow	$35
447	Black Angus Cow	$35
448	6 3/4" Jersey Cow	$35
449	6 3/4" Ayrshire Cow	$48
451	6 1/2" Hereford Cow	$45
452	7" Hampshire Hog	$40
454	4 1/2" Berkshire Sheep	$38
487	4 1/2" Sheep	$45
500	4" Rabbit on Log	$10
521	5 5/8" Deer	$30
526	Pink Poodles, Mom w/Two Puppies on Chain	$45
547	4" Tan and White Colt, Each	$28
551	Small Siamese Cat	$28
00667	6" Pig w/Bow, Glazed	$18
691	4" Dog, Each	$28
711	3 1/2" Foal	$32
750	6 1/4" Hereford Bull	$36
789	6 1/2" Black American Bear	$45
857	4" Horse	$28
860	4" Persian Cat	$20
871	7" Cat and Dog, Luster w/Stones, Each	$30
880	Rabbits, Pair	$33
00996	3 1/2" Snowflake Kitty "Watch Me Grow" - 1993	$18
1006	7 1/2" Horse	$75
01068	6" Elephant, Trunk Up - 1993	$12
01078	4" Elephant, 2 Assorted - 1993	$12
01079	6" Elephant, 2 Assorted - 1993	$12
1081	4" Chipmunk	$22
01219	4" Elephant, 2 Assorted - 1993	$9

ANIMALS (cont'd)

1311	5 1/2" Skunk w/Flowered Hat & Two Babies	$40
1316	2 1/2" Dog w/Mouse	$12
1350	4 1/2" Horse	$28
1397	3" Bear Couple by Marika, Pair	$25
1426	7" Brown Tabby Cat	$32
1435	8" Schnauzer in Show Stance	$38
1439	7 1/2" Schnauzer Dog	$32
1513	3 1/2" Persian Cat, Matte, Each	$14
1514	5" Persian Cat	$20
1515	3 1/2" Persian Cat	$18
1517	6 1/2" Persian Cat	$28
01579	Kitty Snowflake on Ice Skates - 1994	$12
1640	Dog w/Background, Each	$55
1641	Dog w/Background, Each	$55
1653	5 3/5" Poodle, Pearl Luster w/Stones	$18
1811	4 1/2" White Colt w/Black hoofs	$23
01835	6" Brown Rabbit	$18
01836	5 3/4" Koala Bear	$28
01837	5 7/8" Panda Bear Eating Leaves	$28
1838	5 3/4" Squirrel	$45
01839	5 3/8" Raccoon	$18
1850	4" White Cat	$30
1876	3 1/2" Siamese Cat	$22
01878	3 3/4" Elephant	$28
1954	Poodle w/Matte Finish	$22
1970	4 1/2" Elephant	$28
2010	3" Brown Baby Bear	$23
2072	Cat	$20
2149	6" Raccoon w/Baby	$85
2175	7" Basset Hound w/Pup	$32
02181	5 3/4" Palomino Horse	$45
2198	4" Wild Animal, Bisque	$15
2203	9" White and Grey Cat	$55
2211	7" Horse - Each	$75
2212	4 1/2" Colt	$45
02231	2 1/2" Mouse w/Phone on Shamrock	$12
02264	3 1/2" Bunny Ironing	$12
2266	3 1/4" Frog Playing Instrument	$10
02294	3 3/4" Dog - Each	$18
2372	4 3/4" Siamese Cat	$28
2433	4" Rabbits, Pair	$36
02469	3 3/4" Mouse w/Book	$10
02529	3" Pigs, Each	$12
2540	4 1/2" Cat on Pillow	$15
2563	7" Bulldog	$45
2564	3 1/2" Elephant	$25
2565	4" Elephant	$30
2580	3 1/2" Dog in Irish Hat	$12
2673	5 1/2" Elephant	$35
2674	4 1/2" Elephant	$34
2675	3 1/2" Elephant	$33
02666	4 1/2" Chipmunk	$45
02721	3 3/4" Bunny Playing Accordion	$15
2731	4" Dog Playing Instrument, Each	$18
02811	3 1/2" Frog	$12
2817	4" Boxer Puppy, Glazed	$32
2817A	2 3/4" Spaniel Puppy	$35
2817B	4 3/4" Poodle Puppy, Matte Finish	$35
2817C	4 1/2" Terrier Puppy	$35
2818	8" Long Persian Cat Laying Down	$45
2889	3 1/2" Rabbit w/Mouse	$16
2922	6" Cat	$25
2923	5" Longhaired Tabby Cat	$30
2942	5 1/2" Cat on Back	$30
03072	2 1/4" Bear on Stump w/Baby Chick	$12
03072	2 1/4" Bear w/Baby Squirrel	$12
03101	7" St. Bernard	$28
03103	Dog Figurine, Glazed, Each	$20
3110	4 1/2" Spotted Fawn	$18
03138	3" White Cat in Red Shoe	$12

3343	8" Siamese Cat	$32
3347	18" Cat w/Roses	$75
03434	3/1/2" Chipmunk Holding Nut	$14
3451	6 1/2" Horse	$26
3458	4 1/2" Pink Poodle and 2" Puppies on Chain	$32
03584	Mama & Baby Bear, Honey Bears Collection - 1983	$28
03588	Teacher with Pupil, Honey Bears Collection - 1983	$15
03593	Girl Bear Typist, Honey Bears Collection by Marika - 1983	$23
3674	Playful Cat on Back w/Paws Up	$18
3679	4 1/2" Brown Pug	$25
3710	Puppies in a Basket	$23
03790	Baby Bear in Bed, Honey Bears Collection - 1983	$28
03793	2 1/4" Bears Holding Hands - 1983	$18
4032	Siamese Cat Sitting	$15
4039	Siamese Cat	$20
04254	Pig Family "Mother Knows Best"	$32
04407	5" Airedale	$32
4546	3 1/2" Lambs, Pair	$18
04684	3 1/2" "Home Sweet Home" Barnyard Friends Collection, 1984	$19
04714	4 1/2" Dog, Glazed	$28
4747	5" Beaver, Bisque	$36
4748	5" Chipmunk, Bisque	$38
4749	5" Squirrel, Bisque	$36
4751	5 3/4" Koala Bear w/Cub, Bisque	$50
4752	5" Raccoon, Bisque	$38
4753	11" Chipmunks	$110
04845	2 3/4" Grey Tiger Cat w/Green Eyes	$12
04854	2 3/4" Frog, Each	$8
4871	4 3/4" Horse	$20
04882	4 1/2" Unicorn - 1985	$15
04907	2 1/2" Goose w/Ribbon	$12
4910	4 3/4" Panda Bear, Bisque	$45
4912	5 1/2" Black Bear, Bisque	$38
04946	3" Cat, Each	$10
4950	8" Tiger, Bisque	$80
04971	4" Dog w/Red Shoe - 1985	$10
5057	5" Hare, Bisque	$42
5058	5" Red Fox, Bisque	$38
5059	5 1/2" Elephant	$48
05119	2 1/2" Black and White Cat, Glazed	$12
05124	6" Siamese Cat, Each - 1985	$22
05131	3 1/2" Penguin - 1985	$18
5275	5" Boxer	$28
5364	4 3/4" Cat	$15
05419	3 1/2" Fox - 1986	$12
5639	6" Mother and Kitten, Black, Gray, and White, Pair	$25
05794	3 3/4" Thanksgiving Teddy Bears, Pair	$24
06012	4" Mouse in Dress	$15
06064	3" White Sheep w/Bell and Flowers around Neck	$12
06147	5 1/2" Goose w/Pink Ribbon - 1987	$15
06151	7 1/2" Stuffed Cat Figurine w/Satin Bow	$23
6247	5" St. Bernard Pup	$30
06329	2 1/2" Puppies, Each	$18
6364	4 1/2" Cat, Each	$23
6531	Siamese Cat	$28
06536	4 1/2" Buckskin Horse	$24
06656	6" Horse	$12
06657	6" Horse	$12
6658	3 1/2" Tiger Cub	$18
6659	6" Grey Poodle	$42
6661	4" Brown Rabbit	$20
6662	4 1/2" Horse	$20
6664	Rabbits, Pair	$40
6703	6 1/2" Leopard, Bisque	$38
6761	Tiger	$35
6862	4" Cat or Dog w/Large Blue Eyes	$18
6899	12" Black Poodle	$85
6970	4 1/4" Beaver	$22
6970	5" Rabbit	$22
6980	3 1/2" Elephant	$28
6790	Squirrel Eating an Acorn	$22
7059	4" Donkey	$18

7063	3" Lion	$18
7142	6" Buffalo	$32
7143	White Bunnies w/Pink Eyes, Pair	$25
7326	5" Dogs, Each	$35
7328	4 1/2" Dog, Each	$30
07466	3 " Elephant - 1989	$18
07470	6" Mother and Baby Elephant	$32
07593	3 1/2" Birthstone Kitten, Each - 1990	$18
07631	6 1/2" Sitting Dachshund - 1990	$15
7695	3 1/2" Skunk Holding A Flower	$15
7696	3 1/2" Puppy Holding A Gift	$15
7780	4" Fox - 1990	$12
7781	3 3/4" Rabbit - 1990	$12
07832	Mother and Two Piglets, Black & White - 1990	$18
07834	Three Black & White Pigs - 1990	$18
07836	Mother and Piglet by Fence - 1990	$18
07837	Three Pink Pigs - 1990	$18
07891	Unicorn - 1990	$25
7976	5" Boxer Dog	$65
8081	4" Sitting St. Bernard Puppy	$24
8165	7 1/2" Puppy, Each	$38
8181	White Poodle Dogs, 3 Piece Set	$60
8214	4" Basset Hound	$40
8220	5" Elephant	$32
8273	Siamese Cat	$25
8277	2 3/4" Mouse w/Lady Bug	$15
8278	2 1/2" Basset Hound Puppy, Each	$20
8286	4" Dog	$28
08305	2" Frog on Lily Pad, Each	$10
8451	5 1/4" Horse	$32
8743	8 1/2" Tiger, Black, White and Gold	$55
9050	4" Siamese Kitten	$15
9051	3" Terrier Puppies	$15
9248	7" Chipmunk on Log	$30
9446	5" Schnauzer	$28
10126	5 1/2" Dolphin with Starfish and Coral	$15
10910	5 1/4" Unicorn, 2 Assorted - 1996	$11
10911	6 3/4" Unicorn, Musical "Born Free" - 1996	$25
10912	5 3/4" Unicorn, 2 Assorted - 1996	$12
10913	5 1/2" Unicorn, 2 Assorted - 1996	$10
10914	5 1/4" Unicorn, 2 Assorted - 1996	$10
11075	4 3/4" White Cat with Gold Bow	$23
11256	Single Dolphin Pearl Finish	$7
11257	Double Dolphin Pearl Finish	$9
11258	Triple Dolphin Pearl Finish	$12
11305	5 3/4" Dolphin with Coral - 1997	$17
11306	5 3/4" Dolphin with Coral - 1997	$17
11307	5 3/4" Double Dolphin with Coral - 1998	$20
11540	3 3/4" Irish Bear, 3 Assorted	$7
11541	3" Irish Pig, 2 Assorted	$6
11740	4 1/2" Penguin & Baby - 1998	$18
11741	4 1/2" Penguin & Baby - 1998	$18
11742	4 1/2" Penguins Hugging - 1998	$18
11743	4 1/2" Penguins Looking at Fish - 1998	$19
11745	5 1/2" Dolphin, White & Gold - 1998	$20
11747	3 1/2" White Harp Seal - 1998	$18
11748	5" Harp Seal Laying on Ice - 1998	$18
11749	4" White Harp Seal and Baby - 1998	$18
11750	4 1/2" Mother Seal and Baby - 1998	$18
11880	3 1/2" Rabbit	$18
80018	Cats	$18
80089	4 1/2" Pink French Poodle	$25
80108	4 1/2" Pink Poodle with Black Glasses and Collar w/Stones	$30
80204	French Poodle Family, Set	$48
80219	4 3/4" Cats	$30
80248	5 1/2" Elephant w/Gold Accents	$35
80319	4 1/2" Cat	$23
80518	5 1/2" Siamese Cat, Each	$28
80519	4" Elephant, Each	$30
80521	5" Dog, Each	$52
80550	French Poodles w/Stones, 3 Piece Set	$50
80552	6" Poodle w/Bee and Stones	$50

BABY SETS

2706	Singing Bluebird, 3 Pieces	$40
3293	Mr. Toodles, 2 Pieces	$60
3396	Carousel Design, 3 Pieces	$46
3553	Miss Priss, 2 Pieces	$65
04528	Sports Bear, 3 Pieces	$28
05619	Cabbage Patch Doll w/Balloons, 3 Pieces	$28
05620	Child w/Balloons, 3 Pieces	$28
06589	Teddy Bear w/Balloons, 3 Pieces - 1988	$30

BAGS

2056	6" Christmas Shopping Bag	$12
2210	4" Bag w/Violets	$20
02385	4" Bag w/Bluebird	$20
2621	4" Bag w/Flowers and Bows	$20
03733	Money Bag w/Ribbon Tie, Violets	$15
05650	4" Bag, Halloween "Boo" - 1986	$14

BANKS

069	8" Uncle Sam Boy or Girl Bank	$35
087	Frying Pan Bank, "Cooking Like Saving Is An Art"	$45
090	6 1/2" Piggy Bank w/Painted Flowers	$38
00111	5 1/2" Shamrock Piggy Bank	$10
119	6" Owl Bank	$20
00136	6 1/2" Bank, Grandma w/Cat	$18
00137	6 1/2" Bank, Grandpa w/Dog	$18
145	6 3/4" Kewpie Bank	$48
00265	5 1/2" White Piggy Bank	$8
355	5 1/2" Piggy Bank, White w/Applied Pink Roses	$25
379	Piggy Bank, Pink w/Hand Applied Flowers	$52
0423	6 1/4" Pink Hippo Bank	$18
479	6 1/2" Owl Bank, Bisque	$28
479	5 1/2" Mouse Bank, by Marika	$20
00517	6 1/4" White Bear w/Beach Ball - 1992	$15
00618	6" Pink Kitty w/Polka Dot Bow	$25
701	Wishing Well Bank "Drop a Coin, Make a Wish"	$38
713	4" Baby in Cradle	$18
745	5" Piggy Bank	$35
879	4 1/2" Mushroom w/Butterfly and Pixie	$25
882	6 7/8" Uncle Sam Bank	$35
00928	6 1/4" Country Boy or Girl w/Straw Hat	$18
947	5 1/2" Owl Graduate Bank	$18
1122	5 1/2" Piggy Bank, Pearlized w/Forget-Me-Nots	$18
1138	Smiling Pig w/Eyes Closed and Applied Roses	$32
1240	4 1/2" Dog	$18
01281	6" Retirement Old Lady In Rocking Chair	$18
01297	5 1/2" Pink Pig with Pink Flowers	$10
01298	5 1/2" Pink Pig Musical "Brahm's Lullaby"	$25
1342	5" Baby Shoe w/Baby, Luster	$22
1973	5" Bank "Pin Money"	$32
1992	5" Pig w/Forget-Me-Nots	$25
2017	4 1/2" Barrel of Money	$20
2246	6 3/4" Brown Dog	$35
2429	7" Pink Elephant w/Stones	$20
2729	5" Pig dressed in Overalls	$22
2813	6" Pig, Pearl Luster	$15
2936	6 1/2" Pig w/Applied Flowers, Pearl Luster	$32
2987	5 3/4" Piggy Bank	$15
3008	Baby in Cradle	$35
03280	5 1/2" Blue Airplane	$15
03395	6 1/2" Piggy w/Painted Flowers	$20
03616	Pink Monkey w/Moveable Arms	$15
03617	Pink Monkey w/Moveable Arms	$15
03632	6" Pig Eating Corn	$15
03740	5" Clown Bank	$22
03742	5" Bed w/Bear "Our Little Treasure"	$20
03864	White Piggy Bank	$15
3893	Duck, Turtle, or Owl w/Glass Eyes	$12
04130	4" Bag "Bundle of Joy" - 1984	$18

BANKS (cont'd)

04193	6 1/2" Teddy Bear - 1984	$15
4265	7" Man & Woman Retirement in Rocking Chairs, Pair	$42
4266	8 1/2" Man & Woman Retirement in Rocking Chairs, Pair	$38
4267	5" Pig w/Protruding Eyelashes	$15
4293	7 1/2' Lady & Man Retirement in Rocking Chairs, Each	$18
4302	5" Mouse, or Dog w/Glass eyes, Each	$13
04349	6" Girl w/Curly Yarn Hair - 1984	$35
04409	6 1/2" Koala Bear in Pink Dress	$25
4880	5 3/4" Owl Bank	$15
04909	Bunny w/Hat, Dress & Purse - 1985	$35
5010	6 3/4" Graduate Girl "College Fund"	$35
5038	6 1/4" Lady in Mink Coat, "Money Is Everything"	$45
5251	8" Astronaut Bank	$25
5861	4" Purse w/Applied Roses "Pin Money"	$45
5956	6 1/2" Sitting Donkey, Brightly Painted and Glazed	$17
5956	5 1/2" Sitting Teddy Bear, Glazed	$17
5956	5" Green Chipmunk	$18
5956	6" Dog Bank	$18
6090	6 3/4" Stork Bank	$22
6145	7" Clock w/Daisies	$32
06520	5 1/2" Pig with Pink or Blue Bow	$10
06521	4 1/2" Pig with Pink or Blue Bow	$8
06582	9" Pig with Pink or Blue Bow	$25
06483	8" Pig with Pink or Blue Bow	$20
06485	5 1/2" Bear, Quilted Look w/Bow - 1987	$28
06486	3 3/4" Pig w/Flowers & Bow - 1987	$24
6922	7 1/2" Raggedy Andy Bank	$58
07176	6 1/2" Black & White Sitting Pig - 1989	$20
7485	7" Bluebirds Love Nest Bank	$85
07634	6 1/2" Cocker Spaniel Bank	$30
7825	8 1/4" Pink, Green or Yellow Doll Bank	$12
7826	6 1/4" Green or Pink Sitting Doll Bank	$12
07963	7 1/2" Elephant Bank	$30
9635	5 1/2" Miss Pimple Bank	$36
9898	7 1/2" Pig w/Pink Flowers and Bow	$70
10476	4 1/2" Piggy Bank with Pink or Blue Ribbon and Flowers	$10
10477	5 1/2" Piggy Bank with Pink or Blue Ribbon and Flowers	$12
10478	6 1/2" Piggy Bank with Pink or Blue Ribbon and Flowers	$17
10479	7 1/2" Piggy Bank with Pink or Blue Ribbon and Flowers	$20
10480	7 1/2" Musical Pig w/Flowers and Ribbon, "Brahm's Lullaby"	$25
10481	9" Piggy Bank with Pink or Blue Ribbon and Flowers	$25
10482	12" Piggy Bank with Pink or Blue Ribbon and Flowers	$26
10483	5 1/2" Piggy Bank with Pink or Blue Flowers	$10
10484	7 1/2" Piggy Bank with Pink or Blue Flowers	$20
10485	7 1/2" Musical Piggy Bank w/Flowers, "Brahm's Lullaby"	$25
11220	6" Cat Bank	$10
11221	6" Baby Shoe Bank	$10
11251	6" Bear Holding Basketball or Football - 1997	$35
11252	Sport Bear with Basketball	$12
11253	Sport Bear with Football	$12
11254	Sport Bear with Baseball Bat	$12
11255	Fireman Bear Bank	$12
11879	5 3/4" Irish Piggy Bank	$10
13384	6" Lion Wearing Glasses	$55
13574	7" Kangaroo w/Baby Bank	$35
30284	6" Dog, Black w/Bow, Red Ears	$25
90195	6 1/2" Owl w/Rhinestone Eyes	$55
90250	5" Purse, Pink "Pin Money"	$50
90276	7" Puppy w/Green Bow	$40
90338	5" Bird Nest w/Stones	$65

BASKETS

00248	4" Pink Roses w/Blue Ribbon	$12
1355	4" White Wicker Look w/Daisies	$20
02672	3 1/2" White Daisy Pattern	$15
02676	3 1/2" w/Violets	$15
2741	White Basket Weave w/Pink and Blue Flowers	$18
02910	3 1/2" w/Shamrocks	$12
03094	3 1/2" w/Hearts	$12
3095	4" w/Hearts	$13

03098	4" White w/Blue Painted Flowers	$12
03120	3" w/Lily of the Valley	$12
03163	3" Basket w/Violets	$12
03168	3" White Basket w/Floral Design	$10
03538	3 1/2" White Basket w/Pink Flowers	$12
04085	4 1/2" White Basket w/Ribbon - 1984	$15
4597	4 1/2" w/Hot Poppy	$15
4661	5" Fiesta	$15
4915	Two Handled w/Red and Green Stripes	$12
05165	Pink Floral w/Wavy Top - 1985	$17
06129	5" White Wicker Look w/Bow and Flowers - 1986	$18
06140	2 3/4" White Basketweave w/Doves - 1987	$18
06211	5" White Basket Weave - 1987	$12
06234	5" White w/Floral and Gold Trim - 1987	$15
6473	5" Mushroom Forest - 1970	$15
07089	5" White Wicker Look w/Bow & Flowers, Each - 1989	$18
07159	3 3/4" Pink Basket w/Bow - 1989	$12
07763	5" White Wicker Look w/Bow & Flowers, Each - 1990	$18
11079	4 3/4" Shamrock Basket	$8

BATHROOM AND BEDROOM ITEMS

052	4" Tumbler w/Violets	$25
125	Hand Ring Holder	$28
128	Perfume Bottle, Eastern Elegance	$45
233	Perfume Set, Lilac w/Stones, 3 Piece Set	$170
270	Lilac Bisque Toothbrush Holder	$28
279	Tooth Brush Holder, Yellow w/Yellow and Pink Flowers	$12
385	Perfume Set, Only a Rose, 3 Piece Set	$100
00414	6 1/2" Soap Dish, Violets	$14
442	4" Ring and Lipstick Holder	$20
831	5" Apothecary Jar, Nobby Milk Glass w/Applied Flowers	$45
841	2 1/2" Shell Soap Dish, w/Applied Flowers	$18
842	Perfume Set, White Bisque w/Applied Flowers, 3 Piece Set	$90
903	3 1/2" Lipstick Holder	$20
1371	8 1/2" x 1 3/4" Toothbrush Tray w/Daisies	$18
1402	8 1/2" x 1 3/4" Toothbrush Tray w/Floral Design	$18
1444	3 3/4" Ring Holder, Hand	$32
1458	Hand Lotion Dispenser, Pink Dogwood - 1994	$20
1550	2 3/4" Toothbrush Holder, Wild Flowers	$15
1634	5 3/4" Soap Dish, Gold Lily of the Valley	$14
1754	Tumbler, Majestic Gold	$15
1755	Soap Dish, Majestic Gold	$15
1759	Jars, White w/Gold Trim, Cotton and Powder	$65
1770	2 Perfume Bottles & Powder Dish w/Applied Flowers	$110
1818	Lipstick Holder, Angel Soap Dish and Powder Box, Set	$45
1963	Lipstick Holder w/Cherubs	$40
1991	4" Toothbrush Holder, Small Daisy	$18
2286	8 1/2" x 1 3/4" Toothbrush Tray, Floral	$18
2372	6 3/4" Perfume Bottle, Golden Laurel	$32
2373	4 1/2" Lipstick Holder, Golden Laurel	$28
2376	5" Lipstick Holder, Golden Laurel	$28
2401	2 Perfume Bottles, Golden Laurel, Each	$24
2403	4" Tumbler, Golden Laurel	$18
2404	Jars - "Cotton", "Powder", "Things", Golden Laurel, Each	$18
2408	9"x 6" Tray, Golden Laurel	$15
2469	Perfume Set, French Rose, 3 Piece Set	$46
2633	Soap Dish w/Cupid, French Rose	$15
2646	3 3/4" Toothbrush Holder, French Rose	$18
2649	Perfume Set, French Rose, 3 Piece Set	$45
2734	5" Lipstick Holder Shaped Like Swan	$28
2738	Perfume Set, Swan and Flowers, 3 Piece Set	$95
2933	Lipstick Holder, Hand w/Applied Flowers	$22
3253	Powder Dish, French Rose	$18
03296	Ring Holder w/Violets	$10
3381	3 1/2" Lipstick Holder, French Rose	$10
3384	Perfume Set, French Rose, 3 Piece Set	$35
3602	5 1/2" Soap Dish w/Cherubs, Renaissance	$20
4215	Soap Dish and Tumbler	$25
4660	4" Tumbler w/Hand Painted Gold Lily of the Valley	$10
5025	Soap Dish and Tumbler, Rose Design	$22
5066	Shell Shaped Soap Dish	$10
05708	Ring Holder - 1986	$10

5760	5 1/2" Pedestal Soap Dish, Gold Accents	$20
6121	Soap Dish and Tumbler	$32
6124	Soap Dish, Gold Roses or Butterflies	$15
6410	Soap Dish, Pink and Yellow Roses w/Gold Trim	$15
6433	Soap Dish & Tumbler, Petites Fleurs	$25
6875	Soap Dish, Paisley Fantasia	$18
07054	Soap Dish, Mint Green w/Pink Roses	$14
7085	Tumbler, Lt. Blue w/Flowers	$10
7685	Tumbler, Lt. Yellow w/Flowers	$10
7685	Tumbler, Lt. Pink w/Flowers	$10
7686	Soap Dish, Lt. Blue w/Flowers	$12
7686	Soap Dish, Lt. Yellow w/Flowers	$12
7686	Soap Dish, Lt. Pink w/Flowers	$12
8182	4" Tumbler w/Floral Pattern w/Gold trim	$8
8183	Soap Dish, Pink w/Pink & Yellow Flowers	$11
8206	4" Toothbrush Holder w/Blue Flowers	$18
8207	Soap Dish, Pink & Yellow Flowers	$10
90041	4" Powder w/Rhinestones and Flowers	$50
90042	4" Box & Perfume Bottles, White Flowers w/Rhinestones	$135
90043	Perfume Set w/Rhinestones, 2 Bottles, Powder Box, Tray	$145
90046	Soap Dish, White w/Pink Flowers & Gold Trim	$18
90452	Perfume Set, White w/Rhinestones, 3 Piece Set	$140

BEE LINE/HONEY BEE

1278	Teapot	$110
1279	Cookie Jar	$135
1280	Jam Jar	$40
1281	Mug	$22
1282	4 1/2" Pitcher	$40
1284	Egg Cup	$25
1285	Cheese Dish	$45
1286	Three Compartment Dish	$48
1287	Two Compartment Dish	$40
1288	Salt and Pepper	$28
1289	Spoon Rest	$30
1290	Butter Dish	$36
1291	Sugar and Creamer	$55
1527	Wallpocket	$65
1588	Two Compartment Dish	$25
1593	Candle Holders	$23
7892	ESD Jam Jar	$35
21150	ESD Two Compartment Dish	$35

BELLS

0112	Angel Bells, Set of 3 - 1958	$45
00151	Bell with Branch Handle and Applied Flowers	$18
00152	Wedding Bell w/Two Doves & Applied Flowers - 1983	$20
283	3 3/4" w/Two Doves	$11
295	5 1/2" Bell, Antiqued Bisque	$16
418	3" Lilac and Rhinestone	$22
428	4" Bisque w/Hand Painted Flowers	$16
783	4 3/4" Antique Ivory Bisque w/Applied Flowers	$15
785	4" Bell of the Month	$16
1041	2 3/4" White Bisque w/Applied Flowers	$18
1101	50th Wedding Anniversary	$12
01113	3 1/2" Flower Bell w/Butterfly Handle - 1984	$12
1119	Butterfly on Flower	$15
1237	3" Girl w/Lime Green Dress, White Smock & Hat	$12
1306	50th Anniversary Bell	$11
1413	3" Angel Bell	$18
1417	4" Bride and Groom	$12
1434	4" w/Hand Painted Flowers	$8
01919	3 1/2" Trimmed in Gold w/Gold Daisies	$13
1922	Floral w/Gold Handle	$15
1971	Violet Pattern	$16
1990	3 1/2" Floral w/Gold Handle	$13
2012	3 1/2" Floral w/Green Trim	$10
2031	3 1/4" w/Miniature Pink Roses and Pink Trim	$12
02038	3" Angel Bell	$10
02045	4 1/2" Flower Girl Bell	$15
02066	3" Bell, 3 Kinds	$10

2118	25th Anniversary Bell	$12
2119	50th Anniversary Bell	$12
02261	3" Bell of the Month	$10
2558	3 3/4" Boy & Girl Angel Bell, Pair	$20
02598	4" w/Hand Painted Blue Birds on Tree Branch	$10
02600	5" White Glazed w/Blue Bird on Tree Branch	$12
02609	4 1/2" w/Shamrocks	$12
02687	3 1/2" w/Roses "You'll Never Know How Much..."	$14
2839	4 3/4" w/Violets	$18
3196	2 3/4" Bride & Groom	$8
03257	Angel of the Month Bell, 2 sizes	$8
03259	3 1/2" Bell of the Month - 1983	$10
03535	5" Pink Dogwood - 1983	$8
03568	Bell of the Month - 1983	$10
03569	4" Bell w/Flowers and Butterfly	$18
03571	Bird w/Flowers - 1983	$12
04073	4 1/4" w/Applied Roses	$22
04074	7" White Bisque w/Woodpecker - 1983	$15
4199	3 1/2" Bisque w/Applied Flowers	$12
04320	5 1/4" Floral Design - 1984	$12
04576	7" w/Pelican and Flowers, Bisque	$14
4700	4" Bride and Groom, Glazed	$14
04771	50th Anniversary Bell - 1983	$10
04775	5 1/2" Anniversary Bell - 1983	$10
04778	5 1/2" Wedding Bell - 1983	$10
05502	5 1/2" Floral w/Bird Handle - 1986	$22
05503	3 1/2" Tree Branch Handle w/Bird - 1986	$18
05685	Bethlehem Collection - 1986	$11
05686	6" Bethlehem Collection - 1986	$14
05807	5" Wedding Bell w/Rose - 1986	$10
06238	Tulip Shaped w/Pink Flowers - 1987	$10
6452	6" w/Red, Green, Gold Ribbon & Bow - 1987	$14
6476	4 1/2" w/Flowers & Lace Edge - 1987	$12
7054	White w/Flowers Bouquet on Front and Back	$15
07066	Happy Anniversary - 1989	$13
7300	3 3/4" Floral	$12
7685	25th Anniversary Bell, 2 Assorted, Each	$12
07816	5 1/4" w/Dogwood	$15
7965	3" Pink or Yellow Flower, Each	$10
8031	Narcissus Bell - 1984	$15
08143	5 1/2" w/Herons - 1987	$12
8293	3" Pink w/Forget-Me-Nots and Rose Handle	$28
8336	Little Girl w/Pig Tails and Purse, Glazed	$10
8947	2 1/2" Bride & Groom	$18
10583	5 1/4" 25th Anniversary	$9
10594	5 1/4" 50th Anniversary	$9
12261	3" Bell of the Month	$10
13003	6" Glazed Bell w/Applied Pink Flowers - 1999	$14
80112	Angel Girls, 3 Piece Set	$45
90082	2" Congratulations	$15
90460	3" Pink w/Forget-Me-Nots	$20

BERRY HARVEST

291	Three Compartment Dish	$38
292	Two Compartment Dish	$35
293	Handled Relish Dish	$32
294	Cookie Jar	$125
296	Compote	$45
297	Covered Candy Dish	$60
298	Sugar and Creamer	$55
299	Jam Jar	$48
300	Candle Holder	$45
301	Salt and Pepper Shakers	$28
302	Cup and Saucer	$30
303	Dinner Plate	$28
304	6 1/2" Bread and Butter Plate	$20
305	8" Salad Plate	$28
306	6" Bowl	$22
308	14" Platter	$65
309	Cake Plate	$35
310	Egg Cup	$25

BERRY HARVEST (cont'd)

311	Butter Dish	$35
312	Pitcher	$65
313	Spoon Rest w/Salt Shaker	$45
314	Canister Set, 4 Piece Set	$95
315	Spice Jars	$65
316	Oil and Vinegar Bottles	$42
317	Two Tier Tidbit Tray	$75
318	Wall Hanging, Salt Box	$38
319	Wall Hanging, Match Box	$35
430	Teapot	$130
431	Plate w/Handle	$45
434	Wall Hanging, Pitcher and Bowl	$40
572	Snack Set	$28
599	Soup Tureen Tray and Ladle	$125
669	Cup and Saucer	$30
4649	Wall Pocket, Pitcher and Bowl	$45

BIRDS

086	1 1/2" Baby Bluebird, 3 Pieces	$18
121	4 1/2" Owl	$15
00130	3" Two Birds on Tree Branch, Each	$20
00131	2 1/2" Open Winged Bird on Branch	$18
135	9" Blue Cockatoo	$95
135	5 1/2" Oriole, Glazed	$20
139	Wood Duck	$35
140	6 3/4" Bird of Paradise, Each	$80
141	5" Macaw	$50
142	4" Parrot	$38
212	11 1/2" Open Winged Duck	$125
214	5" Mallards, Pair	$50
217	7 1/2" Crane	$50
00224	4" Cardinal, Nest Egg Collection - 1991	$30
00242	4" Bird, 6 Assorted	$13
00246	5" Bluejay, Nest Egg Collection - 1991	$30
00247	5" Birds with Flowers, 6 Assorted	$17
251	Canary on Branch	$18
00376	4" Doves on Branch, Nest Egg Collection - 1991	$30
395	5" Bluebird	$20
395	5" Goldfinch	$18
395	5" Parakeet	$22
395	5" Robin	$20
395	5" Cardinal Head Up or Down, Each	$18
00401	6" Cardinal, Nest Egg Collection - 1991	$30
00427	7" Hummingbird with Morning Glories, 3 Assorted	$65
440	6" Robin on Driftwood w/Flowers	$35
464	4 1/2" Bluebird w/Flowers	$25
464	4 1/2" Parakeet	$23
464	4 1/2" Cardinal, Head Up or Down, Each	$18
464	4 1/2" Hummingbird	$35
465	5 1/2" Hummingbird	$55
465	6 1/2" Parakeet	$32
465	5 1/4" Robin on Cattail Leaves	$40
465	5 1/2" Baltimore Oriole	$48
467	5" Baltimore Oriole w/Baby	$55
467	6" Blue & Green Parakeets	$60
467	5" Cardinal w/Baby	$55
467	5" Red Robin w/Baby	$60
467	Hummingbirds	$60
494	6" Roosters, Pair	$65
504	5 1/2" Glazed Pink Flamingo w/Baby, Pair	$95
00542	2 3/4" Bluebird on Branch - 1992	$18
00550	3" Doves on Branch - 1992	$18
609	5 1/2" Bohemian Waxwing	$25
657	6" Flamingos, Pair	$95
670	8 1/4" Pheasant	$30
743	5" Kingfisher	$18
00749	2 1/2' Bird on Branch w/Flower	$9
00749C	2 1/2" Cardinal	$9
00753	2 1/2" Owl on Branch	$9
00754	2 1/2" Doves on Branch	$9

00755	2 1/2" Duck	$9
760	5 3/4" California Quail, Pair	$65
761	5" Canadian Goose in Flight	$35
763	6" Baltimore Oriole (Planter)	$45
763	6" Parakeet (Planter)	$45
768	5 1/2" Ducks, Pair	$95
769	7 1/2" Pheasant, Pair	$80
776	6 1/2" Baby Bird on Tree Limb w/Flower	$40
796	10" Fighting Roosters, Matte w/Gold Accents, Pair	$50
841	3 1/4" Swan w/Baby Swan	$38
854	8" Roosters Fighting, Pair	$145
855	4 1/2" Hummingbird and Flower (Wall Plaque)	$45
864	5" Bird on Base w/Flower or Nest, Each	$28
866	Owl	$23
907	5 1/2" Woodcock	$35
908	Wood Duck	$35
909	5 1/4" Seagull	$40
910	6" White Pelican	$40
912	7" Bunting	$22
01001	Robin w/Daffodils, Antique Ivory Bisque	$28
01008	2 3/4" Baby Chick	$8
1024	Early American Roosters, Pair	$85
01043	6" Bird on Branch with Flowers, 3 Assorted	$27
01046	6" Hummingbird with Hibiscus	$24
01047	5 1/4" Hummingbird with Azalea	$25
01048	6 3/4" Hummingbirds with Hibiscus	$27
01049	6" Hummingbirds, 2 Assorted	$25
1051	6 1/2" Plymouth Rock Roosters, Pair	$65
1052	6 1/2" Roosters, Pair	$60
1054	9" Quetzal	$150
1056	8 1/2" Toucan	$105
1060	11 3/4" Golden Pheasant	$50
01076	6" Robin on Branch w/Two Flowers - 1993	$27
01083	Rooster & Hen, Pair	$38
01183	8" Blue Jay	$36
1184	5" Thrasher, Purple Martin, Mockingbird, Each	$22
1184	5" Painted Bunting, Flycatcher, House Wren, Each	$22
1251	4" Bird on Tree Branch, Each	$20
01265	4" Bird on Branch, 6 Assorted	$10
1271	7" Bluebird	$45
1273	Doves, Matte Finish w/Gold Accents, Pair	$24
1282	7" Robin	$45
1283	6 1/2" Bohemian Waxwing	$45
1284	7" Cardinal	$45
1288	7" Skylark	$45
1290	6 1/2" Bobolink on Base	$35
01386	8 1/2" Hummingbirds, "Waltz of the Flowers", 2 Assorted	$30
1465	Plymouth Rock Rooster (Planter)	$35
1523	5 1/2" Heron	$38
1528	5 1/2" Long Tail Roosters	$85
1529	5 1/2" Golden Pheasant	$35
1531	5" Crane	$35
1532	5 1/2" Heron	$55
1533	6" Cockatoo	$65
1538	7 3/4" Golden Pheasant	$40
1541	6 1/2" Heron	$45
1542	7 1/2" Cockatoo	$85
1547	8 1/2" Pheasant w/Open Wings, Pair	$50
01591	7" Eagle with Open Wings	$32
01593	5 1/2" Eagle	$30
1637	3 1/2" Baby Bird, Each	$18
1706	7" Bird w/Flowers	$100
1707	5 1/2" Bee Eater	$65
1726	6" Two Owls on Tree Stump	$28
1728	4 3/4" Green Parakeet on Tree Branch	$28
1732	6" Bluebird on Tree Branch w/Acorns	$28
1804	6 3/4" Bluebird on Tree Stump Feeding Baby	$40
01811	6 3/4" Two Robins on a Hollow Log	$40
01886	4" Goldfinch on Tree Stump w/Flower	$28
2002	4" Bobwhite	$22
2004	3 1/2" Baby Robin w/Planter	$35
2005	4" Open Winged Pheasant	$30
2070	Mallard Ducks, Pair	$48

02143	6" Musical Bird Figurine	$45		06302	2" Pair of Swans, Nest Egg Collection - 1987	$18
02203	4" Double Bird with Flowers, 4 Assorted	$10		06304	Bluebird w/Flowers - 1983	$25
02203C	4" Cardinal	$10		06323	3" Robin	$15
2235	6 1/2" Owl	$18		06324	2 1/2" Bird on Branch w/Flower	$16
2291	4 1/4" Dove, Each	$12		06378	3" Bird on Branch w/Flower	$18
2304	Hummingbird, Limited Edition of 1500	$45		06590	5" Duck with Wood Base, Nest Egg Collection - 1988	$32
2335	6" Peacock w/Straight Tail	$55		6609	4 1/2" Bird on Tree Stump	$22
2336	6" Peacock w/Tail Spread	$65		6705	7 3/4" Eagle w/Open Wings	$25
02344	5" White Pelican	$58		06707	5" Hawk, Nest Egg Collection - 1988	$50
02348	2 3/4" Goose w/Hat, Each	$10		6715	4 1/2" Turkey	$25
2396	9" Rooster & Hen, Pair	$45		06874	5" Snow Owl, Nest Egg Collection - 1988	$35
2668	5" Ruffled Grouse, Pair	$75		06881	Baby Robin on Branch w/Flower	$20
02707	5" Hummingbird w/Flower, 2 Assorted	$23		6981	Yellow Ducks, Pair	$38
02727	6 3/4" Owl	$28		7020	7" Bird on Tree w/Flowers	$55
02713	4" Mother and Baby Penguin	$10		7212	Eagle on Rock w/Open Wings	$20
2829	3 1/2" Owl, Glazed	$18		7218	6 3/4" Mockingbird	$50
3072	Roosters, Glazed, Pair	$40		7219	7 3/4" Scissor Tailed Fly Catcher	$56
3209	7" Roadrunner, Each	$40		7456	Mother Bird on Branch w/Baby	$25
03223	7" Owl on Log	$50		7457	6 1/2" Blue Jay, Lark or Goldfinch	$22
03305	3" Baby Bird on Tree Stump, Nest Egg Collection	$22		7674	6" Baby Birds on Branch	$45
03306	3" Double Birds on Tree Branch, 4 Assorted	$9		07721	Hanging Hummingbird with Ornament Holder	$15
3411	Woodcock	$45		8008	6" Robin on Branch Feeding Baby	$65
3414	5" Snow Goose, Limited Edition	$45		8009	Bluebird on Raspberry Vine	$25
3415	5" Red Head Female	$45		8258	3" Bisque Baby Birds	$28
3416	6" Red Head Duck, Limited Edition	$45		8566	3" Bird on Branch, Glazed	$30
3417	5 1/2" Canvas Back Duck, Limited Edition	$45		8846	Pink Flamingo & Baby, Glazed	$55
03477	5 1/2" Rooster	$28		8978	Cardinal Feeding Babies, Glazed	$38
03484	Sitting Hen & Rooster, Pair	$40		8978	Blue Jay Feeding Babies, Glazed	$38
3505	5" Mother Bird w/Fledglings in Nest	$55		9446	3 1/4" Baby owls, Each	$12
03585	8" Rooster and 6" Hen, Pair	$60		10091	14 1/2" Eagle	$120
3597	Roadrunner, Tail Straight	$45		10092	5 3/4" Eagle	$32
3738	7 1/2" Bird on Nest w/Eggs	$65		10093	7" Blue Jay, Musical "Fly Me to the Moon"	$32
03831	4" Doves on Branch - 1983	$22		10093	7" Cardinal, Musical "Moon River"	$32
03832	5 1/2" Peacock, Nest Egg Collection - 1983	$55		10093	7" Bluebird, Musical "Over the Rainbow"	$32
03961	Rooster and Hen, Glazed - 1983	$22		10094	5" Bird on Branch with Flowers, 3 Assorted	$22
03993	4 3/4" Canary, Nest Egg Collection	$25		10447	3" Playing Penguin	$12
03999	5" Owl	$20		10474	8" Bluebird on Branch w/Flowers - 1995	$45
04001	4" Mallard Duck, American Decoy Collection - 1983	$35		10702	7" Hummingbirds with Morning Glories, 3 Assorted	$25
04002	4" Canadian Goose, American Decoy Collection - 1983	$35		10706	8" Hummingbird, Musical "Waltz of the Flower", 3 Assorted	$33
04006	3" Pelican - American Decoy Collection - 1983	$20		10712	6" Chickadee w/Holly	$25
04022	4" Loon, American Decoy Collection - 1983	$25		10713	5" Chickadee w/Holly	$24
04023	2" Canary - 1984	$12		10922	6" Cardinal w/Snow Rose	$25
04024	2 1/2" Pheasant - 1987	$18		11074A	Hummingbird Musical, White and Gold "Waltz of the Flower"	$27
4037	6" White Dove	$35		11074B	Hummingbird Musical, White and Gold "Evergreen"	$27
4206	5" Bird, Each	$18		11302	6" Double Owl on Trunk	$22
04254	Chicken Family, Barnyard Friends Collection - 1984	$16		11304	5 3/4" Rooster Pair, 2 Assorted	$30
04473	7 1/4" Bald Eagle	$35		11308	5" Double Dove	$18
04485	5" Mallard Duck, Pair - 1983	$40		11309	5 1/4" Open Winged Dove	$20
04742	Swan - 1985	$18		11310	4 1/4" Double Hummingbird	$20
04801	4" Open Winged Cardinal on Branch	$18		11311	6" Bird, 3 Assorted	$22
04907	3" White Duck w/Ribbon Around Neck - 1985	$15		11312	6" Cardinal	$22
4954	6" Bird w/Flowers on Base, Each	$50		11313	5" Bird with Baby, 3 Assorted	$24
04957	4 3/4" Bird on Branch w/Flowers - 1985	$18		11314	5" Cardinal with Baby	$24
04967	5 1/2" White Owl - 1985	$23		11315	4 3/4" Double Bird, 3 Assorted	$22
04988	Mallard Duck, Nest Egg Collection - 1985	$23		11316	4 3/4" Double Cardinal	$22
4996	10" Owl on Tree	$130		11317	4 1/4" Open Winged Bird on Branch, 3 Assorted	$10
05134	Doves, Nest Egg Collection - 1985	$23		11318	4 1/4" Open Winged Cardinal	$10
5157	7" Birds on Oval Base	$50		11319	4 3/4" Hummingbirds, "Waltz of the Flowers", 3 Assorted	$27
5158	8 1/4" Goldfinch w/Large Flower	$55		11366	9" Hummingbirds w/Daffodils, 3 Assorted	$45
5159	9 1/4" White Dove	$160		11367	8" Hummingbird w/Lady Eardrop, 2 Assorted	$45
5447	8" White Dove	$65		11368	9" Hummingbird w/Morning Glories, 3 Assorted	$50
5448	7 1/2" White Doves, Pair	$70		11369	6 1/2" Hummingbird w/Hibiscus, 2 Assorted	$30
5466	4 3/4" Doves, Pair	$40		11370	9" Hummingbirds w/Hibiscus, 2 Assorted	$65
05633	4" Eagle	$18		11371	7" Hummingbird w/Rose, 4 Assorted	$30
5763	8" Owl w/Applied Flowers and Leaves	$35		11734	Hummingbird w/Hibiscus	$30
5825	6 1/4" Hummingbird	$52		11768	4 3/4" Bird on Branch w/Flowers - 1985	$13
5900	8 1/2" Cardinal w/Flowers on Base	$65		11769	Hummingbird w/Flowers, 4 Assorted	$10
06608	5" Parakeet	$23		11801	6 3/4" Long Billed Curlew	$37
06007	5" Meadowlark	$18		11802	6 3/4" American Avocet	$37
06046	5 1/2" Swan w/2 Babies	$32		11803	9 1/2" Eagle in Glass Dome, Musical "America The Beautiful"	$70
06058	3" Eagle by Sevilla - 1987	$18		11805	16" Barn Owl	$150
06073	Cardinal	$20		11806	8 1/2" Snow Owl	$50
06141	5" Flamingo, Nest Egg Collection - 1987	$28		11807	6 1/4" Brown Pelican	$30

BIRDS (cont'd)

11808	5" Road Runner	$35
11809	Hummingbirds w/Hibiscus and Dome, "Impossible Dream"	$60
11810	4 3/4" Spotted Sandpiper	$25
11811	6" Sea Gull w/Wave	$33
11812	5" Robin w/Babies and Apple Blossoms	$33
11813	5 1/2" Goldfinch w/Fledglings and Flowers	$37
11814	5" Cardinal w/Holly	$33
11816	8 1/2" Eagle on Tree Trunk w/Base	$35
11818	Hummingbird w/Glass Vase	$10
11819	10 1/4" Double Eagle on Branch	$60
11820	5" Eagle	$50
11822	Rubythroat Hummingbird w/Trumpet	$37
11823	Hummingbird w/Fuschia	$37
11920	Hummingbird w/Tigerlily	$30
11984	Hummingbird w/Babies and Wild Rose	$30
11985	Hummingbird w/Orchid	$35
12331	5 1/4" Eagle	$13
13026	7 1/2" Heron - 1999	$25
13126	6" Hummingbird on Branch w/Flower	$23
13192	2 1/2" Bird on Branch, Each	$18
13210	3 1/2" Baby Cardinals on Flowered Branch - 1999	$25
13211	3 1/2" Baby Mockingbirds on Flowered Branch - 1999	$25
85134	2 1/2" Doves on Leaves, Nest Egg Collection - 1985	$23

BLUEBIRD LINE

057	Wall Plaque, 3 Piece Set	$115
151	5 1/2" Spoon Rest w/Salt Shaker	$175
239	Salt and Pepper Shakers, Bluebirds w/Stones	$145
267	Bank, Bluebird w/Stones	$175
282	Salt and Pepper	$50
283	Wall Pocket, Mr. & Mrs. Bluebirds	$325
284	Baby Set, Mug - 2 Piece set	$125
286	Egg Cup	$58
287	4 1/2" Pitcher	$95
288	Planter, Bluebird w/Rhinestone Eyes	$150
289	Cookie Jar	$350
290	Sugar and Creamer	$95
435	Baby Bowl and Mug- 2 Piece Set	$125
436	Jam Jar	$95
437	Cheese Dish	$325
438	Teapot	$295
734	Musical Teapot	$200
7027	ESD Condiment Jar	$75
7169	ESD Cookie Jar	$125
7170	ESD Sugar & Creamer	$50
7175	ESD Salt and Pepper Shakers	$42
7353	ESD Teabag Holder	$55

BLUE PAISLEY

1972	Coffee Pot	$135
1974	Sugar and Creamer	$45
1975	Two Tier Tidbit Tray	$32
2131	Egg Cup	$35
2133	Cup and Saucer	$22
2141	6" Lemon Dish	$28
2142	5 1/2" Candy Dish, 3 Legged	$35
2154	Small Trinket Box	$10
2169	5 1/8" Ewer Type Bud Vase	$18
2170	6 1/4" Bud Vase	$15
2173	5 1/4" Lamp	$35
2334	Jam Jar w/China Spoon and Plate	$50
2337	9 1/4" Plate	$22
2338	7 1/4" Plate	$18
2339	Cup and Saucer	$25
2340	Snack Set	$22
2341	Compote	$22
2344	5" Round Ashtray	$15
2346	Salt and Pepper	$28
2347	Sugar and Creamer	$65

2348	Tidbit Tray	$18
2349	6 1/2" Nappy	$18
2350	6 1/2" Nappy	$18
2351	Sugar and Creamer w/Tray	$55
2354	Teapot Teabag Holder	$13
2358	Mini Sugar and Creamer	$37
2359	8" Bone Dish	$18
2360	Urn w/2 Ashtrays	$18
2367	3 1/2" Shell Shaped Ashtray	$12
2373	Teapot	$105
2725	Mug	$16
3249	6 1/2" Bonbon	$20

BONE DISHES

106	Heavenly Rose	$28
706	Moss Rose	$12
1825	Rose Heirloom	$23
2623	Magnolia	$18
4186	Forget-me-Not	$14
4262	White Pear and Apple	$18
8245	Antique Ivory Bisque w/Floral Pattern	$15

BOOK ENDS

067	Baseball Glove and Football	$40
249	Golf Club and Tennis Racquet	$40
510	White Cat	$42
518	White Persian Cats	$50
1262	Horses	$75
1681	Horse Head, Bay	$65
1683	Owls w/Glass Eyes	$35
2230	Pheasants	$70
2229	Ducks	$95
3496	Dogs	$40
3729	Siamese Cats	$55
03936	Siamese Cats w/Blue Eyes	$55
04192	Teddy Bears - 1984	$35
4837	Elephants	$35
4837	Poodles	$40
4847	Horses Heads	$45
7484	Dogs	$45
80164	Chinese Boy and Girl, Glazed	$135

BOWLS

00236	7" Octagonal, Floral w/Pink & Gold Trim	$32
381	4" Blue & White w/Oriental Motif	$23
408	6 1/2" Flower, Pearl Luster	$30
425	7 1/2" Swan Center, Only a Rose	$95
486	6 1/2" w/Hand Painted Floral or Fruit Design	$35
822	5" Milk China	$45
878	7" w/Roses, Glazed	$55
960	Double Shell Bowl	$35
1339	Punch bowl, White Bisque	$25
1778	9 1/4" Legged Bowl, White Bisque	$35
1779	9 1/4" in Pink Bisque w/Flowers	$65
2330	8" Swan Shaped Bowl, Bisque	$45
2566	Tomato Design, 5 Piece Set	$65
3566	6" Diameter w/Tab Handles, Renaissance	$38
3575	9 1'2" White Glazed, Renaissance	$48
5125	6 1/2' Flower Shaped, Gold on Edge	$40

BOXES

0026	4" Egg w/Gold Rose	$18
123	3 3/4" Round w/Applied Flower	$23
00151	3 3/4" Irish Hat w/Mouse	$12
00177	Cat w/Red Bow and Applied Flowers	$20
179	3 1/4" Heart Shaped, Red Lid w/Roses	$10
207	2" Pin Box, Antiqued Bisque	$8
212	Heart Shaped, Antiqued Bisque	$19
217	4" Covered Box, Antiqued Bisque	$15

00290	Violet Design - 1991	$14		02389	Heart Shaped w/ Roses "Hugs & Kisses"	$10
308	4 1/4" Round Box, Flower Garland	$21		2400	Golden Laurel, Hinged	$28
335	5" Hinged, Egg-Shaped, Spring Bouquet	$40		2443	2 1/2" Pin Box, Heart or Round, Flower Garden	$32
377	3 1/2" Egg Shaped, w/Applied Flowers	$28		2486	2 1/2" Pin Box, Oval w/Pansies	$18
394	5 1/2" Egg Shaped, Legged, Spring Bouquet	$45		2487	2" Round Basket Weave Box w/Butterfly on Lid	$15
397	4" Heart w/Flowers and Butterfly	$20		2526	Golden Laurel	$40
425	Egg Box w/Hand Painted Flowers	$18		2549	4" Round w/Rose Design	$18
426	4" Egg w/Floral Decoration	$12		2575	3 1/2" Basketweave w/Bird on Lid	$23
455	3" Covered and Hinged, Antiqued Bisque	$15		2615	Shamrock Shaped with Shamrocks	$12
460	50th Anniversary Trunk	$10		2641	2" Pin w/Rose Design	$10
472	4 1/2" Lime Green Egg w/Applied Purple Flowers	$12		2688	Heart Shaped w/Poem to Mother	$12
495	3 1/2" x 4" Gold Edged w/Flowers	$28		2710	3" Pin Box w/Baby on Lid	$10
516	6 1/2" Glazed Egg w/Ribbon & Flowers	$23		2733	3 1/2" Pin, Shaped Like Swan	$18
542	6 1/2" Heart w/Applied Pink Roses	$23		2767	4" Oval, w/Floral Design	$15
550	3 1/4" Round w/Applied Flowers	$20		2771	White Bisque w/Butterfly on Lid	$20
613	4" Egg w/Flowers and Butterfly	$12		2786	3 1/2" w/Christmas Girl Mouse	$15
00617	3" Flower w/Butterfly Handle	$12		2788	3 1/2" w/Christmas Mouse	$15
642	2 1/2" Box of the Month, Antique Ivory Bisque	$10		02874	2 1/2" Heart Shaped w/Flower and Gold Trim	$18
658	Turtle	$12		02984	2" Fan Shaped w/Rose & Ribbon Design	$10
00658	2 1/2" Various Styles on Wooden Base	$13		02984	2" Round w/Rose & Ribbon Design	$10
672	2 1/4" Gift Box w/Silver Ribbon	$14		3107	4" Oval, Silver Wedding Anniversary	$10
673	4" Gift Box w/Silver Ribbon	$18		03177	1 1/2" Heart Shaped w/Flowers	$8
00736	Heart Shaped w/Roses - 1993	$18		3231	Apple Shaped w/Hand Painted Flowers	$33
784	6" Elegant White w/Rose	$20		03262	4 1/2" Box of the Month w/Angel Handle	$12
824	Round, Milkglass w/Applied Flowers	$18		03297	2" Bisque Heart, Purple w/White Lid w/Purple Flowers	$9
00848	4 1/2" Heart Shaped w/Shamrocks - 1992	$12		3375	4" Round w/Gold Accents	$18
872	2 1/2" Box w/Gold Bow	$18		03419	Ladies Picture Hat w/Pink Ribbon and Flower	$13
873	White Box w/Gold Bow	$15		3433	3 1/2" Pin Box, Round w/Birds on Top	$15
923	Gold Flowers & Trim	$39		3447	4" w/Angel of the Month Lid	$30
964	Pink w/Hand on Lid	$45		03678	5" Egg w/Branch Handle and Applied Flowers	$30
1019	3" Heart Shape w/Flowers "I Love You"	$12		03686	Egg w/Branch Handle & Applied Flowers - 1983	$18
1039	Round Pink Bisque w/Applied Forget-Me-Nots	$38		03688	2 1/2" Heart Shaped w/Applied Rose & Lovebirds - 1983	$18
1049	Egg Box, Fleur de Lis	$18		03692	3" w/Bow and Flowers - Each	$12
1055	3 1/2" Lady w/Cake	$30		03694	Egg, Yellow Lace w/Yellow Ribbon & Bow	$35
1223	2 1/2" Box w/Ribbon and Butterfly	$18		03695	Upright Egg w/Bow & Applied Flowers	$25
1263	2 1/2" Footed Shell Shape w/Applied Flowers	$13		03701	3" Heart Shape w/ Teddy Bear Handle	$10
1268	2 1/2" Footed Round or Heart Shape w/Applied Flowers	$13		3780	2 3/4" Pin, Bisque Floral Bouquet	$18
1274	2 1/2" Pin, Floral	$13		03780	Heart Shaped Box w/Applied Flowers	$18
1358	3 3/4" Round Portrait Box with Three Legs	$35		03934	Round Shaped w/Ballet Slippers on Lid - 1983	$15
1377	3 1/2" Heart Shaped w/Gold Bow	$18		04087	4" Egg w/Pink or Yellow Bow & Flowers, Each - 1984	$15
1408	2 1/2" Heart Shaped w/Flowers and Wheat	$10		04089	Lt. Blue Egg w/Purple Bow & Flowers	$24
1429	Decorated Egg, w/Bow	$15		04088	2 1/2" Square w/Applied Flowers - 1984	$10
1485	3 1/2" Egg w/Wheat & Red Poppies	$15		04092	2 1/2" Round w/Applied Flower - 1984	$10
1664	4 Legged Trinket Box with Floral Design	$14		04095	3 3/4" Sunflower - 1984	$16
1681	Box w/Ribbon and Applied Flower	$15		04232	5" Girl Praying "My Rosary" - 1984	$23
1691	6" Egg w/Yellow Ribbon & Flowers - 1963	$35		04238	Heart Shaped - 1984	$16
1782	4" Colonial Lady Pin Box	$20		4245	4 1/2" Egg, w/Bow and Floral Design	$16
1893	3 1/2" Heart Shaped Box w/Floral Design	$12		4473	2 1/2" Egg Shaped Box	$10
01912	Heart Shaped Box, Garden Bouquet	$10		4741	4 1/2" Egg-Shaped Candy w/Flowers and Bow on Lid	$23
1924	2" Heart Shaped Pin Box w/Roses	$10		4742	4 1/2" Egg-Shaped Candy w/Flowers and Bow on Lid	$25
1926	4" Footed Covered Box w/Roses	$25		04943	Basket weave w/Cat on Lid - 1985	$12
1935	5 1/2" Fan Shape Covered Box	$28		5090	3 1/2" Pin Box w/Owl Decoration	$13
1937	3" Fan Shaped w/Roses	$18		5206	3 1/2" Pin Box	$12
1947	4" Footed Covered Box, Violets	$25		5524	4" Egg w/Floral Design	$18
1948	3" Round Box w/Violets	$22		5528	4" Egg Box w/Yellow Flowers	$18
1952	3" Fan Shape Pin Box	$12		06137	3 1/2" Heart Shaped w/Lacy Edges - 1987	$12
1956	Oval Shape w/Flowers	$15		06236	4" Swan w/Pink Flowers - 1987	$18
1958	Pin Box, Snail w/Violets	$25		06838	4" Egg w/Flowers & Ribbon	$12
1959	5 3/4" Fan Shaped w/Violets	$15		6051	Hinged Heart Shaped Box w/Victorian Motif	$28
1963	2" Oblong Shape Pin Box w/Violets	$10		06839	Egg w/Purple Ribbon and Flowers - 1988	$15
1964	2" Pin Box w/Violets	$10		6953	3 1/2" x 5" w/Victorian Motif	$32
1974	4" White Daisy, Footed	$18		6954	3 1/4" Hinged, Grand Piano w/Victorian Motif	$38
01985	2 1/2" Heart Shape Box w/White Daisies	$14		6959	4 1/2" Round Hinged Box, Lavender Rose	$25
2020	5 1/2" Fan Shape Box	$25		07391	3" Round Box, Black w/Pink Roses	$12
2151	2 1/2" Footed Round Box, Flower Garden	$35		7519	3 1/2" Egg Shaped w/Flowers	$15
2163	3" Card Shaped, Viola	$12		7585	2 1/2" Swan w/Applied Flowers, Glazed	$12
2209	5" Egg w/Violets, or Roses	$19		7687	2 1/2" Pale Blue Box w/Blue Flowers	$12
2260	2 1/4" Pin Box, Flowers of the Month	$10		7697	4" Red Heart w/Angel on Lid	$18
2310	2" Three Footed Box, Oblong w/Gold Design	$10		7786	Heart Shaped, 25th Anniversary	$10
2318	5 1/2" w/Gold Bow and Applied Rose, Glazed	$25		07992	3 1/2" Round w/Applied Red Roses	$15
2320	3 1/4" Cat in Yellow Dress	$15		08140	3" Heart Shape w/Herons	$15
2369	Heart shaped box, "A Token of Love"	$10		8187	3 3/4" Heart w/Floral Design	$12
2381	3 1/4" Heart Shaped Box w/Holly	$10		8222	4 1/2" Chair w/Floral Design	$12

BOXES (cont'd)

11155	2 1/2" Hinged Chest - 1997	$17
11156	2 3/4" Hinged Heart - 1997	$17
11157	3 3/8" Hinged Boot - 1997	$17
11158	2 1/4" Hinged Grand Piano - 1997	$17
11159	2 1/4" Hinged Heart - 1997	$17
11160	2 1/4" Hinged Purse - 1997	$17
11161	3 3/4" Hinged Bell - 1997	$18
11162	2 1/4" Hinged Watering Can - 1997	$18
11163	3" Hinged Egg - 1997	$18
11164	2 1/2" Hinged Chest - 1997	$17
11165	2 3/4" Hinged Heart - 1997	$17
11166	3 3/8" Hinged Boot - 1997	$17
11167	2 1/4" Hinged Grand Piano - 1997	$17
11168	2 1/4" Hinged Heart - 1997	$17
11169	2 1/4" Hinged Purse - 1997	$18
11170	3 3/4" Hinged Bell - 1997	$18
11171	2 1/4" Hinged Watering Can - 1997	$18
11172	3" Hinged Egg - 1997	$18
11173	2 1/4" Hinged Box with Ribbon & Roses, Chest - 1997	$17
11174	2 1/4" Hinged Box with Ribbon & Roses, Heart - 1997	$17
11175	2 1/4" Hinged Box with Ribbon & Roses, Boot - 1997	$17
11176	2 1/4" Hinged Box with Ribbon & Roses, Piano - 1997	$17
11177	2 1/4" Hinged Box with Ribbon & Roses, Heart - 1997	$17
11178	2 1/4" Hinged Box with Ribbon & Roses, Purse - 1997	$18
11179	2 1/4" Hinged Box with Ribbon & Roses, Bell - 1997	$18
11180	2 1/4" Hinged Box with Ribbon & Roses, Watering Can	$18
11181	2 1/4" Hinged Box with Ribbon & Roses, Egg - 1997	$18
11180	2 1/2" Hinged Watering Can - 1997	$18
11182	4 1/4" Hinged Chest - 1997	$17
11183	2 1/4" Hinged Watering Can - 1997	$18
11184	3 3/8" Hinged Boot - 1997	$17
11185	3 3/4" Hinged Bell - 1997	$18
11186	2 1/4" Hinged Grand Piano - 1997	$17
11187	2 1/4" Hinged Egg with Roses - 1997	$17
11188	4" Hinged Box with Angel, White and Gold - 1997	$19
11189	4" Hinged, Cape Hatteras Lighthouse - 1997	$18
11190	2" Hinged Box, Flower - 1997	$19
11191	3 1/2" Hinged Box w/Kissing Angels, White and Gold - 1997	$21
11195	2 1/4" Hinged Box, Elephant - 1997	$13
11196	2 1/4" Hinged Box, Cat - 1997	$13
11197	2 1/2" Hinged Box, Toy Soldier - 1997	$13
11198	2 3/4" Hinged Box, Rabbit - 1997	$13
11199	2 3/4" Hinged Box, Teddy Tear - 1997	$13
11208	2" Hinged Box, Daisies - 1997	$13
11209	2" Hinged Box, Tulips - 1997	$13
11210	2" Hinged Box, Roses - 1997	$13
11211	2" Hinged Box, Pansies - 1997	$13
11212	2" Hinged Box, Lilies - 1997	$13
11225	4 1/2" Hinged Round Box, Musical "Edelweiss" - 1997	$35
11227	4 1/2" Hinged Round Box, Musical "Für Elise" - 1997	$35
11322	2 3/4" Hinged Telephone with Ribbon & Roses - 1997	$17
11324	2 3/4" Hinged Box, Telephone Shaped with Roses - 1997	$17
11326	2 2/3" Hinged Box, Telephone Shaped with Violets - 1997	$17
11327	3 3/8" Hinged Box, Boot Shaped with Violets - 1997	$17
11328	2 3/4" Hinged Box, Tea Pot Shaped with Violets - 1997	$16
11329	2 3/4" Hinged Box, Egg Shaped with Violets - 1997	$18
11331	2 1/2" Hinged Box, Grand Piano with Violets - 1997	$17
11332	3 3/4" Hinged Box, Bell Shaped with Violets - 1997	$18
11344	2 1/2" Hinged Box with Butterfly, 3 Assorted - 1998	$16
11345	3 3/4" Hinged Box with Girl, White and Gold - 1997	$18
11346	3" Hinged box with Manger Scene, White and Gold - 1997	$18
11347	3 3/4" Hinged Box with Angel, White and Gold - 1997	$16
11348	3 3/4" Hinged Box with Clown, 2 Assorted - 1997	$17
11351	2 3/4" Hinged Box Dog in Dog House - 1997	$18
11352	3" Hinged Box, Penguin - 1997	$16
11353	2 1/2" Round Hinge Box w/Victorian Motif, 4 Assorted - 1997	$16
11356	3 3/4" Hinged Box, Bride and Groom - 1997	$18
11387	2 7/8" Hinged Heart Shaped Box with Roses - 1997	$18
11388	2 1/4" Hinged Purse with Roses - 1997	$18
11389	2 3/4" Heart Shaped Box with Roses - 1997	$16
11606	Ball Shaped Hinged Box, Blue Bisque Baltic Rose - 1997	$17

11607	Round Hinged Box, Blue Bisque, Baltic Rose - 1997	$17
11609	Ball Oval Covered Box, Blue Bisque, Baltic Rose - 1997	$10
11876	3" Hinged, Limoge Like, Many Varieties - 1998	$18
11981	3" Hinged, Limoge Like, Many Varieties - 1998	$18
20458	"Nest Egg" Box w/Forget-Me-Nots and Stones	$30
40604	Eastern Elegance	$32

BROWN HERITAGE

051	Floral - Pitcher and Bowl	$115
055	Floral - Sugar and Creamer	$65
062	Floral - Coffee Pot	$200
068	Floral - Sugar and Creamer	$65
072	Floral - Cup and Saucer	$38
072	Fruit - Cup and Saucer	$40
113	9" Plate w/Plastic Handle	$55
117	Floral - Compote	$95
185	9" Plate w/Plastic Handle	$55
328	Floral - Miniature Pitcher and Bowl	$38
469	Fruit - Covered Candy Dish	$60
476	Floral - Miniature Teapot	$60
478	Fruit - Miniature Teapot	$60
480	Fruit - Bone Dish	$25
481	Floral - 6 1/4 Plate	$15
561	Fruit - Cup & Saucer	$45
562	Fruit - 7 1/4" Plate	$32
563	Fruit - Bone Dish	$25
563	Floral - Bone Dish	$20
607	Fruit - Salt and Pepper Shakers	$30
613	Floral - Salt and Pepper Shakers	$30
689	Fruit - Compote	$125
703	Floral - Cup and Saucer	$28
1265	Fruit - Tumbleup	$95
1861	Floral - 9" Plate, Circa 1975	$45
1862	Floral - Mini Vase	$14
1864	Floral - Snack Set	$35
1866	Floral - Coffee Pot	$175
1867	Floral - Sugar and Creamer	$65
1869	Floral - Bone Dish	$20
1871	Floral - 8 1/2" Vase w/2 Handles	$65
1873	Floral - Pitcher and Bowl	$58
1874	Floral - Pitcher and Bowl	$55
1882	Floral - 7 1/2" Plate	$25
1883	Floral - Cup and Saucer	$42
2222	Floral - 9" Plate	$38
2222	Fruit - 9" Plate	$40
2635	Floral - Demi Cup and Saucer	$38
2636	Fruit - Demi Cup and Saucer	$38
2720	Fruit - Covered Candy Dish	$45
2760	Fruit - Salt and Pepper	$30
2761	Floral - Jam Jar w/Tray	$75
2762	Fruit - Jam Jar w/Tray	$85
2763	Floral - 5 1/2" Vase	$22
2764	Fruit - 5 1/2" Vase	$28
3112	Floral - Teapot	$155
3113	Fruit - Teapot	$185
3114	Floral - Pitcher	$150
3115	Fruit - Pitcher	$150
3116	Floral - 8 3/4" Vase	$65
3117	Fruit - 8 3/4" Vase	$65
3118	Fruit - 3 1/4" Vase	$18
3118	Floral - 3 1/4" Vase	$18
3288	Floral - 3 1/2" Pitcher and Bowl	$35
3289	Fruit - 3 1/2" Pitcher and Bowl	$35
4239	Floral - 13" Oil Lamp	$225
4277	Floral - 11" Oil Lamp	$210
4283	Fruit - 11" Oil Lamp	$210
5649	Floral - Sauce Boat w/Under Plate	$85
20127	Floral - Nappy, 3 Shapes, Each	$32
20127	Fruit - Nappy, 3 Shapes, Each	$32
20128	Fruit - Coaster	$12
20128	Floral - Coaster	$12
20129	Floral - 2 Tier Tidbit Tray	$85

20129	Fruit - 2 Tier Tidbit Tray	$95
20130	Fruit - Snack Set	$35
20131	Floral - Tidbit Tray	$32
20334	Fruit - 4 1/2" Dish	$30
20334	Floral - 4 1/2" Dish	$30
20591	Fruit - Coffee Pot	$155
20592	Fruit - Creamer and Sugar	$75

BUSTS

219	5 1/2" Kennedy	$45
831	5 1/2" Provincial Boy and Girl, Each	$40
1114	5 1/2" Lincoln	$28
1121	5 1/2" Washington	$25
1131	5 1/2" Robert E. Lee	$38
1146	5 1/2" Ben Franklin	$25
1147	5 1/2" Mendelssohn	$35
1161	5 1/2" Brahms	$30
1166	6" Chopin	$30
1176	5 1/2" Beethoven	$30
2198	5 1/2" T. Roosevelt	$28
2295	5 3/4" Mark Twain	$28
2297	5 1/2" U.S. Grant	$25
2301	5 1/2" Charles Dickens	$25
2303	7" Franz Liszt	$42
2321	7" Mendelssohn	$50
2508	5 3/4" William Shakespeare	$28
2509	5 1/2" Edgar Allan Poe	$40
2511	6" Bernard Shaw	$40
3902	5 1/2" Girl and Boy, White w/Gold - Pair	$45

BUTTER DISHES

3294	6 3/4" Mr. Toodles	$150
3363	7" Daisytime	$20
3739	7 1/2" Pear N Apple	$20
5863	Hot Poppy	$35
5964	Fiesta	$28
6468	7 1/2" Mushroom Forest - 1970	$28
6514	7 3/4" Bossie the Cow - 1970	$25
6724	Fruit Fantasia	$22
7127	Yellow Tulip	$28
7297	Tisket A Tasket	$28
7309	Dancing Leaves	$26

BUTTERFLIES

2317	3 1/4" Butterfly on Flowers, Each	$22
2318	4 1/2" Butterfly on Flower, Each	$28
2319	5 1/2" Butterfly on Flower, Each	$32
2414	5 1/2" Butterfly on Flower - 1983	$24
7213	4 1/2" Butterfly on Flowers	$22
7219	4 1/2" Butterfly on Flowers	$22
07784	3" Butterfly on Flower, 3 Assorted	$12
07785	4" Butterfly on Flower - 1991	$22
10127	3 1/2" Butterfly on Dogwood Branch	$18
13037	2" Blue Butterflies on Branch w/Flower - 1999	$18
13117	1 1/2" Butterfly on Purple Flower - 1999	$25
13118	3" Butterfly on Flower, Buckeye Butterfly - 1999	$28
13121	3" Butterfly on Flower, Black & White Butterfly - 1999	$25

CANDLE WARE

208	Holder - White w/Sponge Gold and Flower, Pair	$55
285	Holder - Pink China w/Gold & Lily of the Valley, Pair	$58
363	Holder - 5 1/2" w/Pink Rose	$40
383	Holder - 5" w/Applied Pink Rose	$38
527	Holder - 6 1/4" Cherubs w/Urns	$38
0645	Holder - 3 1/2" White w/Ribbon Design - 1987	$18
681	Holder - 3 1/4" Shiny Finish, 4 Piece Set	$35
687	Holder - Elegant White w/Applied Rose w/Gold Trim, Pair	$25
688	Holder - Elegant White w/Applied Rose w/Gold Trim, Pair	$18
694	Holder - 25th Wedding Anniversary	

698	Holder - 5" White w/Applied Flowers, Glazed	$35
771	Holder - Pink w/Forget-Me-Nots, Pair	$62
835	Holder - 4" Milk China w/Applied Flowers, Pair	$65
836	Holder - 8" Milk China w/Applied Flowers, Pair	$75
899	Holder - Antique Ivory Bisque w/Applied Flowers	$22
902	Holder - Antique Ivory Bisque w/Applied Flowers	$20
987	Holder - 6" Bird Bath w/Angel and Birds	$30
1103	Holder - 50th Anniversary	$10
1316	Climbers - Angel w/Halo, Noel, Pair	$40
1390	Holder - 3 1/2" White Ware	$30
1453	Climber - 3 1/4" Angel w/Musical Instrument	$15
1593	Holder - Flower Shaped w/Leaves and Bumble Bee	$14
1848	Holder - 3 1/2" White Bisque w/Pink Roses, Pair	$50
1908	Holder - 4" Blue Bisque	$30
2109	Climber - 2 3/4" Pixie, Pair	$20
02326	Holder - 3 1/2" Mouse in Dress	$12
2559	Holder - 4" Angel Boy & Girl, Pair	$22
2588	Holder - 3 1/2" Angel Reading a Book	$15
2773	Climber - 2 1/2" Angel & Devil, Pair	$16
2959	Holder - 6 1/4" Luscious Lilac, Pair	$55
03110	Holder - Silver Wedding Anniversary, Pair	$18
3211	Holder - 2" Milk White w/Applied Forget-Me-Nots, Pair	$50
3256	Holder - w/Small Flowers, Pair	$35
03427	Ring - Girl Praying and Angel Laying on Tummy, Pair	$14
3564	Holder - 3" Renaissance	$18
03772	Holder - Ruffled 25th Wedding Anniversary, Pair	$18
04069	Holder - 50th Anniversary	$14
4745	Holder - White w/Applied Flowers, Pair	$35
5444	Holder - White Bisque w/Applied Flowers	$35
06397	Holder - 4 1/2" Turkeys - 1985	$12
06437	Holder - 5" Duck - 1997	$12
6526	Holder - 3" Renaissance	$18
6940	Holder - 1 1/2" 25th Anniversary, Pair	$20
6941	Holder - 1 1/2" 50th Anniversary, Pair	$20
7112	Holder - 4 5/8" Happy Anniversary	$10
07278	Ring - Angel - 1989	$9
7790	Holder - w/Bell, Flowers and Ribbon	$10
7798	Holder - Anniversary	$15
9958	Holder - 5" White Porcelain w/Pink & Blue Flowers, Pair	$55
10582	Holder - 25th Anniversary	$15
10593	Holder - 50th Anniversary	$15
11059	Holder - Reclining Angel, Milk White Glazed, Pair, 1997	$20
11060	Holder - Standing Angel, Milk White Glazed, Pair, 1997	$20
11061	Holder - Standing Angel, Milk White Glazed, Pair, 1997	$20
11096	Holder - 2 1/2" Votive, Milk White Glazed, Each, 1997	$10

CANDY DISHES

221	4 5/8" Candy Dish w/Lid, Antiqued Bisque	$22
359	6 1/4" Candy Dish, White on White	$15
360	White on White w/Handle	$27
721	4 1/4" White China Swan w/Applied Pink Roses & Gold	$65
772	5" Antique Ivory Bisque, Basketweave w/Applied Flowers	$24
782	7 5/8" Covered Candy Dish, Elegant White w/Gold Rose	$32
997	50th Anniversary Footed Candy Dish with Lid	$18
998	25th Anniversary Footed Candy Dish with Lid	$15
1037	7 1/2" Candy Dish w/ Lid, Ice Pink Bisque w/Applied Flowers	$70
1048	Candy Dish with Applied Flowers	$28
1084	Footed Candy Dish with Lid, Cosmos	$55
1187	6" Candy Dish with Lid, Milk China	$45
1188	5" Candy Dish w/Pink and Blue Flowers	$25
1192	5" Candy Dish with Lid, Milk China w/Roses	$60
1377	5" Footed Candy Dish with Lid, Violet Heirloom	$50
1377	5" Footed Candy Dish with Lid, Rose Heirloom	$50
1519	8" White Bisque Candy Dish with Lid, Applied Flowers	$40
1594	Covered Candy Dish, Antiqued Bisque	$28
1908	4 1/4" Candy on Large Pedestal	$27
1961	4 1/2" Candy Dish, Viola	$27
2089	6 1/2" Candy Dish with Lid, Della Robbia	$35
2210	6 1/2" Candy, Red w/Cherub on Lid	$40
2459	7 3/4" Candy Dish, White w/Blue Grapes	$50
2526	4 1/2" Covered Candy, Golden Laurel	$25
2527	5 1/4" Covered Candy, Golden Lauren	$27

CANDY DISHES (cont'd)

2528	6 1/2" Covered Candy, Golden Laurel	$28
2604	4 1/2" Covered Candy, 25th Anniversary	$18
2606	4 1/2" Covered Candy, 50th Wedding Anniversary	$13
2908	6 1/2" Covered Candy, White Ware	$22
2911	Covered Candy, Fleur de Lis	$18
2931	5" Candy, Shaped Like A Chicken, Yellow	$18
2939	7 1/2" Candy, Luscious Lilac	$80
3030	6 1/4" Covered Candy, Vineyard Line	$18
3549	6 1/4" Covered Candy, Gold Leaf	$40
3766	Covered Candy, Pear N Apple	$18
3781	4 1/2" Round Shaped Candy, Floral Bisque Bouquet	$32
3836	5" Oval Shape Covered Candy Dish, Rose Design	$18
4341	5" Square or Round Candy Dish, Floral Bisque Bouquet	$32
4670	6 1/4" Candy Dish, Floral Mood	$15
4673	5 3/4" Candy Dish, Roses	$20
4669	5 3/4" Candy Dish, Floral Mood	$10
4637	Candy Dish with Applied Flowers	$28
5370	5 1/2" Covered Candy Dish, Violet Heirloom	$50
5511	Covered Candy Dish "Happy Anniversary"	$18
05652	5" Halloween Pumpkin w/Witch Lid	$30
6078	7" Double Handled, Orange & Black	$18
6290	Covered Candy Dish, "Happy Anniversary"	$15
6508	4" Anniversary w/Bells & Gold Trim	$15
6809	Covered Candy Dish Paisley Fantasia	$25
7297	7" Candy Bucket w/Handle & Forget-Me-Nots	$40
7364	5" Candy Bucket w/Handle & Applied Fruit	$40
20429	6 3/4" Pink w/Gold Flowers & Trim	$40

CANISTER SETS

701	Fruit on Vine, 4 Piece Set	$85
1501	Garden Daisy, 4 Piece Set	$60
2616	Raised Clover, 4 Piece Set	$70
3487	Della Robbia, 4 Piece Set	$110
3733	Green Orchard, 4 Piece Set	$115
3761	Pear N Apple, Green, 4 Piece Set	$95
4084	Brown Bag Shaped, 4 Piece Set	$120
4131	Pear N Apple, Gold, 4 Piece Set	$95
4595	Pink Daisy, 4 Piece Set	$75
4612	Blue Country Charm, 4 Piece Set	$150
5254	Fiesta, 4 Piece Set	$120
5308	Hot Poppy, 4 Piece Set	$135
5557	Hens w/Daisies, 4 Piece Set	$80
5930	Fruit & Flower, 4 Piece Set	$75
5948	Carrots, 4 Piece Set	$75
5948	Yellow Peppers, 4 Piece Set	$75
6353	Mushroom Forest, 4 Piece Set	$60
6447	Romance, 4 Piece Set	$95
6561	Mushroom, 4 Piece Set	$90
6721	Fruit Fantasia, 4 Piece Set	$95
7065	Tisket A Tasket, 4 Piece Set	$95
7122	Yellow Tulip, 4 Piece Set	$65
7277	Falling Leaves, 4 Piece Set	$85
7530	Floral Basketweave w/Butterfly, 4 Piece Set	$85
7979	Harvest Pansy, 4 Piece Set	$65

CAROUSEL HORSES

00317	5 1/4" Set of 3	$75
00874	11" Musical Carousel "Carousel Waltz"	$135
01521C	6 3/4" Plays "Camelot"	$35
05500	7" Carousel w/3 Horses	$28
08620	10" Horse on Brass Stand	$60
08621	10" Horse on Brass Stand	$60
08622	10" Horse on Brass Stand	$60
08623	10" Horse on Brass Stand	$60
08624	12" Musical Horse "The Sting" Limited to 2000	$125
08625	12" Musical Horse "Stars & Stripes Forever" Limited to 2000	$125
08626	12" Musical Horse "Carousel Waltz" Limited to 2000	$125
08627	12" Musical Horse "Camelot", Limited to 2000	$125
08637	12" Musical Horse "Beautiful Dreamer" Limited Edition	$125

08638	12" Musical Horse "Chariots of Fire" Limited to 3500	$125
08639	10" Musical Horse "Fascination" Limited to 5000	$100
08640	10" Horse on Brass Stand	$60
08641	10" Musical Horse "Camelot" Limited to 5000	$100
08642	10" Horse on Brass Stand	$60
08643	8" Musical Horse "The Sting" Limited Edition	$85
08645	8" Musical Horse "White Christmas" Limited to 4700	$85
08646	6" Musical Horse "Carousel Waltz" Limited to 6500	$50
08647	6" Musical Horse "Carousel Waltz" Limited to 6500	$50
08658	Merry-Go-Round w/Canopy "Carousel Waltz" Limited Edition	$175
11442	4" Musical Horse on Oval Base "Carousel Waltz" 1 of 3	$36
11442	4" Musical Horse on Oval Base "Camelot" 2 of 3	$36
11442	4" Musical Horse on Oval Base "The Sting" 3 of 3	$36
11445	4" Musical Horse on Round Base "Carousel Waltz" 1 of 3	$36
11445	4" Musical Horse on Round Base "Camelot" 2 of 3	$36
11445	4" Musical Horse on Round Base "The Sting" 3 of 3	$36
11451	7" Birthday Carousel "Happy Birthday to You" 1st of 8 in Set	$40
11452	7" Birthday Carousel "Daddy's Little Girl" 2nd of 8 in Set	$40
11453	7" Birthday Carousel "You are my Sunshine" 3rd of 8 in Set	$40
11454	7" Birthday Carousel "Oh You Beautiful Doll" 4th of 8 in Set	$40
11455	7" Birthday Carousel "Que Sera, Sera" 5th of 8 in Set	$40
11456	7" Birthday Carousel "Talk To The Animals" 6th of 8 in Set	$40
11457	7" Birthday Carousel "Over The Rainbow" 7th of 8 in Set	$40
11458	7" Birthday Carousel "Skaters Waltz" 8th of 8 in Set	$40
11460	4" Horse on Brass Stand, 4 Assorted, Each	$15
11465	4" Rocking Horses, 4 Assorted, Each	$18
66408	12" Horse & Jeweled Carousel Top "The Sting" - 1988	$65

CHEESE DISHES

014	Round Swiss Cheese w/Mouse Handle	$25
916	Plate - w/Cheeses and Mouse	$20
799	9" Tray w/Knife	$30
1419	4 3/4" Barrel w/CHEESE	$22
1862	Plate - w/Cheeses and Mouse	$20
7136	Swiss Cheese Wedge w/Mouse Handle	$25

CHILD WITHIN COLLECTION, THE

11628	"Snowflake" the Snowman	$10
11629	"Flora" the Rose Bouquet	$10
11630	"Chrissy" the Christmas Tree	$10
11631	"Vinney" the Bunch of Grapes	$10
11632	"Sunshine" the Sunflower	$10
11633	"Peanut" the Elephant	$10
11634	"Rudy" the Reindeer	$10
11635	"Elsie" the Cow	$10
11636	"Frosty" the Polar Bear	$10
11637	"Budd" the Frog	$10
11638	"Tweety" the Bird in Nest	$10
11639	"Whiskers" the Rabbit	$10
11640	"Buttercup" the Butterfly	$10
11641	"Buzz" the Bumble Bee	$10
11649	"Pinky" the Watermelon	$10
11650	"Mack" the Apple	$10
11651	"Sweetie" the Strawberry	$10

CHRISTMAS ITEMS

019	Bell, Christmas Snowball	$28
024	Planter, Bloomer Girl	$45
040	Mug w/Red Stripes and Holly	$8
051	8" Planter, Girl w/Muff and Hat in Green	$45
052	Salt and Pepper Shakers, Santa & Mrs. Claus on Sleigh	$25
00052	3" Christmas Mouse w/Bluebird	$12
054/96	Tree Hors D'oeuvre Holder w/Salt and Pepper, 3 Piece Set	$15
072	Little Boy Carolers, 3 Piece Set	$75
072	Little Girl in Christmas Outfit Playing Violin	$30
072	Little Girl in Christmas Outfit Holding Lantern	$30
072	Little Girl in Christmas Outfit Holding Song Book	$30
073	Salt and Pepper Shakers, Mr. and Mrs. Claus	$22
102	4 1/2" Little Miss Mistletoe	$45
107	4" Miss Mistletoe Tying Her Slipper	$35

00129	8 3/4" Old World Irish Santa Musical "Christmas in Killarney"	$35
00147	6" Musical Nativity Scene Waterball "Silent Night"	$50
166	Girl Planter w/Muff and Hat	$25
223	Leaf Shaped Nappy, White Bisque w/Poinsettia	$22
267	6" Children w/Baby Musical "Oh Come All Ye Faithful"	$45
286	Angel Musicians, 3 Piece Set	$75
00314	5 1/2" Holy Family Musical Waterball "Silent Night"	$25
450	8" Santa Clause Wall Plate	$28
492	3"x 6" Planter or Card Holder w/Candy Cane "NOEL"	$35
600	4" Tree Shaped Card Holder	$16
624	Candy Cane Cart Planter or Card Holder	$28
625	3 1/2" Candy Cane Girl Ornament	$20
626	Four Angels w/Hats, Scarves & Mittens on Candy Cane	$60
638	6 3/4" Christmas Carolers Musical "Silent Night," circa 1983	$39
707	3" Candle Climbers, Santa and Mrs. Claus	$25
707	3" Reindeer Candle Holders, Pair	$25
709	Salt & Pepper Shakers, Santa and Deer	$24
722	Angel w/Lamb Musical "Silent Night"	$39
724	Girl in Red Dress w/Fur Trimmed Coat and Muff	$28
725	4 1/2" Planter, Teddy Bear w/Holly and Ribbon	$12
743	2 1/4" Christmas Elf w/Bluebird	$12
00746	3" Bell w/Christmas Mouse	$10
758	5 1/2" Santa Claus	$18
770	7" Christmas Sleigh, Candy Box	$80
771	Head Vase, Christmas Girl w/Muff	$110
868	Mug, Santa on Front w/Mrs. Claus on Back	$25
1086	Planter, Christmas Mouse	$18
1096	8" Plate, Christmas Tree	$30
1146	3 1/4" Bells, Christmas Boy and Girl, Each	$15
1202	9 1/2" Reindeer Card Holder	$30
1259	Angel in Green Dress Playing Musical Instrument, Each	$22
01286	6" Old World Irish Santa	$13
1303	Mug, w/Three Cardinals, Red Ribbon and Holly	$12
1336	4 1/2" Bell, House w/Santa	$28
1383	7 3/4" Santa Decanter Bottle and Six Mugs	$75
1418	3 1/2" Bell, Angel Playing Instrument, Each	$18
1475	4 1/2" Santa Boot	$22
1477	Salt and Pepper Reindeer	$17
1496	6" Planter, Santa on Reindeer	$25
1498	Salt & Pepper, Santa Claus Face	$18
1499	6 1/2" Vase, Christmas Girl Head	$35
1556	4" Salt and Pepper Shakers, Candlestick	$22
1665	4" Christmas Girl w/Gift	$23
1669	3" Salt and Pepper Shakers, Little Deer, Pair	$12
1734	4 1/2" Santa's Helper	$22
1826	Holly Girl w/Muff and Cape	$30
1889	6" Musical Box Christmas Angel	$28
1996	5 1/2" Shelf Sitters, Mr. & Mrs. Santa Claus, Pair	$55
02037	3" Christmas Cat Bell - 1983	$12
02039	3" Christmas Angel Bell - 1983	$12
2056	6" Christmas Shopping Bag	$12
2029	Candle Holders - Holly and Gold Decoration, Pair	$33
2097	Santa Cookie Jar	$110
2246	Salt & Pepper Shakers, Rocking Horse and Drum	$18
2300	4 1/2" Boy Putting On Santa Suit	$25
2305	NOEL Angel Candleholders - Set of 4	$65
2306	Red Boot w/Holly and Gold Buckle	$25
2329	7 1/4" Santa in Chimney Illuminated House	$49
2391	Fan Shaped Box w/Holly and Red and Green Trim	$19
2395	3 1/2" Bell w/Holly and Red and Green Trim	$15
2410	8" Dish, Christmas Tree Shaped w/Santa Face	$25
02477	2 1/2" Animal, Christmas Mouse, Each	$15
2509	Salt and Pepper, Holly w/Green and Red Ribbon	$12
2540	3" Kissing Christmas Cats, Pair	$18
2544	2 3/4" Boot w/Holly	$18
2687	8 1/4" Plate, Decorated Tree	$15
02788	Box w/Dog or Cat Wearing Santa Hat	$15
2886	9 1/2" Plate, Christmas Tree	$16
2914	5" Elf Head Planter	$15
02944	7" Little Shepherd Musical "Oh Little Town of Bethlehem"	$39
3320	Christmas Tree Tidbit Tray	$18
03392	Candy Cane Mug w/Teddy Bear	$14
03641	2 1/2" Christmas Angel Candleholders, Pair	$18

3656	8" Planter, Santa w/Bag	$28
3752	5" Holly Box w/Red Ribbon	$28
03909	Basket w/Holly & Red Ribbon	$12
04160	Kissing Mr. and Mrs. Santa Claus	$10
4164	3" Salt and Pepper Shaker Snow Couple, Pair	$18
4224	7" Santa in Window Illuminated House	$42
4281	Salt and Pepper Shakers, 3" Bell Shape	$16
4284	3 1/2" Mug, Green w/Elf Handle	$10
4370	Rudolph Salt and Pepper Shakers	$15
4405	3" Snow Babies, 3 Piece Set	$45
4709	3 3/4" Snowman Head Mug	$18
04713	Caroling Mice, 3 Piece Set	$20
4799	Girl in Red Skirt and White Boots, Marika's Original, Each	$25
05154	Salt & Pepper, Panda Bears w/Wreath and Candycane - 1985	$12
05414	Kissing Mr. and Mrs. Santa Claus	$18
05594	2 1/2" Angel Ornaments, Set of 3	$45
05658	6" Santa Planter - 1986	$18
05816	Ornament, House Decorated for Christmas - 1986	$15
05877	3 1/2" Candle Holders, Christmas Kitty - 1987	$20
5999	Salt and Pepper Shakers, Santa & Mrs. Claus	$12
6111	4" Napkin Holder, Reindeer w/Christmas Tree	$18
6111	4" Napkin Holder, Christmas Angel	$18
6216	Salt and Pepper Shakers, Christmas Tree Girl	$18
6394	4" Angle Playing Flute	$15
06434	8" Tree Shaped Dish w/Poinsettia Design	$15
6439	7 3/4" Santa w/Reindeer Musical "Jingle Bells"	$39
06454	4 1/2" Candy w/Taffeta Ribbon	$12
6545	Illuminated Snowman	$35
6604	4" Bell, Little Girl in Red Coat w/Song Book	$28
6604	4" Girl Holding a Christmas Tree	$18
6604	4" Girl Holding Poinsettia	$18
6605	Musical Christmas Girl "Jingle Bells"	$32
06644	Kidney Shaped Dish w/Finger Hold, Poinsettia Design - 1988	$18
06758	Salt and Pepper Shakers, Christmas Cat - 1988	$12
6854	3 1/2" Candleholder, Christmas Girl	$12
06987	2 1/2" Santas, 3 Assorted	$8
7047	3 1/2" Candleholder, Pixie Girl, 3 Assorted, Each	$12
7069	Christmas Puppies, Each	$12
7074	Musical Angels, 3 Piece Set	$60
7087	Choir Boys, 3 Piece Set	$60
7167	5 1/4" Planter, White w/Poinsettias	$14
7235	4" Santa/Merry Christmas Mug	$14
07233	Creamer and Sugar, Snow Covered House	$35
07234	Teapot, Snow Covered House	$48
07236	Mug, Snow Covered House	$15
07237	Salt and Pepper Shakers, Snow Covered House & Tree	$15
07675	4 1/2" Round Christmas Box	$14
7696	3 3/4" Christmas Animal	$12
7698	Christmas Girl w/Basket of Holly	$24
7745	6 1/2" Basket, White w/Green Holly and Red Bow	$18
7749	Three Compartment Christmas Tree, White w/Bow and Holly	$24
7750	8" Christmas Tree, White w/Red Bow and Holly	$18
7836	4" Christmas Angel, Set of 3	$20
8024	4 1/2" Candle Holders, White Bisque w/Poinsettia	$45
8025	Applied Poinsettia Bisque Lamp	$32
8026	5 1/2" Candy Dish, Bisque w/Poinsettia	$28
8027	Pitcher and Bowl w/Poinsettia	$28
8029	7" Vase, Bisque w/Poinsettia	$25
8030	Applied Poinsettia Bisque Bell	$12
8073	Boy and Girl Angel Candleholders	$14
8088	Applied Poinsettia Candle Holder	$18
8102	8" Merry Christmas Plate	$25
8139	Salt and Pepper, Mr. & Mrs. Claus in Rocking Chairs	$28
8157	4" Christmas Pinbox, Set of 3	$36
8250	Bell, Girl w/Red Coat Trimmed in White w/Gift	$40
08283	3 1/2" Little Girl in Red Dress w/White Trim	$15
8284	3 1/4" Little Girl in Red & White Suit w/Animal, Each	$15
8745	4 1/2" Candy Cane Kid	$10
10398	Musical Santa and Snowman "Here Comes Santa Claus"	$17
10398	Musical Santa & Snowman "Santa Claus is Coming to Town"	$17
10400	8 3/4" Old World Santa Musical "Christmas in Killarney"	$35
10401	6" Irish Santa	$13
10436	3 3/4" Salt and Pepper Shakers, Mr. and Mrs. Snowman	$9

CHRISTMAS ITEMS (cont'd)

10437	3 3/4" Salt and Pepper Shakers, Santa and Mrs. Claus	$9
10443	3 3/4" Salt and Pepper, Santa and Mrs. Claus in Rockers	$9
10601	Rotating Santa Musical "Santa Claus Is Coming To Town"	$17
10602	Rotating Santa Claus Musical "Jingle Bells"	$17
10603	Rotating Santa Claus Musical "White Christmas"	$17
10604	Rotating Santa Claus Musical "The Nutcracker"	$17
10605	Rotating Santa Claus Musical, "Toyland"	$17
10656	4" Santa Figurines, 4 Assorted	$10
10716	2 1/2" Santa Elves, 4 Assorted	$6
10717	2 1/2" Santa Elves, 4 Assorted	$6
10945	3 3/4" Reindeer, 3 Assorted	$7
11064	6" Snowman Musical "Let it Snow"	$25
11070	6 1/2" Santa and Angels Musical "Here Comes Santa Claus"	$28
11193	2 3/4" Santa Claus Hinged Box	$13
11194	2 1/4" Snowman Hinged Box	$13
11418	Musical Snowman w/Waterglobe "Frosty the Snowman"	$27
11419	Musical Snowman Angels "Hark the Herald Angels Sing"	$25
11420	Musical Snowman Couple "Winter Wonderland"	$25
11421	Musical Snow Couple "We Wish You A Merry Christmas"	$25
11422	Musical Snowman Family "Frosty the Snowman"	$27
11423	Musical Snowman w/Snowchild "Deck the Halls"	$25
11424	Musical Snowman w/Scarf & Hat "Winter Wonderland"	$25
11425	Musical Snowman w/Harp "A Merry Little Christmas"	$25
11426	Musical Snowlady "Let it Snow"	$25
11427	Musical Egg w/Santa "Silver Bells"	$29
11497	Standing Santa	$11
11498	Sitting Santa	$11
11530	Musical, Train/Pond w/Skaters "We Wish You A Merry..."	$40
11712	8" Santa Musical "Have Yourself a Merry Little Christmas"	$25
11713	Drummer Boy Musical "Little Drummer Boy"	$35
11714	7 1/4" Christmas Tree Musical "O' Tannenbaum"	$33
11917	8 1/8" Irish Santa Musical "Have Yourself A Merry Christmas"	$33
12101	Music Box, Santa on Reindeer "Here Comes Santa Claus"	$45
30579	3 1/2" Santa Salt and Pepper Shakers	$12
80109	4 1/2" Christmas Bell	$15
80136	10" Figurine, Sleigh w/Girl and Two Reindeer, Set	$110
90400	3 1/4" Bell, Santa	$25
90401	4 1/2" Bell, Candy Cane Girl	$28

CHRISTMAS/CHRISTMAS CARDINAL

00244	4" Basket	$16
1061	8 1/2" Plate	$18
01062	4" Mug	$12
1063	Mug	$12
1067	Salt and Pepper Shakers	$15
1068	3 1/2" Pitcher and Bowl	$22
1069	5 1/4" Bell	$12
1070	6 1/4" Vase	$15
01198	3 1/2" Tree Shaped Box	$18
1205	3 1/2" Bell	$12
1206	Napkin Holder, Tree Shaped	$20
1207	6 3/4" Nappy Dish	$28
1239	Leaf Shaped Dish	$18
1260	Coffee Pot	$85
1297	Cup and Saucer	$20
1655	Teapot	$110
2055	5 1/2" Shopping Bag	$22
2108	12 1/2" Platter	$48
02279	Heart Shaped Dish	$15
02450	Leaf Shaped Candy Dish	$15
02525	3 1/4" Purse Planter	$15
02597	Pitcher and Bowl	$25
02845	Candleholder	$18
02846	3" Candle Holder	$12
02966	5" Ribbed Dish	$15
03042	3" Basket	$18
4533	7 1/4" Plate	$22
04541	Leaf Shaped Candy Dish - 1984	$15
4550	3 1/2" Tree Shaped Box - 1984	$18
04552	3" Tree Bell - 1982	$12

04555	3" Basket w/Two Cardinals	$16
04556	2" Round Box - 1984	$9
04697	Cup and Saucer - 1984	$18
05975	2 1/2" Round Box w/Two Cardinals	$10
05979	4 1/2" Basket	$14

CHRISTMAS/CHRISTY

00438	6 1/4" Vase	$18
00441	Salt and Pepper Shakers	$16
00442	Footed Candy Dish	$35
00443	Nappy Dish	$18
00446	Heart Shaped Box	$12
00447	7" Mug	$10
00448	7 1/2" Wall Plaque	$20
00449	3 1/2" Pitcher and Bowl	$18
8109	Watering Can Planter	$15
8110	8" Oil Lamp	$45

CHRISTMAS/GOLDEN TREE

1873	Coffee Pot	$90
1875	Two Tier Tidbit Tray	$65
1876	Snack Set	$28
1877	Miniature Creamer and Sugar	$35
1878	Teapot	$65
1880	Creamer and Sugar	$40

CHRISTMAS/GREEN HOLLY

159	6" Box, Candy w/Cover	$25
161	6" Round dish	$22
161	6" Plate	$18
717	Candle Holders, Pair	$30
787	3 1/2" Bell	$18
1187	4" Reindeer	$30
1346	8" Sleigh	$48
1347	7 1/2" Leaf Mint Dish	$25
1348	Dish, Celery	$40
1349	Dish, Two Compartment	$38
1351	Dish, Three Compartment	$45
1352	Dish, Four Compartment	$75
1353	Salt and Pepper Shakers	$20
1355	Creamer and Sugar	$50
1357	6" Teapot	$85
1359	Cookie Jar	$110
1360	Candle Holders and Climbers, 4 Piece Set	$35
1361	5 1/2" Candy Dish	$32
1362	Compote w/Lid	$60
1363	Snack Set	$20
1364	Two Tier Tidbit Tray	$35
1366	Mug	$11
1367	Punch Bowl	$110
2047	Cup and Saucer	$25
2048	9" Plate	$22
2369	18" Platter	$90
2636	18" Platter	$75
2637	10 1/2" Sleigh	$50
2688	11 3/4" Dish, Tree Shaped	$38
2691	8" Dish, Tree Shaped	$22
2693	8 1/2" Vase	$65
2694	8 1/2" Lantern	$125
2695	9" Lantern	$95
3152	Dish, Four Compartment	$65
3750	Bell, Miss Green Holly	$20
3854	15 1/2" Tree-Shaped Tray w/Lid	$85
4229	5 1/2" Hurricane Lamp	$45
4231	8 3/4" Bowl	$38
4369	2" Candle Holder	$12
4621	Small Green Sleigh w/Holly	$38
4859	12" Bell Shaped Platter	$50
4863	5 3/4" Hurricane Lamp	$55
5172	2 Compartment Deep Dish	$30

5173	12" Hors d'oeuvre, 6 Piece Set	$85
5174	Pitcher and Bowl	$25
5178	Bud Vase	$20
5179	3" Boot	$20
5183	Miniature Sugar and Creamer w/Tray	$30
5185	4 3/4" Green Boot Planter	$22
5186	4 3/4" Basket w/Handle	$18
6003	4" Bells - Each	$15
6005	8" Sleigh Planter	$30
6007	Celery Dish	$25
6008	9 1/2" 2 Compartment	$24
6014	5" Round Candy Bowl	$25
6018	9" Round Plate	$25
6027	Candle Holders	$28
6035	Salt and Pepper, Boot Shape	$18
6036	Creamer and Sugar on Leaf Tray	$38
6037	3 1/4" Shoe,	$10
6038	4 3/4" Shoe	$18
9032	4" Pitcher	$12

CHRISTMAS/HOLLY

001	Mug	$7
453	3" Tree Box	$12
743	9" Plate w/Handle	$45
2040	Egg Cup	$32
02451	5" Leaf Shaped Nappy Dish	$9
03028	Cup and Saucer	$12
03030	8" Plate	$18
03031	Mug	$10
03044	7 3/4" Christmas Tree Nappy Dish	$12
03048	7" Bud Vase	$12
03049	5 3/4" Nappy Dish	$15
03051	Napkin Rings, Set of 6	$36
03053	Candle Holder	$12
03057	Bag Planter, w/Red Rope Tie	$12
03059	Small Pedestal Dish	$10
03416	6 1/2" Tree Shaped Dish	$15
03868	5" Round Dish	$9
03879	Oval Dish, Nappy or Soap	$10
4946	6 3/4" Nappy	$14
05246	7 3/4" Tree Shaped Dish	$18
7802	Coffee Pot	$95
7805	7" Plate	$15
7809	Candy Dish	$12
7813	6 1/4" Nappy Dish	$14
7821	Lemon Dish	$15
7940	3 3/4" Pitcher and Bowl	$15
7941	5 1/4" Pitcher and Bowl	$18
7942	7" Vase, Each	$15
7943	Covered Candy Dish	$20
7944	5 3/4" Bell	$14
7945	Candle Holders, Pair	$15
7946	Nappy Dish	$13
7947	Oval Condiment Dish w/Attached Tray	$20
7949	Sugar and Creamer	$28
7950	Cup and Saucer	$18
7951	Demi Cup and Saucer	$18
7954	Two Tier Tidbit Tray	$40
7955	Salt and Pepper Shakers	$18
7956	7 1/2" Compote	$28
8190	Tree Shaped Dish	$18
8192	9 1/4" Dish, Two Compartment	$32
8193	Leaf Shaped Dish	$12
8269	Two Tier Tidbit Tray	$40

CHRISTMAS/HOLLY GARLAND

1402	Snack Set	$35
1802	Cup and Saucer	$30
1803	7 1/2" Salad Plate	$28
1804	9" Dinner Plate	$35
1964	Coffee Pot	$125

1965	Cream and Sugar	$65
1966	Salt and Pepper Shakers	$45
2038	Three Compartment Dish	$75
2039	Jam Jar, Spoon and Plate	$65
2040	Egg Cup	$38
2041	3" Mug	$25
2093	Two Tier Tidbit Tray	$55
2094	Single Tier Tidbit Tray	$32
2095	Nappy Dish	$30

CHRISTMAS/HOLLY & TOUCHES OF CANDY CANE

025	9" Plate	$30
026	Cup and Saucer	$27
027	11" Three Compartment Dish	$50
028	8 1/2" Three Compartment Dish w/Handle	$55
029	Sugar and Creamer	$40
030	Cigarette Box and Two Ashtrays	$32
031	Divided Dish	$40
032	Candle Holders, Divided Handle, Pair	$50
033	Candle Holders, Single Handle, Pair	$37
034	Salt and Pepper	$18
035	Jam Jar w/Spoon, Tray, Salt & Pepper	$65
036	Compote	$35
038	Candy Dish	$38
116	One Tier Tidbit Tray	$18
210	10" Punch Bowl	$55
210	Mugs	$10
211	Mug	$12
725	Cookie Jar	$125
735	Cake Server	$45
738	Two Tier Tidbit Tray	$48
739	Gravy Boat w/Tray	$45
742	Teapot	$135
1293	7" Leaf Shaped Nappy Dish	$22
1294	8" Christmas Tree Nappy Dish	$35
2146	Milk Pitcher	$55
2617	Plate	$22

CHRISTMAS/POINSETTIA

4383	Coffee Pot	$135
4384	Sugar and Creamer	$45
4385	Demitasse Cup and Saucer	$35
4386	Jam Jar w/Spoon	$35
4387	Footed Candy Dish	$45
4388	Teapot	$135
4389	6 1/4" Pitcher	$135
4390	Salt and Pepper Shakers	$23
4391	Two Tiered Tidbit Tray	$58
4392	Cup and Saucer	$35
4394	Nappy Dish	$32
4595	7 1/4" Plate	$18
4396	9" Plate	$30
4397	Snack Set	$38
4398	Bone Dish	$18

CHRISTMAS/TREE WITH PRESENTS

1064	8 1/4" Plate	$15
1066	Mugs	$12
1073	Cake Plate	$25
1074	Pitcher and Bowl Set	$25
1075	Salt & Pepper Shakers	$15
1202	Tree Shaped Napkin Holder	$18
1253	Pedestal Cake Plate	$28
1298	Cup and Saucer	$18
1763	Cup and Saucer, Demitasse	$20

CHRISTMAS/WHITE CHRISTMAS

603	Teapot	$80
604	Sugar and Creamer	$35

CHRISTMAS/WHITE CHRISTMAS (cont'd)

605	Jam Jar	$35
606	Cup and Saucer	$22
608	7 1/2" Plate	$18
610	9" Plate	$25
611	Two Tiered Tidbit Tray	$55
825	Salt and Pepper	$25
1340	Snack Set	$18
1341	Candleholder	$38
1342	Candy Box	$28
1368	11" Tray, Christmas Tree Shaped	$40
1386	Cookie Jar	$75
1387	Mug	$10
1408	Sleigh	$38
2062	9" Bell	$15

CHRISTMAS/WHITE HOLLY

6048	5" Sleigh, Small	$15
6050	6" Round Candy Box	$40
6051	6" Dish, Cookie	$15
6052	5" Candle Holder	$40
6053	3 1/2" Bell	$12
6054	Cookie Jar	$105
6055	8" Planter, Sleigh	$55
6056	Dish, Nappy	$20
6057	12" Dish, Relish	$30
6058	9 1/2" Dish, Two Compartment	$22
6059	Dish, Three Compartment	$25
6061	Salt and Pepper	$20
6062	Sugar and Creamer	$42
6063	Teapot	$125
6064	6" Candy Box	$35
6065	Two Tier Tidbit Tray	$60
6066	Mug	$12
6067	Cup and Saucer	$25
6068	9" Plate	$25
6069	4 3/4" Basket w/Handle	$25
6070	10" Planter, Sleigh	$65
6071	8" Tree Shaped Dish	$22
6072	11 1/2" Dish Christmas Tree Shaped	$25
6073	6" Box, Gift Box Shape	$35
6074	9" Dish, Bell Shaped	$20
6075	Pitcher and Bowl Set	$27
6076	5 1/4" Pitcher and Bowl	$45
6077	5 1/2" Basket w/Handle	$30
7742	Box, Tree Shaped w/Bow	$55
7744	Bell w/Red Bow Handle	$15
7743	Candle Holder w/Bow	$30
7748	6" Pitcher and Bowl	$55
7751	Candy Dish w/Holly Handle	$35

CHRISTOPHER COLLECTION

00129	5" Bride and Groom Musical, "Wedding March" - 1993	$30
00176	6 1/2" Carolers, "Adeste Fideles" - 1982	$30
00177	6" Nativity Scent, "Ave Maria" - 1982	$30
00179	5 1/2" Boy Monk, "Blessed Are the Pure in Heart..." - 1982	$22
00253	Bride and Groom	$28
00330	7" Bell, "Oh Come All Ye Faithful" - 1982	$12
00334	5" Girl Angel Ringing Bell, "Joy to the World" - 1982	$25
00491	5" Ballerina, "Rejoice in the Lord" - 1992	$20
00493	Girl w/Cat, "Jesus & I Love You" - 1992	$18
00498	Girl w/Doll in Rain Gear, "God Cares for You" - 1992	$18
00499	Girl w/Bird, "Jesus is My Friend" - 1992	$18
00501	Girl Pushing Bear in Buggy, "Life Begins w/Jesus" - 1992	$18
00502	5" Girl Feeding Kitten, "God is Always With You" - 1992	$18
00503	Girl w/Baseball Cap and Bag, "Have Faith in the Lord" - 1992	$18
00505	Black Girl Holding Candle, "Jesus Lights Up My Life" - 1992	$18
00506	Black Girl Ballerina, "Rejoice In The Lord" - 1992	$18
00507	Dark Skinned Girl Holding Dove, "Jesus Is My Friend" - 1992	$18
00508	Dark Skinned Girl Jumping Rope, "Trust in the Lord" - 1992	$18
00509	Dark Skinned Girl w/Cat, "Jesus And I Love You" - 1992	$18
00512	Dark Skinned Girl Artist, "Jesus Colors My World" - 1992	$18
00540	Baby on Blanket w/Pillow, "Jesus Loves You" - 1991	$18
00599	Girl Holding Cat, "God's Love Embraces You" - 1992	$18
00944	Bell w/Love Birds and Pink Bow Handle	$18
00945	5 1/2" Bell w/Love Birds and Yellow Bow Handle	$18
01066	4 1/2" Ballerina - 1993	$15
03217	Girl Sleeping w/Cat "Hobos"	$20
03217	Girl Carrying Dog and Bag "Hobos"	$20
03229	5" Boy, "Thanks Unto The Lord" - 1982	$25
03230	5" Girl, "Thanks Unto The Lord" - 1982	$25
03252	5" Wedding Couple, Pair	$40
03269	6" Piano Babies, Pair	$85
03369	4" Bell, "Happy Anniversary"	$14
03426	3" Girl Angel w/Instrument - 1982	$15
03427	2" Angel Candle Huggers - 1982	$25
03428	4" Bell w/Angel, Pink, Yellow or Blue	$12
03429	Box w/Angel on Lid - 1982	$20
03431	4" Bell, Mary and Joseph w/Baby - 1982	$18
03443	3 3/4" Girl Angel w/Book - 1982	$18
03443	3 3/4" Girl Angel Playing Violin - 1982	$18
03448	Birthday Girl Series - 1982	$10
03452	4" Girl w/Squirrel, "Good Friends Have a Special..." - 1982	$20
03454	4 1/2" Girl on Log w/Dog, "To You with Love" - 1982	$22
03455	3" Girl or Boy, "Now I Lay Me Down to Sleep"	$28
03456	4" Girl Feeding Ducks, "Life's Little Pleasures..."	$23
03457	4 1/2" Little Girl Sewing, "Lord Bless Our Work"	$22
03458	4" Girl w/Dog, "To You With Love"	$18
03459	5" Little Girl w/Chickens, "Seeds of Kindness..." - 1982	$20
03460	5" Little Boy w/Chickens, "Seeds of Kindness..." - 1982	$22
03461	5" Girl w/Duck "Seeds of Kindness..." - 1982	$22
03463	5" Girl, "Love Makes All Things Beautiful" - 1982	$20
03464	4 1/4" "Little Miss", Each - 1982	$18
03465	4 1/2" "Never Leave Me" - 1982	$18
03467	4 1/2" Girl w/Dog, "Be My Pet" - 1982	$18
03474	4 1/2" Country Friends, "Of All The Joys ..." - 1982	$20
03476	5 1/2" Boy & Girl at Shrine, "Blessed are the Pure... - 1983	$24
03481	Madonna	$32
03482	Musical Bell w/Nativity Scene, "Silent Night" - 1983	$18
03505	Mary and Baby w/2 Angels, Holy Treasure Series - 1983	$35
03546	Girl Kneeling by Bed, "Now I Lay Me Down to Sleep" - 1983	$22
03550	Musical Nurse Figurine, "A Spoonful of Medicine..." - 1983	$35
03554	4 1/2" Bride and Groom - 1983	$22
03555	3" Praying Girl or Boy, First Communion - 1983	$24
03556	3 1/2" Praying Girl, First Communion - 1983	$24
03561	3" Baby's First Christmas	$12
03562	3" Bell w/Angel Handle - 1983	$12
03572	6 1/2" Bell, Jesus on Cross	$18
03600	5" Girl w/Clown Doll, "Caren's Clown"	$22
03666	7 1/2" Plate, Madonna & Baby Jesus - 1983	$18
03705	4" Bell, "The Lord Bless You and Keep You" - 1983	$16
03708	3 3/8" Box, Bride & Groom, "The Lord Bless You..." - 1983	$25
03746	Little Baby Girl w/Ribbon - 1983	$30
03796	Picture Frame w/Boy or Girl Graduate - 1983	$18
03802	4 1/2" Bell w/Boy Graduate Handle - 1983	$18
03803	3 1/2" Girl Graduate - 1983	$25
03804	3 1/2" Girl Graduate - 1983	$22
03805	3 1/2" Graduate - 1983	$25
03806	3 1/2" Graduate Nurse -1983	$23
03807	4" Bell, Bride as Handle - 1983	$15
03809	5" Frame Bride and Groom - 1983	$20
03811	6" Frame Boy w/Teddy Bear, "Smile God Loves You" - 1983	$18
03823	3" Kneeling Angel in Pink Holding Candle - 1983	$12
03823	3" Kneeling Angel in Blue Holding Harp - 1983	$12
03825	Angel w/Infant, "Baby Jesus, Lord of All" - 1983	$28
03827	4" Bride and Groom Kids	$25
03841	4" Boy w/Squirrels, "The Biggest Share of Happiness..."	$24
03842	3 1/2" Girl, "Love and Special Friends Are Blessings"	$25
03843	5" Boy w/Dogs, "One Can Never Be Alone..." - 1982	$30
03844	Girl Knitting, Musical, "Thank Heaven for Little Girls" - 1982	$32
03845	4 1/2" Boy w/Dog - 1982	$25
03846	4 1/2" Boy w/Lamb, "The Lord is My Shepherd" - 1982	$28
03848	4" Girls Praying, "Prayer Changes Things" - 1982	$22

03849	5 1/4" Girl Praying, "Unto Thee Oh Lord..." - 1982	$23
03850	4" Girl w/Goose, "God Is Love" - 1982	$25
03850	4" Girl w/Goose, "Please Stay Near You Are So Dear"	$25
03898	3 1/2" Girl w/ Doll, "Dolly"	$15
03911	4 1/2" Girl of the Month, "Smile, God Loves You" - 1983	$25
03912	Birthday Girl of the Month, Musical "Happy Birthday" - 1982	$35
03914	3 3/4" Boy of the Month - 1983	$22
03924	Madonna - 1983	$22
03925	8 1/2" Madonna - 1983	$25
03926	6 1/2" Madonna - 1983	$22
03927	Madonna - 1983	$22
03979	4 1/2" Girl Doing Laundry, "Lord Bless Our Work"	$22
04030	Kissing Angel - 1984	$18
04031	4" Bell, Bride as Handle	$14
04032	4 1/2" Bride and Groom - 1984	$22
04076	3 1/2" Angels at Manger - 1984	$18
04078	6 1/2" Madonna and Child - 1984	$28
04268	Boy Kneeling In Prayer, "Praise the Lord" - 1984	$20
04270	3 3/4" Boy, "Praise the Lord"	$15
04452	5" Angel Playing Mandolin	$18
04454	7 1/2" Bride Music Box	$45
04455	4 1/2" Bride & Groom, "We've Only Just Begun" - 1982	$45
04466	3 1/4" Figurine, Wedding Couple	$22
04502	Madonna and Child - 1984	$55
04503	6" Camel	$30
04580	Bell, Bride and Groom	$10
04587	Music Box, Train Shape w/Boy and Girl, "On the Road Again"	$55
04588	Music Box, Boy and Girl on Train Cart, "Side by Side"	$45
04589	Music Box, Boy and Girl on Cart, "Country Roads"	$45
04594	6" Cow	$20
04633	Girl w/Dog, "The Lord Will Provide" - 1984	$28
04633	Boy w/Dog, "Trust in the Lord" - 1994	$28
04634	Musical, Wedding Couple, "We've Only Just Begun" - 1984	$38
04635	4 1/2" Figurine, Hobo Wedding Couple	$28
04636	4 1/4" Box, Covered w/Small Bride and Groom	$22
04637	5" Bell, Bride & Groom, "We've Only Just Begun"	$25
04638	4 3/4" Frame, House Shape w/Bride and Groom	$28
04639	4" Figurine, Hobos, 2 Assorted	$28
04640	4" Figurine, Hobo Girl	$28
04641	4" Figurine, Hobo Boy	$28
04642	6" Music Box, Suitcase w/Boy and Girl, "Side by Side"	$55
04649	Little Girl Bathing Dog - 1984	$28
04649	Little Girl w/Kittens, "Love Always Has Time for Others"- 1984	$28
04650	6" Music Box	$60
04657	Bell, Child Angel Praying	$12
04666	3 3/4" Madonna - 1984	$35
04978	3" Bell, Boy or Girl Praying	$10
04981	4" Bride and Groom - 1985	$22
04982	Cake Topper, Heart w/Wedding Bells - 1985	$16
04983	4" Bride and Groom - 1985	$22
04984	4 1/2" Bride and Groom - 1985	$22
04985	4" Bride and Groom - 1985	$22
05071	Cross w/Child - 1985	$18
05100	6 1/2" Ballerina - 1985	$24
05189	10" Last Supper	$55
05325	3 1/2" Girl w/Duck, Little Treasures - 1985	$20
05326	3 1/2" Boy w/Duck, Little Treasures - 1985	$20
05381	2 1/2" Camel Laying Down - 1985	$28
05412	3" Girl Figurines w/Easter Animals - 1986	$18
05420	4" Barefoot Angel Playing Instrument, Each - 1986	$20
05421	Nativity Set, 9 Pieces - 1986	$165
05422	First Communion, Little Girl Praying - 1986	$18
05635	3 1/2" Sleeping Angel - 1986	$18
05683	7 1/2" Cross w/Boy or Girl	$15
05687	Bell, Plays "Adestes Fideles" - 1986	$28
05690	Nativity Set, Bethlehem Collection - 9 Pieces	$125
05691	4 3/4" & 6" Angels, Each	$32
05808	5" Anniversary Bell w/Ribbon - 1986	$12
06051	7 1/2" Nurse w/Baby - 1987	$32
06117	6" Camel	$32
06368	4" First Communion Girl - 1987	$24
06374	4" Groom Carrying Bride	$22
06509	6" Christ w/Kneeling Girl, "First Communion" - 1987	$38

06538	7 3/4" Angel - 1987	$28
06557	5 1/2" Cow, Lying Down - 1987	$25
06580	3 3/4" Kneeling Angel - 1988	$18
06856	6 3/4" Bell, Manger Scene - 1988	$22
07265	3 1/2" Mary, Joseph & Baby, "Flight to Egypt" - 1986	$25
07318	7 1/2" Nurse w/Baby - 1989	$30
07400	5" Flower Girl of the Month	$28
07464	4 1/2" Angel Playing Mandolin - 1989	$22
07487	Little Girl Bottle Feeding Pig - 1990	$23
07488	Little Girl or Boy w/Dog and Cats - 1990	$22
08021	6" Angel - 1983	$25

COASTERS

289	Gold Roses, Each	$4
2904	Fleur de Lis, Set of 4 w/Wire basket	$28
20128	Fruit or Floral, Set of 6	$40

COFFEE POTS

124	Eastern Star	$85
247	Striped	$75
1075	Rose Heirloom	$185
1077	Cosmos	$125
1506	Garden Daisy	$55
1708	Rose Heirloom, Coffee or Chocolate Pot	$225
2160	Silver Wheat	$55
2445	Orange and White, or Beige and White	$38
2485	Floral Clover	$32
2518	Magnolia	$145
2690	Heavenly Rose	$175
2910	Fleur de Leis	$65
3028	Vineyard	$65
3122	Floral w/Short Spout	$165
3166	Moss Rose	$95
3186	Pink Cotillion	$85
3191	Blue Cotillion	$85
4580	Spring Bouquet	$85
6315	Lavender Rose	$95
6508	Anniversary	$55
6570	Pink Rose Cascade	$85

COLONIAL VILLAGE COLLECTION

00120	10" Tree	$5
00121	8" Tree	$4
00122	6" Tree	$4
00123	5" Tree	$4
00142	US Flag Pole with Base	$8
00214	The Major and the Mrs.	$12
00215	Carol and Amy on Park Bench	$11
00216	Two Horse Open Sleigh	$15
00217	2 1/2" Nurse Sarah Miller	$10
00218	The Parkers Caroling	$11
00219	Cast Iron Clock	$13
00221	Mr. and Mrs. Anderson on Park Bench	$13
00222	Kenneth Hurst and Sparky	$12
00227	Village Green Gazebo	$15
00228	Stern's Stable	$40
00229	Vanderspeck's Mill, Retired 1992-1996	$45
00230	Main Street Church	$48
00231	San Sebastian Mission Church, Retired 1992-1995	$48
00232	Elegant Lady Dress Shop	$55
00233	County Courthouse	$40
00267	Jake and Olivia Ardmore	$14
00268	Melany, Scott and Taffy	$18
00269	Devinci Brother Carolers	$18
00300	3" Trees	$5
00301	5" Trees	$6
00303	7" Trees	$7
00309	Nativity w/Wisemen and Shepherd	$16
00310	Nativity Scene	$10
00457	Votive Fire House	$10

COLONIAL VILLAGE COLLECTION (cont'd)

00458	Rover and His House	$10
00528	Children's Chorus	$8
00584	Lamp Post	$9
00585	Traffic Signal	$9
00587	Cobblestone	$38
00657	Tommy Reed	$10
00658	Kimberly Johnson	$10
00659	Jeffrey Sawyer	$10
00660	Hockey Player Stanley Reed	$10
00661	The Griffiths, Marv, Liz and Mary Lou	$15
00664	A Christmas Tradition, Chestnut Roaster	$15
00665	Miles O'Keefe, Lighthouse Keeper	$9
00666	Hunter Josh Engles	$10
00667	Conductor Edward Clark	$10
00668	Mr. Hobbs	$10
00669	Carolers "Phil, Tony and Jim"	$15
00670	Bell Ringer Old Ben	$10
00715	St. Peter's Cathedral	$65
00716	Kirby House	$96
00717	Burnside House	$55
00718	Joseph House	$55
00719	Mark Hall	$45
00721	Doctor's Office	$42
00722	Baldwin's Jewelry Shop, Retired 1993-1997	$48
00723	Winslow's Curios	$45
00724	Dentist Office	$40
00725	Green Grocer	$45
00948	The Wood Fence	$6
00961	Cow	$7
00962	Horse	$7
00963	Mr. and Mrs. Fletcher (Bride and Groom)	$15
00964	Father Christopher	$10
00965	Brother Andrew	$10
00966	Sister Mary Margaret	$10
00967	Baker Jacques Le Rousse	$10
00968	Butcher Mr. White	$10
00969	Barber Sam	$10
00972	Willie Karensky	$8
00973	Tom and Betsy	$15
00974	Zack and Mary	$15
00975	Ambulance	$12
00976	Don's Colonial Dairy	$45
00977	Postal Express	$15
00988	Rosamond House	$40
00989	Springfield House	$40
01001	Brown's Book Shop	$43
01002	Village News	$45
01003	Black Sheep Tavern	$45
01004	Village Hospital	$40
01005	White's Butcher Shop	$45
01006	Real Estate Office	$48
01007	Smith and Jones Drugstore	$50
01008	Mundt Manor	$55
01028	2 3/4" Metal Gate	$3
01029	4 7/8" Metal Gate	$4
01030	Street Signs	$10
01166	5" Tree w/Snow	$4
01167	7" Tree w/Snow	$4
01168	9" Tree w/Snow	$5
01170	Lighted Christmas Tree	$28
01320	Notfel Cabin	$45
01321	Savings and Loan	$38
01322	The Cabinet Maker	$40
01323	Rainy Days Barn	$35
01324	O'Doul's Ice House	$42
01325	Patriot's Bridge	$28
01328	Historical Society Museum	$48
01329	Queensgate	$55
01337	Lenny Mullen, Newspaper Delivery Boy	$8
01338	Sean O'Doul, Ice Man	$8
01339	Jay Olson, Reporter	$8
01340	Edwin Hope, Printer	$8
01341	Emery Walling	$8
01342	Libby Thacher, Teacher	$9
01343	Abigail Mason, Librarian	$8
01344	Russ Brody	$8
01345	Natalie Brody	$8
01346	Sandy and Ellen	$11
01347	Tommy O'Doul Delivering Ice	$15
01390	For Sale Sign	$5
01392	U.S. Mail Box	$4
01393	Mark Clemens	$7
01511	Betsy Ross Flag	$5
03327	Applegate House - Members only Piece	$65
05820	Church of the Golden Rule	$38
05821	Lil Red Schoolhouse	$38
05822	Train Station, Retired 1987-1989	$165
05823	General Store, Retired 1987-1988	$175
05824	Welcome Home, Retired 1987-1997	$45
05825	Old Stone Church	$45
05826	Express Train - 3 Piece Set	$40
05827	Eberhardt Family - 6 piece Set	$60
05828	Mark, Carrie and Nickki Caroling	$14
05829	Brian and Friend	$10
05890	King's Cottage, Retired 1987-1997	$48
05891	Nelson House, Retired 1987-1989	$210
05892	McCauley House, Retired 1987-1988	$170
05893	Penny House, Retired 1987-1988	$165
05894	Ritter House, Retired 1987-1989	$170
05895	Charity Chapel, Retired 1987-1989	$330
06094	Millinery Shop	$45
06330	Ghost House	$165
06332	Halloween House	$100
06333	Faith Church, Retired 1988-1991	$175
06334	Friendship Church, Retired 1988-1994	$60
06335	Old Time Station, Retired 1988-1997	$27
06336	Trader Tom's General Store	$38
06337	House of Blue Gables, Retired 1988-1995	$38
06338	Stone House	$45
06339	Greystone House, Retired 1988-1995	$45
06341	Ritz Hotel	$143
06342	Firehouse, Engine Co. No 5	$35
06343	Post Office	$38
06344	Police Station	$42
06345	State Bank, Retired 1988-1997	$45
06346	Johnson's Antiques, Retired 1988-1993	$75
06456	The Hay Ride	$18
06457	Veterinarian Wagon	$18
06458	Old Fire Pump Wagon	$15
06459	The Cab	$18
06460	One Horse Open Sleigh	$15
06461	Matt's Milk Wagon	$15
06470	New Hope Church, Musical "Adestes Fideles"	$375
06522	6 Assorted Lighted Churches, Each	$28
06546	Mike O'Brien, Newspaper Boy	$8
06547	Allison Davis	$8
06548	Dick's Delivery	$11
06549	Lisa and Selina	$14
06550	Kevin Banks	$8
06551	Pamela Hendley	$6
06552	Gary Barnes, Ice Skater	$9
06553	Monica Banks	$8
06554	The Stone Church Carolers	$22
06734	The Cates Family, Gerald, Katherine, Michael and Spot	$18
06735	Mrs. Notfel	$8
06737	Nina and Filippe	$14
06738	Miss Mary Nagy	$8
06739	Merrymaker Ed	$8
06740	Billy O'Malley	$10
06741	Ivan Zelinski, Lamplighter	$8
06743	Station Master, 2 piece set	$11
06744	Carolers Steven and Stacy	$14
06747	Gull's Nest Lighthouse	$35
06748	Maple Street Church, Retired 1989-1993	$65

06749	Village School, Retired 1989-1991	$110
06750	Cole's Barn, Retired 1989-1994	$65
06751	Sweetheart Bridge	$21
06752	Library	$30
06887	Kolenkos Family Caroling	$28
06897	Bijou Theatre, Retired 1989-1990	$195
06898	Village Bakery	$48
06899	Quincy's Clock Shop	$55
06900	Village Apothecary, Retired 1989-1991	$110
06901	Barber Shop	$48
06902	Major's Manor	$40
06904	Capper Millinery	$60
06987	Santa's Helpers, 3 Assorted, Each	$6
07084	Skating Pond	$18
07085	Stone Bridge	$8
07090	Metal Park Bench	$10
07091	Picket Fence	$4
07092	Park Bench	$7
07125	The Colonial Village Flyer - 3 Piece Stationary Train	$31
07124A	Ghost House	$95
07124B	Witch House	$95
07322	Dashing Through the Snow	$14
07323	Alex, David and Jerome	$15
07324	Paddy Wagon	$23
07325	Convenience Outhouse	$12
07326	Mr. Capper and Patches	$10
07327	Ryan and Ericka Sanderson	$12
07328	Peter and Patty Ritter	$14
07329	Good Samaritan Band, Set of 6	$48
07330	Officer Casey	$8
07331	Fireman Bud Michaels	$8
07333	First Church	$45
07334	Fellowship Church	$35
07335	Victoria House, Retired 1990-1993	$60
07336	Hampshire House, Retired 1990-1996	$40
07337	Nob Hill, Retired 1990-1995	$55
07338	Ardmore House, Retired 1990-1995	$55
07339	Ships Chandler Shop	$135
07340	Hardware Store, Retired 1990-1996	$55
07341	Country Post Office, Retired 1990-1994	$50
07342	Coffee and Tea Shoppe	$65
07343	Pierpont-Smithes Curios, Retired 1990-1993	$125
07344	Mulberry Station	$38
07476	Smith's Blacksmith Shop, Retired 1991	$245
07477	Toy Maker's Shop	$55
07478	Daisy's Flower Shop. Retired 1991-1996	$50
07479	Watt's Candle Shop, Retired 1991-1994	$135
07481	Sweet Shop	$40
07482	Belle Union Saloon. Retired 1991-1994	$65
07483	Blacksmith Abe Smith	$12
07716	Mailman	$9
07726	Mini Lamp Posts	$7
07727	Single Lamp Post	$5
07776	Postman Frank Pendergast	$8
07777	Reverend O'Toole	$8
07778	Sylvester Sweeney, Chimney Sweep	$8
07821	Letters for Santa, 3 Piece Set	$24
07824	Bonnie and Charles Cole and Spot	$12
07825	Mary and Jack Cobb	$14
07826	Michael and Missy	$14
07827	Annette, Rebecca and Frosty	$14
07828	The Vanderspeck Kids	$14
07829	The RFD Mailbox	$5
07838	Colonial Village Music Boxes, 4 Assorted, Each	$35
07866	Sign...Entering, Leaving Colonial Village	$12
07923	Iron Hand Pump	$7
07924	Doc Mitchell	$9
07925	Victorian Gazebo	$22
07926	The Well	$10
07927	Sanderson's Mill	$52
07960	North Point School	$35
07961	Brenner's Apothecary	$48
07962	Village Inn	$48
08010	Ryman Auditorium - Special Licensed Edition	$95
10329	Queensgate	$35
10388	Ice House	$30
10389	Dairy House	$30
10391	Lattimore House - 1996 Members Only Piece	$75
10392	Treviso House	$45
10393	Franklin College	$40
10394	Hermitage	$38
10395	Stable	$35
10397	Fairbanks House	$38
10614	Fire Wagon	$18
10615	Carl and Linda Sellers	$15
10616	Fireman Tom	$8
10617	Worthington Phipps, Inn Keeper	$9
10618	Bertha Silvers	$8
10619	Laurie Silvers	$8
10620	Charlotte LaRousse	$8
10621	Ira Robertson	$8
10622	Joshua Corcione-Keller	$8
10623	Silas Notfel Statue	$8
10714	The Travelers	$25
10715	The Fairbanks Family	$45
10719	The Hayride	$15
10732	Trading Post	$42
10735	St. Paul's Church	$38
10825	Village Law Office	$35
10826	Potter House	$45
10827	The Variety Store	$40
10828	Montrose House	$48
10829	Ashton House - 1997 Members Only Piece	$65
10835	3 Piece Colonial Band	$26
10836	Becky, Billy & Bobby	$18
10838	Clark's Charcoal Wagon	$18
10872	Photo Studio	$35
10874	Election Stand	$8
10949	9 1/2" Tree	$5
10950	7" Tree	$4
10951	6" Tree	$4
10952	5" Tree	$4
10956	Michael Bradley, Jr., Photographer	$6
10957	Fisherman	$6
10958	Wilbur Winston, Mayor	$10
10959	Jason Green, Grocer	$6
10960	Zack Peters, Cabinet Maker	$22
10961	Band Director	$6
10962	Morton Manchester, Lawyer	$10
10963	Band Wagon	$12
10964	Santa	$10
11030	Sawyers Creek Mid-Year	$35
11259	Cooper's Shop	$40
11260	Grand Opera House	$40
11262	Berkley House	$45
11263	Blue Bell Flour Mill	$38
11266	Showboat, 7 piece Set	$125
11270	Captain Harrison	$6
11273	Nicole and Puff	$6
11274	Jeb Carter	$6
11275	Josephine	$6
'11276	Mr. Clemmons	$6
11278	Jason Cook	$6
11279	Mark and JR	$6
11280	Mary and Annabelle	$6
11282	Jasper Cook	$18
11283	David Bell	$17
11531	Seth Gordon	$6
11532	Jennifer	$6
11534	Fishing Lodge	$40
11573	Julia	$45
11582	Fence with Haystack and Pumpkins - Autumn Colors	$15
1588	Mooncrest	$65
11991	Hillside Church, Limited Edition 1991-1991	$110
11992	Lakehurse Limited Edition 1992-1992	$100
11993	St. James Church- Limited Edition 1993-1993	$100

COLONIAL VILLAGE COLLECTION (cont'd)

11994	Mount Zion Church - Limited Edition 1994-1994	$100
11995	Wycoff Manor - Limited Edition of 5500 1995-1995	$85
11996	Brookfield - Limited Edition of 5500 1996-1996	$80
11997	Sir George's Manor - Limited Edition of 5500, 1997-2000	$70
11998	Trinity Church - 1998 Limited Edition	$77
12112	Barn and Silo - Limited Edition of 1200	$100
12114	Christmas Wishes	$25
12218	Cotswold - 1999	$45
13537	Village Lighthouse - 2000	$40

COMPOTES

003	Cherubs w/Gold Trim	$40
096	Violets	$45
109	Heavenly Rose	$40
112	Golden Wheat	$32
231	Reticulated, Lilac and Rhinestones	$85
592	Violets w/Lattice Rim	$42
695	Floral w/Butterflies	$18
712	Rose Design w/Lattice Rim	$15
713	Rose Design	$15
757	Tiffany Rose	$90
913	Elegant Rose w/Hand Held Base	$95
1083	Cosmos	$50
1656	Violets or Roses	$15
1950	Della Robbia	$28
2027	Latticed w/Gold Accents	$18
2053	Rose Bouquet	$18
2310	Pink w/Applied Flowers	$35
2330	Violet Bouquet w/Lattice Rim	$48
2356	Fleur de Lis	$28
2427	Golden Laurel	$24
2604	Applied Fruit	$105
2604	Applied Forget-Me-Nots	$105
2524	Golden Laurel	$18
3561	Renaissance	$25
3563	Milk Glass Renaissance	$18
4328	Pear N Apple, Green	$22
5090	Fiesta	$18
5760	Floral Design w/Gold Edging	$25
6405	Paisley Fantasia	$25
7145	White Milk Glass w/Scalloped Edges	$18
7278	Dancing Leaves	$24
20053	Fruit or Floral	$28
20332	Lattice w/Fruit Design	$28
20333	Milk Glass w/Roses or Violets	$28
20406	Violets	$80
20438	Mardi Gras	$105
24653	Violets w/Gold	$38

COOKIE JARS

078	Owl, Marked Italy	$95
130	Mushroom w/Caterpillar on Lid	$65
396	Boy's Head	$275
397	Girl's Head	$275
1173	Scottish Girl	$275
1174	French Girl	$275
1370	Pixie Baby	$125
1378	Wheat Poppy	$42
1674	Fruit Basket/Tutti Fruit	$95
1692	Thumbelina	$175
1742	Della Robbia	$70
2097	Santa	$110
2264	Milkglass w/Fruit Design	$48
2360	Chef Girl	$225
2361	Chef Boy	$300
2366	Dutch Girl	$200
2833	Apples	$65
3236	Mr. Toodles	$225

3319	Grape	$90
3361	Daisytime	$80
3702	Pennsylvania Dutch	$200
3725	Man on Elephant	$48
3762	Green Orchard, Green	$70
3969	Elf Head	$350
4021	Mrs. Toodles	$175
4130	Green Orchard, Gold	$58
4131	Pear N Apple, Green	$65
04190	Bear	$75
4335	Pear N Apple, Gold	$65
4602	Gold Country Charm	$75
4611	Blue Country Charm	$75
4628	Brown Owl	$45
4856	Pink Daisy	$55
5256	Fiesta	$45
5399	Hot Poppy	$50
5557	10" Chicken	$45
6193	Brown w/Colored Daisies	$45
6494	Blue Chrysanthemum	$85
6352	Mushroom Forest	$50
6382	Renaissance	$50
6594	Bossie the Cow	$65
6722	Fruit Fantasia	$70
6760	Yellow Tulip	$65
7065	White Wicker w/Applied Fruit Handle	$58
7128	Tisket A Tasket	$60
7277	Falling Leaves	$48
7239	ESD Chef Boy	$250
7525	Love Birds in Bird House	$65
7794	Mouse w/Cheese	$45
7975	Harvest Pansy	$55
12730	"You Can Never Over Decorate" 1999	$38
20489	Pear w/Cover	$95
21865	ESD Dutch Girl	$125
22072	ESD Dutch Boy	$275

COUNTRY HIGHJINKS COLLECTION

01516	Goat & Chickens," That's What Friends are For" -1994	$15
01541	3" Dog Meeting Baby Duck - 1994	$15
01542	2" Puppies w/Bucket of Fish - 1994	$15
01547	3" Cat and Dog - 1994	$15
01549	3" Lamb in Haywagon w/Hen - 1994	$15
01550	3" Dog in Hen House - 1994	$15

CUP AND SAUCER

061	Jumbo "Good Morning Darling"	$12
107	Eastern Star	$18
108	Peach Colored w/Pink Roses and Gold Accents, Pearl Luster	$35
110	Pedestal w/Floral Design	$32
111	After Dinner w/Floral Design	$20
124	After Dinner w/Rose Design	$18
186	Jumbo, Dad	$16
187	Jumbo, Mom	$16
250	Elegant Rose w/Gold Trim	$38
253	Gold and Brown Striped	$12
270	4 5/8" Demitasse Cup and Saucer, Floral Pattern	$28
271	Gold Leaf and Filigree	$15
272	Gold Pattern	$14
276	50th Anniversary	$15
281	25th Anniversary	$10
328	His and Her Half Cups	$18
354	Pine Cone	$15
368	Tea, Floral	$20
438	Multi-Colored Rose Bouquet	$22
446	Pink Rose on Black Background	$30
510	Demitasse Cup and Saucer w/Purple Flowers	$18
546	Green, Gold and White	$45
546	Pink, Gold and Cream w/Pink Roses	$45
673	Hand Painted Over All Floral Design	$45

684	Rose w/Gold Trim	$18
687	Spring Bouquet	$22
688	Demitasse Spring Bouquet	$25
705	Demitasse Moss Rose	$32
780	Four Seasons	$42
801	Green w/Floral Design, Gold Trimming	$30
911	Footed Floral or Fruit	$45
912	Tea, Decorated in a Beautiful Floral Pattern	$50
922	Floral	$28
975	Fruit or Roses	$45
976	Floral	$35
1076	Rose Heirloom	$28
1076	Violet Heirloom	$28
1079	Cosmos	$35
1085	Jumbo, Grandfather	$16
01138	Mug Cup and Saucer, Rose Design - 1993	$15
1246	Floral Pattern	$25
01248	Red Cardinal	$20
1317	Happy Anniversary	$22
1350	Blue Rose Chintz	$20
1350	Yellow Rose Chintz	$20
1356	4 1/2" Demitasse Cup and Saucer, Victorian Couple	$25
1378	Rose Heirloom	$32
1378	Violet Heirloom	$35
1423	Demitasse w/Rose Pattern, Pearl Luster	$25
1424	Floral w/Pearl Luster	$32
1523	CALIFORNIA, The Golden State	$15
1642	Greek Key Design, Demitasse	$14
1643	Gold Inside, Demitasse	$12
1701	Rose w/Gold Trim	$22
1705	Footed Rose Design - 1994	$28
1707	Pedestal Rose Design - 1994	$22
1709	Mug w/Saucer, Rose Design - 1994	$18
1798	After Dinner, Two Tone w/Flowers	$28
1826	Rose Heirloom	$28
1827	Rose Heirloom Custard Cup and Saucer	$38
1977	Golden Wheat	$17
2021	Demitasse Floral Crackle	$22
2034	Multi Colored Small Floral	$12
02036	Demi Violet	$22
2042	Tea "For a Special Friend"	$20
2042	Tea, Black w/Pink Rose	$45
2058	Floral, Pearlized w/Reticulated Saucer	$30
2119	Pink Floral	$19
2119	Blue Rose Chintz	$28
2119	Yellow Rose Chintz	$22
2120	Blue Rose Chintz, Demitasse	$25
2120	Pink Floral, Demitasse	$22
2157	Wheat, Demitasse	$10
2167	w/Blue Jay	$32
2169	w/Pheasants	$32
2300	Ribbed w/Violets	$40
2320	Cup of the Month, Each	$30
2337	Eastern Star	$22
2370	Demitasse, Orange and White	$12
2416	Solid Color Mug w/White Saucer, Each	$12
2420	Pearlized, Solid Color Cup & Saucer, Each	$12
2421	5" Demitasse	$25
2521	Magnolia	$32
2524	Magnolia, Demitasse	$30
2548	Golden Laurel	$23
2552	Flower Design	$13
2593	Jumbo "Mother"	$22
2594	Jumbo "Grandma"	$18
2595	Jumbo "Dad"	$22
2596	Jumbo "Grandpa"	$18
2619	Pine Cone	$18
02683	Tall Irish Coffee Cup and Saucer	$15
2722	Fruit Design, Signed Geo. Z. Lefton on Inside	$55
2723	Floral Design, Signed Geo. Z. Lefton on Inside	$55
2755	Pink Cup w/Floral Pattern	$17
2756	Heavenly Rose, Demitasse	$42

2758	Heavenly Rose	$45
2773	Floral, Geo.Z. Lefton Signature	$45
2791	Dogwood	$25
2829	Cup of the Month	$20
2864	Tea on a Pedestal	$18
2870	Golden Wheat	$17
2878	Rose w/Gold Accents	$18
2904	Cream Background w/Painted Flowers, Pearl Luster Inside	$20
2908	Violets	$32
2994	Pink Stripe, Demi	$12
2996	Tea, Violets w/Three Legs	$35
3016	Apples	$16
3170	Moss Rose	$20
3183	"To My Mother"	$15
3189	Pink Cotillion	$28
3200	Jumbo Dad	$30
03318	Mug w/Saucer, Floral w/Pink Accents	$18
3372	Vineyard Line	$16
3408	Pink Cup w/White Handle	$12
3450	French Rose, Demitasse	$15
3451	French Rose	$15
3776	50th Anniversary	$13
4177	Forget-Me-Not	$25
4256	Ornate, Floral	$38
4935	50th Anniversary	$13
5383	Heirloom	$28
5507	Happy Anniversary	$12
6120	Mustache	$38
6324	Footed w/Pink Roses and Gold Trim	$28
6698	White Milkglass w/Grape Design	$18
6806	Paisley Fantasia	$25
06970	Multi Color w/Pink Flowers - 1998	$14
7110	Fruit w/Reticulated Saucer	$32
7238	Rose and Violet Chintz	$22
7285	Blue Daisy	$15
8035	Floral Chintz	$24
9000	Floral Design	$18
9004	Floral Design	$32
9009	Flower of the Month	$25
10579	25th Anniversary	$14
10590	50th Anniversary	$14
10967	Violet w/Mug Cup	$22
13017	Irish Lace	$10
20327	Floral Design or Fruit Design	$45
20335	Roses w/Half Circle Trim	$28
20335	3 Legged w/Flower	$28
20355	Floral	$28
20583	Pedestal w/Portrait and Reticulated Saucer	$40
20583	Footed w/Portrait and Reticulated Saucer	$40
20583	Pedestal w/Portrait and Reticulated Saucer	$32
20583	Footed, Pink and White w/Pink Roses	$32
20602	Wheat Design	$18

DAINTY MISS

040	7" Cookie Jar	$175
040	Cookie Jar, Grey Hair	$250
040	Cookie Jar, Blonde Hair	$250
321	Teapot	$170
322	Sugar and Creamer	$80
323	Jam Jar w/Spoon	$80
325	Spoon Rest w/Salt Shaker	$125
439	Salt and Pepper Shakers	$60
648	Teapot Shaped Teabag Holder	$32
1276	Three Compartment Dish w/Dainty Miss Handle	$150
1277	10" Two Compartment Dish	$200
6767	5" Wall Hanging	$95
6820	ESD Sugar and Creamer	$65
6823	ESD Jam Jar w/Spoon	$80
7797	Head Vase	$110
7952	6 1/2" Wall Plate	$95
8677	9 3/4" Divided Dish	$110

DECANTER SETS

991	8 1/2" Monk w/6 mugs, Set	$50
1383	Santa w/Mugs, Set	$60
1691	7" Old Fashion Man	$38
1688	7 1/2" Bum w/Cups, 7 Piece Set	$65
1955	7 1/2" Dog w/Cups, 7 Piece Set	$65

DECORATIVE ITEMS

087	White Birdbath w/Birds and Applied Pink Roses	$48
194	Pink or White Glazed Swan w/Applied Purple Flowers	$38
197	Swan, Lilac and Rhinestone	$38
342	Milk Glass Swan w/Applied Flowers	$24
459	3 1/2" Gold Heeled Shoe w/Lace and Roses	$75
651	2 1/2" Shoe, Antique Ivory Bisque w/Applied Flowers	$18
714	6 1/4" Double Hands	$65
721	Console Set w/Pink Roses, 3 Piece Set	$80
723	Console Set w/Pink Roses, 3 Piece Set	$75
775	Shoe, Antique Ivory Bisque w/Applied Flowers	$20
784	Shoe, Antique Ivory Bisque w/Applied Roses	$20
846	3" White Milk China Swan w/Applied Flowers	$38
847	White Milk China Swan w/Applied Flowers	$40
923	Dish, Rippled Edge w/Sponge Gold Accents, Rose Design	$20
1063	Swan w/Applied Flowers	$75
1201	5 1/2" Swan, w/Applied Flowers	$45
1204	4 1/2" Shoe, White or Pink	$22
1388	White Bisque Swan w/Wings Up	$38
1518	3 1/2" Ring Holder, Hand w/Flowers	$28
1761	High Heeled Shoe w/Flowers	$18
1787	5" Double Hands w/Pink Flowers	$38
2453	4" Shoe w/Pale Blue Grapes	$18
2640	3 1/2" Hand on Heart Shaped Dish, French Rose	$25
2669	5" Swan w/Multi-Colored Applied Flowers	$55
2933	Bisque Hand w/Applied Flowers	$15
2960	4" Luscious Lilac Shoe	$18
2961	2 1/2" Luscious Lilac Shoe	$18
2968	7" Luscious Lilac Boot w/Applied Flowers	$38
3258	Console Set w/Applied Flowers, 3 Piece Set	$75
3277	3" Bisque High Heel Shoe w/Flowers, Pink or White	$18
4198	7" Double Hands w/Applied Flowers	$45
4344	7" Hands w/Applied Flowers	$45
5665	6" Swan w/Applied Flowers	$25
6077	4 1/2" Bird Bath w/Birds and Applied Flowers	$35
8058	4" Swan, Pink Porcelain w/All Over Floral Decorations	$45
8059	5 1/2" Swan, White or Pink w/All Over Floral Decorations	$55
50430	3 1/2" Shoe, Mardi Gras w/Stones on Heel, Each	$35

DENTURE HOLDERS

1162	4" w/HIS on Lid, Antique Ivory Bisque	$24
1163	4" w/HERS on Lid, Antique Ivory Bisque	$24
2653	4" Denture, HERS, French Rose	$24

DISHES

001	5 1/2" Green and Yellow Leaf w/Applied Butterfly & Flower	$32
218	Two Compartment, Floral	$25
232	6" Latticed w/Lilacs and Rhinestones	$32
352	Two Compartment, Pine Cone	$16
366	Two Compartment, Raised Roses	$32
367	Three Compartment, Raised Roses	$38
368	8 1/2" Candy w/Roses	$27
377	5 1/2" w/Lady & Gentleman	$32
473	Three Compartment w/Flowers and Butterfly	$38
474	Two Compartment, w/Flowers and Butterfly	$30
486	6 3/4" Bonbon	$38
492	Two Compartment, Daisytime	$36
681	5 1/2" Leaf w/Hand Painted Flowers	$25
695	8" Three Compartment w/Pixie, Pearl Luster	$38
696	7 1/2" w/Pixie, Pearl Luster	$35
726	6" Square Pedestal Dish w/Applied Rose	$35
744	Leaf Plate w/Floral Design, Each	$28

759	Nappy, Floral Design w/Butterfly	$15
782	7 1/2" Nappy Dish, Elegant White	$18
783	9" Three Compartment, Elegant White	$28
792	4" Dish w/Playing Card Suit and Flowers	$48
1085	6" Bonbon w/Handle, Cosmos	$22
1105	50th Anniversary Nappy Dish	$14
1160	12" Dish w/Compartments, Fruit Design	$32
1169	10" Brown Leaf Dish	$10
1308	Three Compartment, Celery Line	$38
01370	Nappy Dish w/Two Hummingbirds - 1994	$18
1379	6" w/Handle, Rose or Violet Heirloom	$20
1380	8 1/4" Bonbon, Rose Heirloom	$30
1543	4" x 2" Dish w/Colonial Couple Scene	$25
1544	4 1/2" Dish w/Colonial Couple Scene	$28
1596	10" Three Compartment, Country Squire	$38
1824	9 1/4" Two Compartment, Rose Heirloom	$45
1860	Leaf Shaped, Pink w/Roses & Gold	$35
1860	Nappy w/Fruit	$22
1962	Three Compartment, Della Robbia	$40
1970	Heart Shaped w/Violets	$15
1980	Three Compartment w/Raised Pink Roses	$58
2010	6" Heart Shape w/Gold Bow	$15
2023	8" Bluebirds Bonbon	$45
2045	7" Latticed, Gold Wheat Design	$18
2085	Pink w/Sponge Gold and Raised Roses	$65
2090	Three Compartment Dish, Della Robbia	$40
2091	Two Compartment Dish, Della Robbia	$38
2332	Two Compartment, Pink w/Roses	$38
2334	Bonbon, w/Violets in Relief, 3 Shapes, Each	$35
2349	6 1/2" Nappy	$18
2356	8" w/Lattice Edging, Fleur de Lis	$23
2514	6 1/2" Nappy, Eastern Star	$12
2560	7 1/2" Victorian w/Violets	$75
2613	6" Leaf Nappy Dish w/Clover	$12
2618	6" Lemon Dish, Magnolia	$22
02636	5" Shamrock Shaped Dish w/Shamrocks	$21
2665	10" "Grape" Dish	$32
02686	4" Heart Shaped Dish "You'll Never Know…"	$10
2803	5 1/4" Shell Shape, To a Wild Rose	$28
2874	8" Square w/Violets or Roses	$45
2914	Three Compartment, Pink, Leaf shaped w/Roses in Relief	$35
2991	5" Square Dish w/Fancy Edges, Orange	$18
3033	Grape Design	$35
3153	8" Pink w/Gold and Floral Design	$18
3155	8" Pink w/Gold and Floral Design	$18
03287	6" Leaf Nappy Dish w/Violets	$16
3368	5 1/2" Gold Leaf	$11
3844	4" Heart Shaped w/Flowers and Butterfly	$15
4129	12" Two Compartment, Pear N Apple	$28
4187	6" Nappy, Forget-Me-Not	$12
04294	5 1/2" Leaf Shaped Nappy - 1984	$12
04381	40th Anniversary - 1984	$10
4591	Nappy, Spring Bouquet	$12
4653	4" x 6" 25th Anniversary	$14
4670	6 1/2" Ruffled Edge w/Floral Design	$25
4672	4 1/2" Ruffled Edge w/Floral Design	$18
4674	6 1/2" Dish w/Two Compartments	$22
4814	4" Latticed Heart Shaped w/Roses or Violets	$22
5204	Three Compartment, Rose Design	$35
5205	Shell Shaped Dish w/Floral Design	$15
5208	Pineapple Dish w/Roses	$15
5370	Shell Shaped w/Floral Design	$24
5374	Double Leaf Dish w/Stem Handle, Rose Pattern	$20
5762	8" Two Compartment	$24
5763	7 1/2" w/Gold Pattern and Edging	$20
5764	Shell Shaped w/Floral Design and Gold Accents	$42
6433	Leaf Shaped Nappy w/Floral Design	$18
6577	7 1/2" Nappy Dish, Lavender Rose	$26
7050	6 1/2" Floral Design, Two Compartment w/Handle	$20
7052	Petite Fleurs	$28
7056	Three Compartment Dish w/Handle and Gold Trim, Floral	$27
7161	3" Fruit Shapes w/Flowers, 4 Piece Set	$20
7164	Shell Shaped w/Floral Design	$24

7165	Nappy, w/White, Pink and Yellow Roses	$17
7294	Nappy, Light Blue w/Pink Dogwoods	$18
07814	5" Round Dish w/Dogwood	$21
8183	Nappy, Green w/Pink and Yellow Flowers	$15
8242	Footed w/Floral Design and Sponge Gold	$75
8245	Antique Ivory Bisque w/Basketweave & Raised Flowers	$23
08309	Leaf Shaped w/White Flowers	$12
8312	Leaf Shaped, w/Flowers	$12
10584	Nappy Dish, 25th Anniversary	$15
10595	Nappy Dish, 50th Anniversary	$15
11081	5" Shamrock Shaped Dish w/Shamrocks	$13
20032	8 1/2" Double Bonbon, Pink	$55
20127	6" Nappy, Fruit Design, Each	$32
20197	8" Double Compartment, Wheat Design	$35
20225	5" Leaf Shaped Nappy, Eastern Star	$18
20313	9" Three Compartment, Golden Wheat	$35
20334	4 1/2" Fruit or Floral	$20
20567	Nappy, Eastern Elegance	$38
20569	3 Compartment, Eastern Elegance	$65
30132	Nappy, Dark Fruit	$22
99200	2 Compartment, Hand Painted Flowers	$18

EASTER ITEMS

00116	Mother and Baby Chick in Easter Bonnet	$12
00162	3" Egg w/Chicks	$10
00162	3" Egg w/Two Rabbits in Bed	$10
00162	3" Egg w/Two Chicks in Bed	$10
425	Egg Planter w/Chick	$18
500	3 1/2" Rabbits on Log	$12
544	3" Chick Painting Egg	$10
547	Chick Hatching From Egg	$12
548	Egg Box w/Chicks	$15
644	3" Duckling w/Egg	$10
970	Easter Egg	$15
971	5" Candy Box w/Chicks	$18
01113	Egg Box with Girl Bunnies, 3 Assorted	$8
01114	Egg Box with Boy Bunnies, 3 Assorted	$8
1299	4" Wallpocket, Girl in Bunny Costume w/Eggs	$32
01355	3" Duckling w/Egg, Each	$12
1429	Box, Decorated Egg w/Bow	$15
1439	4" Bunny Child & Decorated Egg Planter	$16
01467	4" Easter Egg	$18
01492	3" Easter Bunnies, Set of 3	$28
1601	3 1/2" Egg Urn, Different Colors, Each	$10
1771	5" Candy Box, Chick Hatching Out of Egg	$15
2204	4 1/2" Candy Box, Egg w/Chick Handle	$15
2265	4" Figurine, Girl Pushing Carriage, 3 Assorted, Each	$18
2581	5 1/4" Egg Box w/Easter Bunny	$15
2579	3 1/2" Egg Box, Duck Hatching out of Easter Egg	$22
02738	3 3/4" Egg w/Easter Bunny - 1983	$10
02741	3 1/2" Box, Chick Popping Out of Easter Egg	$22
2785	2 1/2" Box, Egg Shaped w/Chick	$20
2951	5 1/2" Box, Easter Chick w/Flowers	$22
3005	Easter Egg Candy Dish	$26
3429	Easter Egg Box w/Roosters and Chicks	$18
03684	Large Egg w/Rabbit	$13
03685	4" Easter Egg w/Rabbit	$12
03690	Egg Box Decorated, Each - 1983	$15
03691	Egg Box, Chick on Lid w/Bow Handle	$18
4139	Easter Egg w/Chick	$10
4365C	6 3/4" Musical Rotating Egg w/Chick "Easter Parade"	$40
04373	3 1/2" Bunny Pulling an Egg Cart	$15
04374	4" Chick Pulling a Cart	$15
4419	3 1/2" Box, Baby Chick Hatching From Easter Egg	$15
04731	Little Girl in Bunny Suit Holding an Easter Egg - 1984	$18
4741	3 1/4" Egg w/Bow and Flowers	$14
04758	3 1/2" Egg w/Bunny	$18
5196	4 1/2" Box w/Bunny on Lid	$18
05439	3 1/2" Bunny Painting Eggs	$12
5468	Chick w/Half Easter Egg, Planter	$16
5469	3 1/2" Rabbit w/Painted Tulip	$10
5540	Egg w/Bunny Eating Carrot	$15

5549	3 1/2" Open Egg w/Chick and Flowers	$15
5815	4" Broken Egg w/Rabbit Girl	$30
07138	3 1/2" Little Girl Rabbit Carrying Flowers	$18
7141	4 1/4" Bunny Napkin Holder w/Chicken Salt & Pepper, Set	$25
7171	5" Footed Floral Egg Planter	$18
07792	Basket w/Easter Bunny and Egg - 1990	$15
07793	Bunny on Egg Looking into Basket - 1990	$14
07794	4 1/2" Egg Box w/Rabbit	$18
7880	4 1/2" Egg Planter w/Chick	$15
8213	Egg Box, Heather Girl	$18
8214	2 1/2" Salt and Pepper Shakers, Heather Girl	$18
8215	3 1/4" Egg Box, Heather Girl	$18
8216	4 1/2" Egg Box, Heather Girl	$20
10110	Egg Box with Bunny and Ribbon Handle, 3 Assorted	$8
10111	Egg Box with Chick and Ribbon Handle, 3 Assorted	$8
10112	4" Egg Box with Rabbit Eating Carrot, 3 Assorted	$10
10128	3 1/2" Easter Bunny w/Eggs, Each - 1995	$15
10129	3 1/2" Mom & Dad Easter Bunny w/Baby, Each - 1995	$15
10486	Musical Geese "Easter Parade", 6 Assorted	$9
10775	Egg Box with Ribbon and Flowers, 3 Assorted	$10
10776	Egg Box with Ribbon and Flowers, 3 Assorted	$10

EGG CUPS

521	Double, Daisy Line	$10
1448	Floral Design	$17
02611	Daisies or Violets	$15
3295	Mr. Toodles	$30
07833	White Daisy	$15
07833	Violets	$15
20121	Golden Wheat	$12

ELEGANT ROSE

634	Cup and Saucer	$36
676	Salt and Pepper	$28
700	Teapot	$135
866	Miniature Teapot	$65
928	5" Dish	$15
931	13 1/2" Lamp	$150
938	Compote w/Hand Held Base	$75
958	Sugar and Creamer, Dresden Type	$65
1806	Jumbo Cup & Saucer	$30
2048	Egg Cup	$35
2124	Snack Set	$30
2125	Three Legged Cup and Saucer	$35
2275	Ribbed Sugar and Creamer	$95
2276	Ribbed Sugar and Creamer	$65
2323	Teapot	$95
2351	Three Compartment Tidbit Tray	$25
2564	Sugar and Creamer, Stacked	$85
2907	Cup and Saucer	$30
2912	Miniature Sugar and Creamer	$35
2930	Miniature Sugar and Creamer	$55
2992	10" Hors d'oeuvre Plate	$50
4829	Ribbed Teapot, Sugar and Creamer, Set	$125
6964	Candle Holders, Pair	$15

ENGLISH COLLECTION

07543A	Brown Heritage Floral Musical Teapot "Memories"	$60
07543B	Misty Rose Musical Teapot "Memories"	$60
07543C	Lavender Rose Musical Teapot "Memories"	$60
07543D	Summer Daisy Musical Teapot "Memories"	$60
07543E	Rose and Violet Musical Chintz Musical Teapot "Memories"	$60
07543F	Green Heritage Musical Teapot "Memories"	$60
09011	Cup and Saucer, 12 Assorted Floral, Each	$17
09012	8" Plate, Floral, 6 Assorted, Each	$17
09029	Mugs "To Mother", 6 Assorted	$11
09033	Cup and Saucer, 6 Assorted Fruit, Each	$22
09034	Cup and Saucer, 6 Assorted, Each	$26
09901	Teapot, 6 Assorted Floral	$35
09903	Teapot, 6 Assorted Floral	$35

ENGLISH COLLECTION (cont'd)

09906	Teapot, 2 Cup Floral, 6 Assorted, Each	$26
09907	Teapot, 6 Assorted Fruit	$37
09912	8" Plate, Floral, 12 Assorted, Each	$17
09914	Cup and Saucer, 6 Assorted, Each	$20
09916	Cup and Saucer, Fruit, 6 Assorted, Each	$20
09917	7 3/4" Plate, Fruit, 6 Assorted, Each	$20
09918	Cup and Saucer, 6 Assorted Floral, Each	$22
09919	Teapot, 2 Cup Floral, 6 Assorted, Each	$27
09920	Cup and Saucer, 12 Assorted Floral, Each	$17
09921	Mugs, 12 Assorted Floral, Each	$11
09922	8" Plate, 12 Assorted Floral, Each	$17
09923	Teapot, Purple Lilac	$37
09924	Teapot, Pansy	$37
09925	Teapot, Violet	$37
09926	Teapot, Summertime Rose	$37
09927	Cup and Saucer, Purple Lilac	$17
09928	Cup and Saucer, Pansy	$17
09929	Cup and Sauce, Violet	$17
09930	Cup and Saucer, Summertime Rose	$17
09934	8" Plate, Summertime Rose	$17
09936	Mug, Pansy	$12
09937	Mug, Violet	$12
09938	Mug, Summertime Rose	$12
09939	Cup and Saucer, 12 Assorted Floral, Each	$17
09940	Mug, 12 Assorted Floral, Each	$11
09941	Cup and Saucer, Flower of the Month	$17
09943	Cup and Saucer, Lilac Mist	$17
09946	Teapot, 6 Assorted Floral	$35
09947	Teapot, Lilac Mist	$37
09949	Teapot, Fruit Design, 6 Assorted, Each	$27
09950	Mug, Covent Garden, 4 Assorted, Each	$12
09951	Mug, Topiary, 3 Assorted, Each	$12
09952	Mug, Floral, 3 Assorted, Each	$12
09953	Mug, Delta Blue, 3 Assorted, Each	$18
09954	Mug, Vineyard, 3 Assorted, Each	$18
09955	Cup and Saucer, Fruitopia by Royal Winchester, 6 Assorted	$27
09956	Cup and Saucer, Blue Onion, 3 Assorted, Each	$22
09957	Cup and Saucer, 12 Assorted Floral, Each	$17
09958	Cup and Saucer, England's Pink Rose	$28
09959	8" Plate, England's Pink Rose	$28
09960	Cup and Saucer, England's Red Rose	$28
09961	8" Plate, England's Red Rose	$28
09962	Cup and Saucer, Chelsea, 6 Assorted, Each	$25
09964	Teapot, England's Pink Rose	$45
09965	Teapot, England's Red Rose	$45
09966	Teapot, Chelsea, 6 Assorted, Each	$45
09967	Teapot, English Garden	$55
09968	Cup and Saucer, Herbal	$19
09969	Cup and Saucer, English Garden	$25
09970	8" Plate, English Garden	$25
09971	Sugar and Creamer, English Garden	$40
09972	Teapot and Cup, Stacking Herbal	$45
09973	Teapot and Cup, Stacking Violet	$45
09974	Cup and Saucer of the Month, January	$19
09975	Cup and Saucer of the Month, February	$19
09976	Cup and Saucer of the Month, March	$19
09977	Cup and Saucer of the Month, April	$19
09978	Cup and Saucer of the Month, May	$19
09979	Cup and Saucer of the Month, June	$19
09980	Cup and Saucer of the Month, July	$19
09981	Cup and Saucer of the Month, August	$19
09982	Cup and Saucer of the Month, September	$19
09983	Cup and Saucer of the Month, October	$19
09984	Cup and Saucer of the Month, November	$19
09985	Cup and Saucer of the Month, December	$19

FESTIVAL

2613	Teapot	$145
2615	Sugar and Creamer	$55
2616	Cup and Saucer	$28

2617	Jam Jar w/Tray and Spoon	$45
2619	Snack Set	$25
2620	7" Plate	$18
2621	9" Dinner Plate	$28
2622	Demitasse Cup and Saucer	$35
2624	Two Tier Tidbit Tray	$85
2626	Salt and Pepper	$25
2627	8 1/2" Bone Dish	$15
2630	3 1/2" Coaster, Set of 4 in holder	$28
2632	Nappy Dish	$25
2935	Coffee Pot	$155

FIGURINES

001	Bloomer Girl	$70
005	4 1/2" Boys Bowling, Set	$75
021	8" Calypso Dancers, Pair	$125
00030	8" Chef	$55
050	4" Children, "I Would Like To Be"	$35
00062	8" Waitress	$45
113	2 1/2" Red Devil w/Gold Spear	$25
00117	3 1/2" Girl Holding Cat	$18
118	Girl Holding 2 Baskets, Each	$30
00124	Nurse Figurine - 1991	$15
125	7 1/2" Boys in Barrel	$95
125	4 1/2" Flower Girl, 3 Assorted, Each	$40
127	10" Colonial Couple, William & Mary, Pair	$300
127	4 1/2" Chinese, Sitting Boy and Girl w/Stones, Pair	$55
129	6 1/2" Chinese Man and Woman, Pair	$90
131	Mythical Ladies, Each	$35
133	6 1/2" Girls w/Flowers, Each	$38
138	3 1/2" Boy Climbing Fence w/Dog	$10
148	Scottish Girl in Kilt Playing the Bagpipe, Hummel Like	$65
149	7" Lady in Yellow Dress Sitting under Rose Arbor	$45
00153	3" Shamrock Girl w/Friend	$12
157	4 1/2" Bloomer Kicking Up Leg	$50
00175	5" Girl "Thanks Unto The Lord"	$22
00178	4 1/2" Boy w/Walking Stick	$12
181	7" Soldiers, Each	$70
00204	3 1/2" Girl w/Bunny in Cart "Where Ever we Go..."	$18
00205	3 1/2" Boy & Girl w/Cat "Loving is Sharing"	$18
00206	3 1/2" Girl Friends "Friends Find Ways For Loving Days"	$18
00208	4 1/2" Little Girl w/Cat and Dog "Giving is Loving"	$18
00255	4 3/4" Communion Figurines, Boy or Girl, Each	$8
227	5 3/4" Tom Sawyer	$42
229	5" Farmer Boy or Girl w/Flowers, Each	$18
230A	5 3/4" Andorra Collection, Boy w/Rabbit, by Marika	$18
230B	5 3/4" Andorra Collection, Girl w/Frog on Log, by Marika	$18
00234	Graduation Boy - 1991	$8
00236	Graduation Girl - 1991	$8
237	6 1/2" Old Man Holding Rabbit w/Dog	$65
278	6" Oriental Man in Traditional Robe, Belt and Hat	$40
280	6" Oriental Peasant Lady Feeding Bird	$45
281	7" Teacher w/Pupils	$75
291	Monk Figurines, Each	$12
00302	3 3/4" Bride and Groom	$15
302	8" Old Man and Woman w/Gold Clubs, Pair	$85
303	8" Man w/Camera	$40
305	3" Pixie, Pearl Luster	$12
00324	3 1/2" Kitten in Hat w/Mouse	$15
00325	3" Hunting Dog w/Rifle and Duck	$15
326	Little Adorables, Limited Edition of 720, 5 Piece Set	$250
00329	3 1/2" "Care For Me and Keep Me Near"	$20
331	4" Baby of the Month	$20
00331	5 1/4" Boy or Girl	$25
333	6" Lady Figurine w/Hat	$50
334	4 1/4" Flower Girl, Each	$30
335	6 1/4" Flower Girl, Each	$45
337	10" Colonial Couple, Brian and Hildegard, Pair	$250
340	6" Girl w/Flowers	$45
344	8" Colonial Woman, "Old Masters"	$90
345	8" Colonial Man and Woman, Pair	$160
346	6 1/2" Boy and Girl Standing Beside Tree Limb	$55

355	6 3/4" Girl w/Flower Basket, Each	$45
359	9 1/2" Man w/Top Hat and Long Coat	$65
363	4 3/4" American Children Series, Each	$36
364	4" Girl w/Teddy Bear	$36
370	4 1/2" Bloomer Girl w/Blue Dress and Hat	$48
370	9" Colonial Lady	$75
374	8" Provincial Couple w/Duck and Chicken, Pair	$125
375	8" Peasant Girl w/Hen and Basket	$75
387	8" Pinkie and Blue Boy, Pair	$125
388A	5" Lefton Colonial Man	$36
392	4 1/2" Dancing Girls, Each	$35
393	5 1/4" Chinese, Pair	$70
398	6" Lady w/Basket of Flowers and Large Hat	$55
400	8 1/2" Lady	$100
403	8 1/4" Lady Dressed in White w/Floral Design	$150
403	4" Shamrock Girls, 3 Piece Set	$60
404	7" Photographer	$50
406	7" Lawyer	$50
407	8" Boy and Girl Figurines w/Fruit, Pair	$48
408	Old Man Feeding Rabbit	$65
409	Old Woman Feeding Chickens	$65
411	6 1/2" Marilyn Monroe	$175
412	Lady w/Flowing Dress, Scarf and Flower Basket	$67
432	Man in Book Stall Reading to Dog	$95
439	5 1/2" Chinese, Pair	$55
444	5 3/4" Ballerinas, 3 Piece Set	$90
457	6 1/2" Lady & Man, Pair	$150
458	6" Colonial Man & Woman, Pastel Bisque, Pair	$90
459	Colonial Man and Woman, White w/Gold	$100
460	6 1/4" Lady w/Umbrella and Man w/Hat in Hand	$140
461	6" Lady w/Hat and Shawl, White and Gold, Pair	$70
462	6" Lady w/Shawl	$65
463	6" Lady w/Ruffled Dress, Hat and Shawl	$65
463	Lady, Spanish Dancer	$75
493	6 1/2" Siamese Dancers, Pair	$110
00494	4 1/2" Boy and Girl Figurine	$15
00497	4 1/2" Girl of the Month	$15
538	8 1/4" English Bobbie	$55
540	7" Lady Carrying Pails on Shoulders	$75
567	8" Colonial Man and Woman, Pair	$175
576	4" Bloomer Girls	$55
582	8" Porcelain Man, White and Gold, Pair	$230
583	5 1/2" Lady and 6" Man, White and Gold, Pair	$150
585	7 1/2" Victorian Lady w/Umbrella	$135
0598	4" Girl Reading to Old Man, Marked Marika's Original	$45
606	7" Old Lady Mending Boys Pants	$65
612	8" Lady, Matte Finish	$55
615	8" Lady Dressed in Pink	$95
615	4 1/2" Red Riding Hood	$40
628	7 1/2" Old Man w/Donkey	$55
629	7" Lady Doctor	$32
632	4" Flower Girl of the Month, Each	$32
654	7" Girl Reading to Her Puppy	$35
662	5 1/2" Girl w/Bluebird, Marika's Originals	$25
692	5 1/4" Girl w/Flowers and Two Pink Poodles	$36
693	6 1/2" Girl Figurines w/Flowers, Each	$60
707	3 1/2" Unbreakable Lace Ballerina	$85
727	8" Provincial Boy and Girl Playing Instruments, Pair	$65
737	4 1/2" Girl	$40
751	8" Lady, White, Pink and Gold	$125
00756	Little Girl Figurines, Each - 1992	$18
758	10" Lady in White	$75
764	6 3/4" Old Woman on Park Bench Feeding Birds	$65
767	7 1/4" Fisherman, by Marika	$50
768	Old Woman Sewing While Cat Watches	$55
779	3 3/4" Pixie	$18
795	4 1/2" Bloomer Girl, Amelia	$35
797	4 1/2" Bloomer Girl w/Bonnet Carrying Gift	$45
799	3" Girl Dressed As Bunny	$19
00811	4 1/2" Couch w/Cat	$25
828	5 1/2" Piano Babies, Each	$45
837	8" Dentist	$55
840	Tailor Measuring Man for Pants	$40
843	4 1/2" Bloomer Girl, Each	$50
844	6" Becky Thacher, Bisque	$50
845	6" Tom Sawyer, Bisque	$65
850	6" Colonial Man and Woman, Pastel Bisque, Pair	$95
851	6" Lady in Rose Chintz Dress	$50
851	7 1/2" Colonial Lady w/Fan and Flower Basket	$95
858	8" Piper Boy, Bisque	$55
860	9" French Empire Lady	$90
867	7 1/2" Colonial Woman w/Umbrella	$90
869	2" Country Boy w/Bird	$10
869	8" Colonial Lady, Maude	$90
903	4" Girl Powdering Nose	$22
901	3 3/4" "Little Seamstress"	$25
945	5" Kneeling Boy and Girl, Pair	$110
954	9" Oriental Girl, Pearl Finish, Pair	$110
963	4 1/2" Irish Lad Playing Banjo	$28
977	4 1/2" Girl w/Bird	$22
977	4 1/2" Boy w/Shovel	$22
985	5 1/2" Flower Girl of the Month	$65
986	7 1/2" French Provincial Boy and Girl	$125
989	4 1/2" Pastel Tinted Babies	$55
972	6" Child on Pull Toy Horse	$58
1003	4 3/4" Girl Frolicking, Antique Ivory Bisque	$32
1004	5" Amelia, Antique Ivory Bisque	$40
1009	Huckleberry Finn w/Fishing Pole, Glazed	$85
1052	4" Story Dolls, Figure Named on Base, Each	$48
1055	4" Devil Kissing Angel	$55
1061	9" Lady Holding Her Hat	$150
1062	6" Lady Wearing Hat, Holding Shawl	$85
1098	Bloomer Girl	$48
1102	5 1/2" Ole King Cole	$60
1103	5 3/4" X 6 1/2" Old Woman In A Shoe	$180
1104	8" Rock-A-Bye Baby	$140
1105	7 1/4" Old Mother Hubbard	$110
1106	5 1/2" Little Miss Muffet	$65
1107	Mary Mary Quite Contrary	$45
1107	7" Lincoln Standing	$75
1108	8" George Washington Standing	$85
1108	5 3/4" Little Bo Peep	$45
1109	Hickory Dickory Dock	$55
1110	5 1/2" American Children	$36
1119	5 1/2" Man With Whiskey Bottle	$32
1129	5 1/4" Modern Woman, All White	$55
1149	7" Colonial Couple Holding Flowers, Pair	$95
1187	5" Spanish Girl	$80
1188	Girl Figurine w/Real Lace "FiFi"	$55
1191	4" Pixie on Mushroom Watching Frog	$13
1206	4" Girl w/Poodle	$18
1210	4" Girls Going To School	$25
1211	5 1/2" Oriental Man Playing Flute, White	$32
1225	6" Lady w/Full Skirt	$30
1232	5 1/4" Bloomer Girl Scared By Mouse	$45
1233	4" Praying Boy and Girl, Pair	$30
1234	5 " Bloomer Girl w/Mouse	$50
1240	5 1/4" Barefoot Boy w/Fishing Pole and Fish	$30
1247	6 1/4" Peter, Peter, Pumpkin Eater	$65
1248	6" Patty Cake, Patty Cake	$65
1249	4 1/2" Little Boy Blue	$65
1250	5 3/4" Humpty Dumpty	$65
1251	5 1/2" Mary Had A Little Lamb	$45
1252	5 1/2" This Little Pig Went To Market	$65
1254	6" Sing A Song Of Six Pence	$150
1255	6 1/4" Simple Simon	$95
1256	5 3/4" Jack and Jill	$110
1257	4 3/4" Hi Diddle Diddle	$65
1260	Three Little Kittens	$60
1274	8" Lady w/Purse and Parasol, Pink and Gold	$125
1347	8" Teacher at Blackboard, by Marika	$100
1375	5 1/2" Pocahontas and Powhatan, Pair	$75
1412	4" Bloomer Girls, Each	$45
1425	Nuns Playing Baseball, 3 Piece Set	$60
1428	Nun Bowling, 3 Piece Set	$60
1432	3 1/4" Sports Devils, Each	$28

FIGURINES (cont'd)

1433	6" Japanese Geisha Girls, White	$120
1448	4 1/2" Girl in Flowered Dress and Hat Holding Bird	$28
1450	4 1/4" Happy Birthday	$28
1450A	4" Lady in Pink Polka Dot Dress w/Hat	$32
1450B	4" Lady in Blue Dress Carrying Flowers	$32
1451	10 1/2" Lady	$95
1460	6" Lady, Pastel Bisque	$70
1460	6" Lady w/Full Skirt	$55
1460	7" Lady w/Baby	$85
1461	5" Boy or Girl Sitting On Logs, Pair	$40
1461	Boy w/Slingshot	$25
1461	Boy w/Basket of Apples	$25
1464	5" Girl w/Basket	$55
1470	8 1/2" Lady in Pastel Colors	$145
1470	6 1/2" Oriental Couple	$70
1471	8 1/2" Lady w/Umbrella	$120
1473	4 1/2' Mother Goose Line	$60
1474	4 1/2" Pussy Cat, Pussy Cat	$48
1475	5" There Were Two Blackbirds	$60
1481	8" Old Man in Black Cap and Gown	$55
1489	6" Girl In Green Dress w/Two Flower Baskets	$65
01491	3 1/2" Girl	$18
1498	6" Lady w/Strapless Dress Carrying Flower Baskets	$48
1529	3 1/2" Girl Hugging White Cat	$15
1529	3 1/2" Boy w/Squirrel	$15
1553	4 1/2" Girl and Duck	$18
1553	4 1/2" Boy and Pig	$18
1554	4 1/2" Girl in Purple Dress w/Purse	$18
1568	5 1/4" Colonial Boy and Girl Shelf Sitters, Pair	$40
1569	6" Gay Nineties w/Umbrella	$125
1570	6 1/4" Victorian Lady w/Umbrella	$145
1571	6" Girl w/Umbrella and Purse	$80
1572	5 3/4" Gay Nineties, White Trimmed In gold	$125
1573	7 1/2" Gay Nineties In Pink	$140
1574	7 1/2" Gay Nineties w/Umbrella	$150
1581	6" Wine Maker	$55
1583	4 1/2" Girl Playing Heart Shaped Cello - 1963	$30
1588	8" Old Woman Selling Flowers	$75
01592	4 1/2" Boy or Girl Gardeners	$18
1622	4 1/2" Nurse w/Thermometer and Clipboard	$45
1627	4" Nurse in Pink Dress	$28
1631	Chinese Boy and Girl	$85
1698	4" Bloomer Girls, Each	$55
1700A	5" Girl Figurine w/Bird on Lamppost	$40
1700B	5" Girl Figurine w/Flowers on Trellis	$40
1700C	5" Girl Figurine w/Bird on Mailbox	$40
1701	4 1/2" Oriental Man and Woman	$50
1702	4 1/4" Bloomer Girl	$60
1703	6 1/2" Lady Figurine, Each	$50
01797	Graduate Girl or Boy w/Diploma	$15
01798	4 1/2" Graduate Boy or Girl, Each	$18
1806	6" Baby w/Rattle	$38
1821	7 1/2" Blackjack Player	$65
1853	4 1/2" Girl of the Month	$28
1858	8" Veterinarian w/Dog	$75
1859	8 1/2" Baker Figurine	$45
1859	6 1/4" Lady w/Hat and Flower Basket, Blue	$60
1866	8" Chiropractor	$45
1868	5" Girl w/Umbrella, 3 Assorted, Each	$35
01869	8" Doctor	$28
1870	8 1/4" Girl Skier	$60
1871	8" Man and Woman Golfer	$55
1874	8" Lady, Margaret or Elizabeth, Each	$135
01881	3 3/4" Clown	$20
1887	7 3/4" Lady w/Shawl and Umbrella	$85
1888	7 3/4" Lady w/Shawl	$80
1927	6" Baby Boy and Girl, Pair	$60
1928	4 1/2" Praying Boy and Girl	$15
1944	9" Chinese Couple, Pearl Finish, Pair	$65
1985	8 1/2" Colonial Lady w/Purse	$55
1999	4 1/2" Chinese Figurines w/Rhinestones, Pair	$32

2006	7 1/2" Lady w/Garland of Flowers	$42
2041	Spirit of '76, 3 Piece Set	$145
2043	4" Girl of the Month	$28
2044	2 3/4" Girl of the Month	$22
2048	4 1/2" Girl of the Month	$30
2075	7 1/2" Colonial Man and Woman, Pair	$135
2076	8" Colonial Man and Lady, Pair	$185
2077	7 1/2" Colonial Man and Woman, Pair	$150
2091	5" Young Woman w/Ruffled Dress	$65
2098	6 3/4" Chinese Boy and Girl w/Stones	$75
2146	6 1/4" Clown, Set of 3	$99
2164	4 1/2" Chinese w/Musical Instrument	$35
2168	9" Chinese w/Musical Instrument, Pair	$75
2172	8 1/2" Oriental Lady w/Mirror	$48
2175	9" Chinese, Pair	$75
2176	5 1/2" Chinese Boy and Girl w/Stones, Pair	$55
2184	3 3/4" Girl Holding Heart	$15
2197A	3" Farm Boy or Girl w/Animals, Pair	$30
2197B	3 1/8" Children w/Geese, Pair	$30
2197C	3 1/8" Children w/Pets, Pair	$30
2221	8" Policeman	$40
2222	7" Lady Typist	$65
2225	5 3/4" Nurse	$20
2245	8" Accountant Figurine CPA	$45
2245	6" Teenager w/Suitcase	$45
2246	7" Lady Typist	$65
2256	10 1/2" Colonial Man and Woman	$350
2256	3 3/4" Girl Holding Gift	$18
2265	4" Girl Pushing Carriage	$22
2287	4 1/2" Baby Girl in Pink Dress and Bow in Hair	$35
2298	7 1/4" Shoemaker at Work	$65
2300	5 1/4" Boy of the Month	$35
2322	4" Bloomer Girls, Pair	$95
02328	7 1/2" Man in Black Robe	$35
2339	4 1/4" Baby Girl	$20
2340	6" Girl w/Two Flower Baskets, Each	$38
2347	Victorian Man w/Hat and Coat, Woman w/Hat and Fan	$38
2349	6 1/4" Man w/Walking Stick	$45
02350	Boy or Girl w/Dog, Each	$22
2353	6" Girl w/Yellow Flowers on Dress and Hat	$45
02355	4 1/2" Clown w/Ball	$15
02356	Clown Figurine, Each	$15
02375	2 1/2" Little Girl w/Cat, Each	$12
2383	4 1/4" Girl in Pink Dress Holding Flowers	$15
2397	4" Nurse, Each	$28
2431	6 1/4" Woman in Flower Stall	$95
2432	6 1/4" Man in Book Stall	$95
2435	6 1/4" Woman w/Fruit	$75
2436	6 1/4" Old Man Reading Paper	$90
2470	3" Girl w/Wreath	$12
2480	"The Watch Maker"	$45
2482	8" Librarian, by Marika	$40
2484	8" Colonial Man and Woman	$110
2498	3" Little Girl Sunbather	$12
2503	5 1/2" Lady in Green Dress w/Umbrella	$40
2504	7 1/4" 1777 Artillery Soldier	$35
2506	7 1/4" 1799 Cavalry Figurine	$35
02529	4 1/2" Hummel-Like Boy and Girl	$50
02539	Hummel-Like Boy and Girl, Each	$35
2544	5 1/4" Children, Each	$40
02546	7" Old Woman w/Boy	$45
2550	7" Old Couple Sitting on Brick Bench	$55
2554	7 1/2" Old Shoemaker	$65
2556	Old Couple Playing Checkers	$85
02559	8" Old Fashioned Barber	$45
2563	7" Piano Lesson	$95
2568	7" Old Ladies Gossiping	$50
2570	4" Girl Carrying Gift	$24
2570	8" Football Player	$45
2571	6" Old Man and Woman w/Vegetable Basket	$22
2573	7" Schoolmarm w/Sleeping Boy, by Marika	$69
2585	5" Boy and Girl, Shelf Sitters, Pair	$35
2614	4" Boy or Girl Graduation	$12

02623	Gibson Girls	$85
2642	4 1/2" Girl w/Flowers	$25
2643	4 1/2" Girl w/Umbrella, Pearl Luster	$25
02719	5 1/2" Girl w/Flowers, Each	$15
02722	4" Barefoot Boy w/Fishing Pole and Dog	$35
2729	3 1/2" Girl w/Bonnet and Patchwork Apron	$18
2730	3 1/2" Girl w/Basket and Chicks	$15
02731	3" Boy w/Dog	$18
02732	3" Girl w/Lamb	$18
02732	3" Boy w/Squirrels	$18
2732	5" Colonial Man and Woman, Pair	$85
2739	5 1/2" Nurse	$28
2775	8" Baseball Player	$35
2777	7 1/2" Football Player, by Marika	$38
2779	4 1/4" Girls w/Flowers	$20
02781	3" Little Boy w/Puppy	$18
2787	4 1/4" Baby Girl	$38
2791	5" Hummel Like Graduating Boy or Girl, Each	$18
2795	4 1/2" Boy and Girl Shelf Sitters, Pearl Luster, Pair	$25
2804	7 1/4" Woman Washing	$50
2807	6 3/4" Man w/Boy Fishing	$95
2817	4 1/2" Girl w/Flower, Each	$25
2820	6" Lady	$40
2821	4 1/2" Girl	$22
2824	10" Pinkie and Blue Boy	$175
02891	4" Little Girl At Fence w/Duck	$18
02891	4 1/2" Girl w/Rabbit	$18
2891	4 1/2" Girl On Fence Holding Next Of Eggs	$18
2891	4 1/2" Boy On Fence w/Bird	$18
2892	5" Barefoot Farm Boy w/Girl	$22
2902	4 1/2" Nurse	$28
2949	5" Angel Leading Donkey w/Child Jesus	$18
3045	7" Colonial Man and Woman, Elaine and Norman, Pair	$145
3046	7" Colonial, George w/Pillow and Mildred w/Hat, Pair	$170
3047	8" Colonial, Jeanne and Adrien	$130
3048	8" Colonial Victoria and Albert	$150
3049	8" Pinkie and Blueboy, Glazed, Pair	$120
3056	3 1/2" Baby w/Squirrel	$25
3058	4" Girl in Bisque	$40
3074	9" Colonial Man and Woman, Pair	$175
3080	4" Bloomer Girl, Each	$55
3081	5 1/4" Four Seasons, Each	$50
3082	Dante and Eugene w/Birds, Each	$45
3083	6 1/2" Beatrice, Matte, Each	$55
3109	Praying Children, Pair	$38
03114	3 3/4" Pilgrim Girl	$10
3119	5 1/2" Boy Holding Dog	$23
3120	3 1/2" Baby in Pink Holding Teddy Bear	$22
3120	3 1/2" Baby in Blue Holding Rabbit	$22
3139	7" Flower Girls w/Hats	$38
3141	Girl in Yellow Dress w/Flower Basket	$28
3205	7 1/4" Lady w/Lace and Applied Flowers	$75
3210	5 3/4" Four Seasons Double	$65
03218	3 1/4" Girl w/Pet, Each	$12
03221	3 1/4" Girl w/Birds	$12
03222	3 1/4" Girl w/Lamb	$12
03222	3 1/4" Boy w/Duck Stealing Boy's Cap	$12
03226	3 1/4" Child w/Bird and Animal	$18
03227	3 1/4" Boy and Girl w/Cat	$18
3244	4 1/2" Sitting Boy and Girl	$38
3254	3 1/2" Pixie, Pearl Luster	$15
3296	4" Gardening Pixies	$15
03327	2 1/2" Boy and Girl	$12
3422	6 1/2" Old Man Playing Guitar for Dog	$55
3428	5 1/2" Colonial Boy and Girl, Pair	$35
3436	7 3/4" Musicians	$45
3437	7 1/2" Pioneer Man and Woman, Pair	$65
3499	5 1/2" Boy and Girl Sitting, Each	$85
3502	7 1/2" Colonial Boy w/Watering Can	$38
3503	6" Boy w/Dog and Girl w/Kitten	$70
3507	8" Man and Woman, Le Pas Regence, Pair	$150
3508	8" Man and Woman "Le Pas De Fantaisie"	$160
3522	4" Leprechaun	$15

3572	6" Gay Nineties Lady w/Floral Muff	$85
3595	7" Babies	$60
3646	Girl in Chair Eating Homemade Ice Cream	$15
03648	4" Girl w/Chicken "Sharing is Caring"	$20
03650	5" Nurse w/Thermometer	$28
3658	10" Colonial Man and Woman, Pair	$250
3660	10" Colonial Man and Woman, Each	$125
3661	8" Colonial Girl w/Grapes	$60
3662	8" Colonial Man and Woman, Pair	$165
3663	7" Colonial Boy and Girl, Pair	$125
03668	3" Girls w/Hearts, Each	$12
3678B	1851 Military Cadet	$48
3678C	1813 Infantry Soldier	$48
3678F	1871 Major General	$48
3678H	1832 Line Officer	$48
3678J	1796 Drummer	$48
3697	5" Lady w/Umbrella, Gay Nineties	$85
3701	4 1/2" Bloomer Girl	$55
03713	3 1/4" Girl or Boy w/Turkey - 1983	$15
3757	4 1/2" Ribbon Girl w/Bird	$30
3825	4 3/4" Man in Chair, "Old Masters"	$55
3826	4 3/4" Lady in Chair, "Old Masters"	$55
3839	5" Sleeping Huckleberry Finn w/Fishing Pole, by Marika	$55
3840	5 1/2" Boy Fishing	$55
03841	4" Boy or Girl Graduation	$25
03843	5" Boy w/Dogs "One Can Never be Alone…"	$23
03845	4 1/2" Boy and Dog	$32
03848	4" Kid Praying	$32
03851	Girl in Nightgown & Cap, "Evening Prayers" by Marika	$25
03851	5 3/4" Girl "Evening Prayer"	$28
03852	4 1/2" Girl and Boy, Pair	$55
03891	4 1/2" Boy of the Month	$18
03897	3 1/2" Kneeling Child w/Doll	$18
03898	4" Child w/Doll "Dolly"	$24
3913	5" Scottish Boy and Girl, Shelf Sitters, Pair	$48
03914	3 3/4" Monthly Birthday Boy, Each	$15
3930	6 1/2" Scottish Boy and Girl w/Bagpipes, Pair	$40
03949	5" Child Praying	$32
3986	7" Boy and Girl Sitting on Tree Limb, Old Masters Series	$140
3987	7" Girl Gathering Flowers, Old Masters Series	$55
3988	6" Boy in Red, Old Masters Series	$55
3989	7" Lady w/Flower Basket, Old Masters Series	$65
3990	7 1/2" Boy and Girl, Old Masters, Each	$65
04036	4" Circus Clown on Ball - 1984	$18
4038	Bloomer-Type Girl in Yellow Dress w/Big Hair Bow	$35
4045	8" Young Man w/Dove	$55
4047	7" Bisque Girl w/Basket	$80
4053	8" Provincial Boy	$65
4054	8" Provincial Boy and Girl, Pair	$115
4062	Boy or Girl Graduate	$15
4140	7" Dancing Boy and Girl, Pair	$80
4146	6 1/4" Old Man and Woman	$95
4200	4" Girl of the Month	$25
4227	4 1/3" Lady w/Hat and Flowers, Glazed	$45
4232	7" Michelle or Margot	$55
4232	6 1/2" Lady Figurine	$22
04233	8" Pinkie & Blue Boy, Pair	$85
4243	5" Provincial Boy and Girl, Pair	$70
04266	4 3/4" Sitting Clown, Each - 1984	$28
04368	3" Irish Boy or Girl - 1984	$14
04415	4 1/2" Graduate	$18
04425	8" Optometrist	$36
04429	8" Waitress	$36
04431	8" Dentist, Bisque	$36
04422	8" Doctor	$40
04460	Girl at Blackboard "School Days"	$26
4461	St. Patrick's Day Irish Boy or Girl, Dollhouse Original	$15
04467	4" Farm Boy or Girl w/Dog	$18
04471	4 3/4" Shepherd Boy	$15
4476	8" Lady Lifting Skirt	$70
4490	9 1/4" Soldier "Artillery"	$80
4494	8" Lady, Green Dress	$80
4506	Hummel Like Girl Watering Flowers	$14

4506	Hummel Like Girl w/Lamb Going To Town	$14
4508	9" British Sailor, "The Captain"	$65
4518	8 1/4" French Lady w/Milliner Box	$65
4530	9 1/2" Soldier, "1863 Cavalry"	$65
4535	6 1/2" Man and Woman Sitting on Chair	$95
4600	8" Man Sitting at Desk	$55
4638	4 3/4" Girl in Pink or Blue, Marked "Marika's Original"	$32
4648	4 3/4" Boy w/Musket	$25
4649	5 3/4" Girls on Chair	$25
4662	3 1/4" Girls	$20
4662	7 3/4" Girl w/Flower Marked "Marika's Original"	$50
4699	4 3/4" Girl w/Flowers Marked "Marika's Original"	$35
4704	4" Nurses	$45
4705	4" Girl Leprechaun	$12
4706	4 1/4" Leprechaun Smoking a Pipe	$12
4707	4 1/2" Nurse Holding Baby	$28
4715	6" Old Woman Holding Dog	$105
4718	6 3/4" Old Shoemaker	$95
4719	6" Old Woman Holding Cat	$105
4723	7 1/2" Old Woman Reading To Children	$65
4724	2 Old Women	$70
4728	4 1/2" Old Man and Woman on Bench	$32
4733	Girl w/Basket of Flowers	$20
4735	4 1/2" Girl w/Mirror and Napkin	$27
4760	4 1/2" Sitting Ballerina, Each	$25
4762	8 1/2" Man Holding Hat w/Top Coat	$45
4770	5 1/4" Girl w/Basket, Marika's Originals	$22
4791	4 1/2" Bloomer Girl w/Umbrella	$45
4797	6" Twin Girl w/Smaller Child	$35
4802	6" Elf on Mushroom, Spins and Rocks, 2 Pieces	$55
4833	4" Bloomer Girl	$55
04857	7 1/4" Clown, Glazed - 1985	$18
4881	5 1/2" Girl and Boy on Seesaw	$45
04894	Little Girl and Rabbit -1985	$14
4903	4 1/2" Colonial Children on Love Seat	$55
4906	5" Pixie on Mushroom	$23
4908	11" Napoleon on Horse	$225
4952	8 1/2" Colonial Lady	$45
5014	Bunny, 3 Piece Set	$18
5048	5" Girl w/Doll	$32
5050	6 3/4" Girl w/Flower Basket	$50
5051	6" Boy or Girl Leaning on Tree w/Dog	$45
5080	4 3/4" Girls	$20
5081	Boy and Girl Playing Hide and Seek	$18
5084	6 1/4" French Artist	$30
5086	7" Sitting Old Woman w/Fruits and Vegetables	$75
5087	6 1/2" Sitting Old Man Playing Cards	$75
5088	6 1/4" Kitchen Scene w/Man and Lady	$105
5089	8" Modern Boy and Girl	$90
5091	6 3/4" Old Woman w/Donkey	$70
5096	6" Dutch Girl	$22
05097	Musical Clowns, 3 Assorted	$30
05100	6 1/2" Ballerina by Marika	$28
05136	6 1/2" Clown w/Mouse - 1985	$28
05138	3 1/2" Sitting Clown - 1985	$25
5144	9" Modern Lady	$40
5146	4 1/2" Girl of the Month	$38
5151	7 1/2" Colonial Man and Woman w/Flowers, Pair	$170
5152	7 1/2" Colonial Man and Woman	$95
5153	5 1/2" Little Girl	$20
5154	4 1/2" Flower Girl	$35
5154	4" Girl Leprechaun	$30
05183	3" Clown Playing Instrument, Pair by Marika	$60
05198	4 1/2" Clown - 1985	$18
5200	China Man Holding Mandolin, Bisque	$38
5240	7" Old Man and Woman Sitting on Bench	$125
5241	8" Old Man Sitting w/Boy	$125
5296	7 1/2" Woodcarver w/Boy	$95
5306	5" Boy Carrying Pig	$23
5306	5" Girl Carrying Goose	$23
5306	51/4" Provincial Boy and Girl	$20

5309	6 1/4" Girl w/Books, Suzanne	$26
05323	6 1/4" Clown - 1985	$35
5339	6" Girl in Ruffled Dress	$38
5340	5" Boy and Girl w/Parrot, Pair	$60
5341	8 1/4" Woman w/Hat	$45
5358	7 1/2" Colonial Couple	$175
5378	6" Kneeling Boy w/Sheep	$40
5436	8" Old Woman Cutting Old Man's Hair	$65
5441	5" Lady w/Hat, Gloves and Applied Floral Dress	$55
5488	5" Girl Holding Bird, marked "Marika's Original"	$45
5489	5 3/4" Girls, marked "Marika's Original"	$45
5490	4" Girl w/Dog	$23
5495	4 1/2" Girl w/Candle Praying	$18
05516	6 1/2" Clown, Glazed, Sevilla Collection	$40
05517	5 1/2" Clown w/Umbrella, Glazed - 1986	$20
5543	5" Farm Children w/Animals, Pair	$38
5555	7" Piano Teacher	$45
5575	6" Boy or Girl w/Flower Basket	$35
5592	7 1/2" Old Woman Sewing Pants Still on Boy	$60
5593	7" Colonial Man and Woman in Chairs, Pair	$125
5600	6" Praying Girl w/Sheep	$40
5604	6" Lady w/Flower Basket and Full Skirt	$60
5640	5" Brown Haired Baby Boy Holding Bottle	$45
5640	5" Blonde Haired Baby Girl Holding Honey Jar	$45
5641	8" Man and Woman w/Jugs	$110
5643	6" Provincial Boy and Girl w/Goose	$110
5664	Provincial Boy and Girl w/Buckets of Fruit, Pair	$145
5667	5 1/2" Boy and Girl in Overalls, Pair	$65
5682	8 1/4" Professor	$60
5687	6 3/4" Country Doctor	$75
5688	6 3/4" Typist	$75
5701	2 Old Women Whispering	$105
5707	3 1/2" Girl w/Flowers, Dollhouse Original by Marika	$20
5708	6" Girl Peeking over Fence	$15
5741	7 1/2" Jeanne w/Umbrella	$125
5742	7 1/2" Lady, "Fifi"	$125
5743	7 1/2" Louise	$125
5744	8" The Book Worm	$65
5744	Suzette, Deep Color Porcelain	$150
5745	7 1/2" Madaline	$175
5746	8 1/4" Chef	$55
5747	8" Doctor	$55
5748	8 1/2" Boy and Girl, Bisque, Pair	$130
5749	7 3/4" Boy and Girl w/Round Base, Pair	$80
5752	8" Man and Lady on Stands	$120
5755	6 1/4" Old Woman w/Ducks	$85
5756	5 1/2" Old Couple on Park Bench Playing Cards	$85
5758	4 1/2" Animals w/Girl Eating Ice Cream Cone	$30
5765	8" Provincial Boy and Girl	$110
5804	8" Judge	$55
5805	8" Salesman	$55
5806	8" Bartender	$55
5808	8" Boy and Girl, Pair	$95
5810	7 1/2" Boy and Girl, Pair	$95
5820	7" Colonial Man and Woman, Pair	$110
5821	7" Colonial Boy and Girl, Pair	$85
5822	7" Provincial Boy and Girl, Pair	$90
5823	7 3/4" Provincial Boy and Girl, Pair	$110
5827	5" Boy and Girl w/Musical Instrument, Pair	$65
5828	6 1/2" x 5" Double Boy and Girl	$60
5832	9 1/2" Man and Woman	$135
5896	7" Provincial Boy and Girl, Pair	$90
5897	8 1/2" Provincial Boy and Girl, Pair	$250
5899	8" Double Colonial Boy and Girl	$85
5901	7 1/4" Old Woman w/Donkey	$45
5946	7 1/2" Boy and Girl, Pair	$75
5965	5 1/4" Provincial Sitting Boy or Girl	$58
5967	7 1/2" Boy or Girl	$65
5968	8 1/2" Provincial Boy and Girl, Pair	$115
5975	9 1/2" Boy & Girl w/Birdhouse and Birds	$35
05989	4" Grandfather and Girl on Bench, by Marika	$22
05989	4" Grandmother and Boy on Bench, by Marika	$22
06014	2 3/4" Girl Holding Shamrocks	$18

06017	3" Girl with Cat	$15
06020	2 1/2" Sitting Girl w/Ball	$12
06020	2 1/2" Sitting Girl Kissing Bunny	$12
06021	Boy and Girl, "Togetherness is Happiness"	$15
06024	3 1/4" Girl w/Ruffled Dress and Hat	$14
06025	2 1/2" Sitting Girl in Large Bonnet	$12
06027	Two Girls Waving Bye, "Fare Thee Well"	$18
06028	Boy and Girl w/Dogs, "A Sweet Thought"	$28
06029	8" Girl w/Flowers	$28
06031	8" Girl Runner	$28
6093	7" Girl w/Flowered Gown	$35
6098	7 3/4" Boy and Girl, Bisque, Pair	$105
6107	4 1/2" Old Man and Woman on Bench	$32
06107	3" Irish Pixie	$5
6141	7 1/2" Provincial Boy and Girl, Pair	$95
6142	7 1/2" Lady	$55
6152	8 1/2" Nurse	$50
6158	4 1/2" Girl Kissing Boy, Dollhouse Original by Marika	$22
6159	4 1/4" Boy and Girl, Dollhouse Original by Marika	$20
6160	8" Old Man and Woman	$110
6184	4" Girls w/Baby Buggy, Dollhouse Originals by Marika, Pair	$40
6203	4" Leprechauns, 3 Assorted	$23
6228	4 1/2" Girl of the Month, Dollhouse Original by Marika	$18
06343	4" Boy of the Month	$23
6348	Old Man Shoveling Coal in Stove	$69
6393	4 1/2" Pixies	$18
6528	4" Girl w/Flowers	$25
06561	5" African American Bride and Groom - 1988	$18
6584	5 1/2" Girl w/Dog and Umbrella	$55
6598	4 1/2" Boy and Girl, marked "Marika's Original", Pair	$30
6643	4 1/2" Girl w/Flower Basket, Pearl Luster	$32
6646	7 1/2" Beggar Man on Park Bench	$58
6651	Man Bowling	$27
6651	8" Man Playing Baseball	$32
06688	Baby Girl in Pink on Half Moon - 1988	$18
06688	Baby Boy in Blue on Half Moon - 1988	$18
6700	Boy Playing Flute	$32
6714	6 1/2" Girl Collecting Apples	$38
6718	4 1/2" Girl Holding Puppy or Kitten, Each	$28
6760	8" Old Man and Puppet Show	$45
6819	8 1/4" Doctor	$36
6886	7" Old Tailor at Sewing Machine	$85
6986	5 1/2" Glazed Girl Holding Cat or Dog, Each	$45
6988	7 1/2" Provincial Girl and Boy, Pair	$65
7017	4" Girl Baking w/Dog	$20
7039	Lady w/Pink Shawl, Floral Hat and Dress	$85
7087	4" Choir Boys, 3 Piece Set	$30
7110	8" Chimney Sweep	$90
7111	8" Clown w/Monkey	$90
7135	4 1/4" Boy Getting Haircut	$28
7136	4 1/2" Girl Bent over Washtub	$25
07152	7 3/4" Nurse, 2 Assorted	$20
7223	7" Provincial Man and Woman w/Tray of Flowers, Pair	$100
7225	8 1/2" Provincial Man and Woman, Pair	$135
7226	8 1/2" Provincial Man and Woman, Pair	$135
7227	Girl of the Month	$40
7251	Barefoot Boy and Girl w/Bird, Pair	$70
7269	7" Old Couple Discussing Their Golf Score	$40
7270	5 1/2" Veterinarian w/Poodle	$75
07271	8" Old Man Feeding Chickens	$55
07277	4" Graduation Boy or Girl	$9
07319	2 1/2" Juggling Clown - 1989	$15
07320	2 1/2" Sitting Clown - 1989	$15
07330	2 1/2" English "Bobbi" - 1989	$14
7450	Old Fashioned Baker	$55
7451	Stockbroker	$65
7453	6 1/2" Boy and Girl Picking Apples, Each	$45
7454	5 3/4" Boy Reading Story to Bird	$28
07479	8 1/2" Nurse Soaking Feet - 1990	$35
07490	4" Sports Boy, Each	$15
07491	8 1/2" Fireman - 1990	$28
07492	9" "Bobbi" Policeman - 1990	$28
07499	4" Leprechaun, 6 Assorted	$6

7501	Hummel Like Skiers - Each	$22
7502	4 1/2" Boy & Girl Skiing - Each	$15
7513	4" Girl Artist	$18
07531	4 1/2" Ballerina	$12
7535	5" Girl or Boy w/Flowers, Dollhouse Original by Marika	$28
7537	5" Boy w/Dog in Wheelbarrow, by Marika	$30
7537	5" Girl at Mailbox w/Letter, by Marika	$30
7541	4" Little Boy and Girl, Pair	$18
07547	Leprechaun Figurines, 3 Piece Set - 1990	$24
07554	Sitting Clown - 1990	$18
07553	5" Clown Playing Guitar	$15
07557	7" Clown w/Dogs	$18
7559	6" Girl Nurse Holding Baby Bottle, Glazed	$28
7563	9 3/4" Provincial Lady Lifting Skirt	$70
7600	6" Birthday Girl Series	$25
7603	7" Voice Teacher w/Pupil	$95
7604	6 3/4" Hobo w/Wine Bottle	$79
7677	8" Lady w/Umbrella	$75
7678	3 3/4" Boy or Girl Baby In Shoe, Each	$22
7738	5" Irish Boy and Girl, Each	$15
07773	2 3/4" Flower Girls, 1990	$12
7776	7 1/4" Cobbler at Bench Working	$80
7777	Old Man Reading Story to Little Girl	$55
7799	5 3/4" Old Lady Painting	$95
7800	6" French Artist	$68
7808	8" Colonial Lady w/Fan	$75
07819	6" Boy or Girl	$22
07820	Girl Washing Little Boy	$15
07821	4" Boy and Girl on a Seesaw	$18
07821	4 3/4" Children in a Kissing Booth	$20
7852	Man & Child on Park Bench	$20
7852	Woman & Child on Bench Sewing Quilt	$20
7853	7 1/2" Old Woman Knitting w/Baby	$45
7855	5 1/4" Man or Lady on Park Bench, Each	$30
7900	8" Dentist	$35
7901	7" Old Man and Boy on Bench Playing Chess, by Marika	$75
7987	8" Boy Sitting On Wooden Crate	$25
7988	4 1/2" Boy or Girl on Fence Feeding Bird	$15
8001	5 1/2" Children	$30
8005	5 1/2" Girl w/Bloomers	$32
8006	6" Girl Playing Croquet or Boy Playing Baseball	$20
8008	6" Boy and Girl Blowing Bubbles	$22
8014	8 1/4" Colonial Man and Woman, Pair	$135
8016	8 1/4" Colonial Man and Woman, Pair	$135
8017	7 1/4" Girl on Tree Stump w/Animal	$70
8149	Irish Shamrock Girl	$18
8155	4" Old Man and Woman on Park Bench	$65
8180	10" Colonial Man & Woman, Pair	$165
8252	3" Country Boy or Girl w/Bunnies	$15
8262	Provincial Woman w/Purple Hat Playing Mandolin	$55
8266	5" Curly Haired Choir Boy	$18
8267	3 1/4" Pink or Blue "Bow Girl"	$15
8274	8" Lady Figurines w/Stippled Gold Fuzz on White, Each	$135
8569	6" Gay Nineties Lady	$95
8570	6" Gay Nineties Lady	$85
8571	6" Gay Nineties Lady w/Muff and Purse	$95
8572	6" Gay Nineties Lady	$115
8573	7 1/2" Gay Nineties Lady, Each	$125
8574	8" Gay Nineties Lady, Each	$135
8613	Girl w/Bunny	$25
8691	8" Gay Nineties Lady w/Umbrella	$150
8692	8" Gay Nineties Lady w/Umbrella	$185
8693	7 1/2" Gay Nineties Lady	$95
8696	5 1/5" Gay Nineties Lady w/Umbrella	$150
8805	5" Boy Playing Banjo for Rabbit	$28
8819	3 3/4" Girl Talking on Phone	$18
8948	4" Girl w/Ponytail and Miniature Identical Doll	$65
8950	4" Nurse	$42
9570	6" Gay Nineties Lady w/Umbrella	$135
9571	Gay Nineties Lady w/Purse and Umbrella	$120
10005	4 1/2" Figure w/Rhinestones	$35
10008	5 1/2" Oriental Man and Woman w/Stones, Pair	$90
10009	9 1/2" Chinese Man and Woman w/Stones, Pair	$165

FIGURINES (cont'd)

10083	9" Oriental Man w/Hat	$45
10160	5 1/2" Nuns Playing Tennis, 3 Piece Set - 1956	$150
10228	7 1/4" French Lady w/Fan and Shawl, Applied Flowered Dress	$90
10229	7 1/4" French Lady Holding Purse, Applied Flowered Dress	$90
10268	8" Chinese Man and Woman w/Lanterns, Pair	$125
10269	8" Japanese w/Fan	$95
10289	10 1/2" Lady w/Umbrella	$175
10290	10 1/2" Lady w/Umbrella	$175
10292	10" Spanish Dancers, White, Black, & Gold, Pair	$125
10293	8 3/4" Siamese Dancers, Pair	$175
10298	7 1/2" French Lady w/Rhinestones	$75
10299	7 1/4" French Lady	$75
10307	Lady Figurines, Each	$60
10337	6" French Lady w/Stones	$60
10402	3" Irish Pixies, 3 Assorted	$6
10484	10 1/2" Chinese Couple w/Stones, Pair	$135
10485	10 1/2" Chinese Couple, Pearl Luster, Pair	$195
10491	Boy Praying, Lil Country Folk Collection "Pray Today" - 1995	$22
10496	Girl w/Doll, Lil Country Folk Collection "I Love Thee" - 1995	$22
10497	Girl w/Rabbits, Lil Country Folk Collection "Count Thy Blessings"	$22
10498	Girl Gardener, Lil Country Folk "Bloom Where..." - 1995	$22
10530	4 1/4" Kissing Couple, Pair	$60
10531	4" Flower Girl	$45
10532	Waitress Bloomer Girl	$80
10534	7 1/2" Lady w/Umbrella, Pink	$145
10535	7" Lady w/Umbrella, Pink or White	$145
10566	6 1/4" Lady w/Muff	$85
10571	4" Chinese w/Stones, Pair	$65
10600	8" Chinese Ladies, Pair	$135
10616	Man Carrying Buckets - 1995	$15
10624	3" Leprechauns, 3 Assorted	$7
10659	6" Clown w/Umbrella - 1995	$18
10659	6" Clown w/ Ball - 1995	$18
10659	6" Clown w/Bow Tie - 1995	$18
10667	3" Clown with Horn - 1995	$9
10667	3" Clown with Balloon - 1995	$9
10667	3" Clown with Flower - 1995	$9
10668	2 1/2" Sitting Clown Playing Violin - 1995	$9
10668	2 1/2" Sitting Clown Playing Horn - 1995	$9
10668	2 1/2" Sitting Clown Holding Shoes - 1995	$9
10669	4 1/2" Clown with Saxophone and Bird - 1995	$11
10669	4 1/2" Clown with Rabbit in Hat - 1995	$11
10669	4 1/2" Clown with Birds - 1995	$11
10669	4 1/2" Clown Playing Violin - 1995	$11
10669	4 1/2" Clown With Hat Trick - 1995	$11
10669	4 1/2" Clown Playing Concertina - 1995	$11
10774	1st Communion Girl w/Mesh Veil, Each - 1996	$15
10822	5" Pilgrims, 2 Assorted, Each	$10
10823	4" Pilgrims	$8
10824	4" Pilgrims	$8
10840	4" Pilgrims	$8
10841	5" Pilgrims	$10
10844	8" Nurse in Green Uniform, 3 Assorted	$20
10863	Ballerina by Yamada, 3 Different Poses, Each	$15
11139	8" Male Nurse in Green Uniform	$20
11140	6" Nurse w/Baby	$10
11483	Snow Girl on Sled	$10
11484	Snow Boy and Girl on See Saw	$10
11485	Snow Boy and Girl with Skis	$11
11486	Snow Boy Skating	$9
11487	Girl with Snowman	$10
11488	3 1/2" Snowman on Snowboard	$12
11489	3 1/2" Snowman Carrying Skies	$12
11490	3 1/2" Snowman on Skies	$12
11491	3 1/2" Fallen Snowman w/Ice Skates	$12
11492	3 1/2" Snowmen on Ice Skates	$12
11493	3 1/2" Snowcouple on Ice Skates	$10
11494	3 1/2" Snowman on Skies	$10
11495	3 1/2" Snowmen Carolers	$10
11496	3 1/2" Snow Couple	$10
11499	2" Indian "Indian Mother Holding Baby"	$10

11500	2" Indian "Indian w/Fur"	$10
11501	2" Indian w/Peace Pipe	$7
11502	2" Indian "Sitting Indian w/Gold Deco on Hair"	$10
11503	2" Indian "Sitting Indian w/Red Band in Hair"	$10
11504	Mother and Daughter Indians	$11
11542	3 1/2" Irish Pixie, 3 Assorted	$7
11543	3 1/4" Irish Leprechauns	$7
13020	Girl Ballerina in Pink - 1999	$25
21266	4 1/2" Oriental Man w/Mandolin	$30
12268	9" Oriental Figurines w/Lanterns	$135
25564	6 1/2" Girl Playing Mandolin	$32
25661	8" Politician	$55

FLORAL CHINTZ

2119	Cup and Saucer	$55
2120	Demitasse Cup and Saucer	$50
8033	Coffee Pot	$155
8034	Sugar and Creamer	$55
8035	Cup and Saucer	$25
8036	7" Plate	$15
8037	9" Plate	$28
8038	6 1/4" Pitcher and Bowl	$65
8039	5 1/4" Pitcher and Bowl	$55
8040	3 1/2" Pitcher and Bowl	$25
8041	Nappy Dish, 3 Assorted Shapes, Each	$18
8042	Footed Candy Dish w/Lid	$48
8043	7" Compote	$22

FRAMES

271	5" Yellow or Pink w/Floral Design	$18
668	7" Pink w/Floral Design	$18
669	5" Blue w/Floral Design	$18
779	4 3/4" Antique Ivory Bisque w/Applied Flowers	$18
00858	Red and Gold Heart Design	$15
1192	25th Anniversary	$12
1372	7" Oval Opening w/Daisies	$12
1373	4 3/4" Shasta Daisy	$18
1375	6 1/4" Heart Shaped, Shasta Daisy	$35
1899	4 3/4" Floral	$12
1918	4" White Bisque	$20
1919	3 1/2" Picture	$18
1932	4 3/4" Single	$18
1933	7" Double, Wild Rose	$48
01954	4" x 5" w/Violets	$18
02618	4" x 5" w/Shamrock Design	$14
2717	3 1/4" Double, White w/Gold	$15
03127	4" x 5" w/Floral Design	$18
3157	5 x 7 w/Violets	$15
03174	5" Square w/Flowers	$15
03261	Angel of the Month - 1983	$18
03483	5 1/2" Alphabet	$20
03530	5" Glazed w/Floral Design	$12
3535	4 1/2" w/Flowers "To Mother"	$12
03542	2 3/4" Frame w/Flowers	$12
03797	5" Graduation Girl - 1983	$15
4112	4" w/Roses	$10
4113	5" w/Roses	$15
04285	4"x 3" w/Hand Painted Flowers	$15
4480	5" w/Applied flowers	$18
04495	5" x 7" Oval Opening w/Floral and Gold Design	$14
04674	5 1/2" w/Violets and Gold Boarder	$12
04806A	4 1/2" Apple Shaped Frame w/Boy and Girl Doll	$12
04806B	4 1/2" Heart Shaped Frame w/Dolls and Dog	$12
05025	3 1/2" w/Balloons and Teddy Bear	$12
06258	Artists Palette w/Bear Holding Brush "Our Baby," 1987	$10
7221	Oval w/Cherubs	$75
07254	7 1/4" Oval Double w/Floral Design	$28
10587	5" Frame, 25th Anniversary	$9
10598	5" Frame, 50th Anniversary	$9
11075	4" Shamrocks	$8
11600	Heart Shaped Blue Bisque Frame, Baltic Rose	$10

11602	Blue Bisque with White Roses, Baltic Rose	$18
11603	Blue Bisque with White Roses, Baltic Rose	$12
13013	Irish Lace - 1999	$14
90161	6 1/2" w/Applied Pink Roses, Glazed - 1956	$35
90511	4" w/Applied Roses and Rhinestones	$25

FRUIT BASKET/TUTTI FRUIT

1657	Salt and Pepper	$28
1658	Two Compartment Dish	$28
1659	Three Compartment Dish	$32
1662	Four Compartment Dish	$38
1663	Serving Bowl	$32
1665	Egg Plate	$35
1666	7 1/8" Butter Dish	$35
1667	Creamer and Sugar	$55
1668	Teapot	$75
1669	Condiment Set w/Spoon and Tray	$50
1670	Large Pitcher	$55
1671	Medium Pitcher	$45
1672	Gravy Boat	$38
1673	Oil and Vinegar	$50
1674	Cookie Jar	$95
1675	Covered Casserole	$55
1676	Canister Set, 4 Pieces	$120
1677	Cigarette Box and 2 Ashtrays	$28
1678	Compote	$32
1679	Egg Cup	$18
1680	Jam Jar	$38
1682	Salad Bowl w/Salad Fork and Spoon	$55
1686	Three Compartment Dish	$65
1890	Candleholders	$22
1891	11" Chip and Dip Plate	$38
1893	Plate w/Handle	$45
1894	Celery Dish	$28
1895	Teapot Teabag Holder	$28
1896	Two Tier Tidbit Tray	$55
1952	Candy or Nut Dish	$28
21198	ESD Teapot	$60
21203	ESD Salt and Pepper Shakers	$25
21214	ESD Round Covered Cheese Dish	$38
21216	ESD Jam Jar w/Tray	$30

FRUITS OF ITALY

621	Cookie Jar	$60
623	Jam Jar	$25
1175	Teapot	$65
1176	Coffee Pot	$95
1177	Sugar and Creamer	$22
1178	Two Compartment Dish	$20
1179	Three Compartment Dish	$22
1205	8 5/8" Compote	$28
1207	Salt and Pepper	$15
1208	6 1/2" Pitcher	$15
1209	Mug	$10
1211	11 1/4" Relish Tray w/Twist Handle	$18
1212	Two Tier Tidbit Tray	$45
1335	Covered Candy Dish	$38

GARY PATTERSON COLLECTION, THE

11690	4" Ornament, "Hook Line and Sinker"	$10
11691	4 3/4" Ornament, "Great Outdoors Man"	$10
11692	3 1/2" Ornament, "King of the Hill"	$10
11693	3 3/4" Ornament, "King Pin"	$10
11694	3 7/8" Ornament, "Super Fan"	$10
11695	4" Ornament, "World's Greatest Golfer"	$10
11696	4" Ornament, "Tennis Ace"	$10
11697	2 1/4" Ornament, "Fisherman Santa"	$10
11698	3 3/4" Ornament, "Santa Hockey Player"	$10
11699	4" Ornament, "Wishes and Dreams"	$10
11751	6" "Sports Fan"	$40

11752	4" "Now What?"	$25
11753	6" "Thrill of Victory"	$40
11754	6" "Up The Creek"	$24
11755	4" "Tips Up"	$25
11756	4" "#1 Dad"	$25
11757	8" "The Hazard" Water Fountain	$65
11758	4" "Super Mom"	$25
11759	6" "Art of Casting"	$40
11760	4" "Golf Lover"	$25
11761	4" "Fully Equipped"	$25
11762	6" "Mr. Fix It"	$40
11763	6" "It's Only A Game"	$40
11764	4" "Super Fan"	$25

GLASSWARE

00673	6" Glass Christmas Tree, Clear	$14
00790	7" Frosted Glass Angel, 3 Assorted	$30
00791	4" Glass Angel, 3 Assorted	$20
01169	5" Glass Animal Paperweights, 6 Assorted	$15
01301	6" Glass Christmas Tree, Green	$14
01302	6" Glass Christmas Tree, Red	$14
01508	5" Angel, 3 Assorted	$19
01509	Paperweight Shell	$18
05698	7" Glass Angel	$20
05726	4" Butterfly Box w/Gold Butterfly	$18
05728	2" Round Crystal Box w/Butterfly	$20
05734	2" Heart Box w/Gold Butterfly on Lid	$12
05997	5 1/2" Elephant Paperweight	$25
06820	3" Flower Box w/Gold Flower on Lid	$12
06953	4 1/2" Box w/2 Birds on Lid - 1998	$23
07714	4 1/2" Seal	$18
07715	10" Blue Dolphin	$28
07897	8 1/2" Glass Angel	$25
07898	5 1/2" Glass Angel	$17
07899	4 1/4" Glass Angel	$12
07978	5" Dolphin w/Wave	$22
10425	Glass Plaque - Walrus	$24
10426	Glass Plaque - Whale	$24
10427	Glass Plaque - Orca	$24
10429	Glass Plaque - Penguin	$24
10435	Sea Urchin Paperweight	$22
10865	6" 25th Anniversary Glass Tray	$13
10866	6" 50th Anniversary Glass Tray	$13
11867	6" Happy Anniversary Glass Tray	$13
11868	8 3/4" 25th Anniversary Glass Tray	$19
11889	8 3/4" 50th Anniversary Glass Tray	$19
11890	8 3/4" Happy Anniversary Glass Tray	$19
11035	2" Pitcher, White Glass	$22
11378	3 1/2" Pink Glass Bird	$15
11379	3 1/2" Blue Glass Bird	$15
11380	2 1/2" Green Glass Frog	$15
11381	2 1/2" Pink Glass Rabbit	$15
11382	5 1/2" Pink Glass Rabbit	$15
11383	4 1/2" Blue Glass Cat	$15
11383	3" Sitting Cat, Blue Glass	$22
11385	7" Woman Golfer, Limited Edition - 1997	$70
11386	7" Man Golfer, Limited Edition - 1997	$70

GOOD NEWS BEAR COLLECTION

11032	3 1/2" Good News Bear & Noah's Arc (Psalm 116:15)	$15
11033	3 1/2" Good News Bear Backpacking (Psalm 51:10)	$15
11034	3 1/2" Good News Bear Flying Kite (Romans 12:12)	$15
11035	3 1/2" Good News Bear By Fence (Psalm 62:1)	$15
11036	3 1/2" Good News Bear Picnicking (Psalm 51:10-17)	$15
11037	3 1/2" Good News Bear In Quilt (2 Cor.1:3-5)	$15
11038	3 1/2" Good News Bear At School (Psalm 27:11)	$15
11039	3 1/2" Good News Bear Painting (Eph.2:10)	$15
11040	3 1/2" Good News Bear Gardening (James 3:18)	$15
11041	3 1/2" Good News Bear Picking Flowers (Matthew 6:25-34)	$15
11042	3 1/2" Good News Bear Cheerleader (Psalm 100:1)	$15
11043	3 1/2" Good News Bear in Raincoat (Psalm 55:8)	$15

GREEN HERITAGE FLORAL - 1960

510	Coffee Pot	$150
578	Ornate Sugar and Creamer	$60
719	7 1/4" Cake Plate w/ Gold	$30
731	3 1/4" Pitcher Vase, 3 Assorted, Each	$15
748	5" Vase, 3 Assorted, Each	$20
792	Teapot	$165
796	Water Pitcher	$125
1151	Demitasse Cup and Saucer	$30
1152	Jam Jar	$50
1153	Two Tier Tidbit Tray	$65
1266	Tumbleup	$125
1860	Leaf Shaped Nappy, 3 Assorted - Each	$22
2274	7" Compote	$35
3065	Coffee Pot	$150
3066	Sugar and Creamer	$70
3067	Cup and Saucer	$35
3068	7 1/4" Plate	$25
3069	9" Plate	$35
3070	2 1/4" Salt and Pepper	$28
3071	Snack Set	$28
3708	6" Bone Dish	$22
4053	5" Footed Candy Dish	$50
4072	8 1/2" Vase, 3 Assorted, Each	$50
4169	11" Oil Lamp	$210
4171	13" Oil Lamp	$225
4172	4 1/4" Pitcher and Bowl	$55
4577	3 1/2" Pitcher and Bowl	$38
4578	5 1/4" Pitcher and Bowl	$60
4579	6 1/4" Pitcher and Bowl	$65
4998	4 1/2" Pitcher	$17
5206	3" Round Pin Dish	$15
5207	2 3/4" Ring Holder	$20
5649	6" Gravy Boat and Dish	$75
5695	Vase	$28
6069	9" Plate	$35
6131	6 1/4" Candy Dish	$48

GREEN HERITAGE - 1987

02069	9" x 7" Tray w/Handles	$40
05680	Cup and Saucer	$28
05850	9 1/2" Coffee Pot	$75
05851	4" Sugar and Creamer	$40
05852	Cup and Saucer	$28
05853	Demi Cup and Saucer	$25
05854	Cup and Saucer	$25
05855	7" Plate	$22
05856	9 1/4" Plate	$25
05857	6 1/2" Teapot	$60
05858	9" Scalloped Cake Plate	$35
05860	Pitcher Vase	$18
05864	6 1/2" Vase	$18
06075	Salt and Pepper Shakers	$25
06076	Tumble Up	$65
06077	Water Pitcher	$68

GREEN HERITAGE - 1999

12367	7" Pitcher	$25
12369	9" x 7" Dresser Tray	$45
12370	9" Round Plate	$32
12371	8 1/2" Two Handled Vase	$30
12378	Candleholder, Pair	$40
12829	2 1/2" Heart Shaped Box	$18
12830	6" Compote	$32
12831	5" Egg Planter	$22
12832	6 1/2" Nappy Dish	$18
12833	Leaf Nappy Dish	$18

GREEN HERITAGE - FRUIT

6272	Water Pitcher	$65
6275	Snack Set	$35
6276	Cup and Saucer	$30
6279	Pitcher and Bowl	$33
6280	Pitcher and Bowl	$35
6283	7" Nappy, Each	$25

HEAD VASES

041	7" Lady's Head, "Scarlett"	$125
046	6" Lady's Head, "Margo"	$85
051	5" Glazed Head, "Scarlett"	$90
063	7" Lady's Head, "Elaine"	$95
541	6 1/2" Lady's Head	$60
611	5 1/2" Man and Woman, Glazed, Pair	$125
624	5 1/4" Lady's Head	$45
641	5" Lady's Head w/Protruding Lashes and Roses	$75
1086	6" Lady's Head w/Jewelry, Pearl Luster	$85
1115	5 1/2" Blonde w/Jewelry	$85
1229	5 1/2" Lady's Head	$45
1232	3 3/4" Young Girl w/Hat	$35
1282	Young Girl w/Long Red Hair and Hat	$112
1343	6 1/2" Lady's Head, Each	$52
1458	8 1/2" Lady's Head	$65
1736	5 1/2" Lady's Head	$125
1843	6" Lady's Head, Pearl Luster	$75
2143	6" Lady's Head w/Flowers in Hair and Long Lashes	$65
2149	6" Lady's Head	$80
2251	6" Blonde Haired Lady's Head, w/Gloved Hand	$55
2258	4 1/2" Lady's Head w/Broach and Protruding Lashes	$80
2358	6" Lady's Head w/Broach and Protruding Lashes	$80
2359	6 1/4" Lady's Head w/Rose and Protruding Lashes	$65
2424	4 1/2" Lady's Head, Pearl Luster	$60
2536	6" Long Haired Blonde w/Gloved Hand	$60
2568	6 1/2" Lady w/Pearl Necklace & Earrings, Pearl Luster	$65
2666	6 1/2" Lady w/Long Lashes and Applied Yellow Rose	$48
2705	6" Lady's Head	$65
2900	6" Lady's Head Resting on Hands, Protruding Lashes	$125
3130	4 1/2" Lady's Head w/Long Lashes	$43
3140	6" Lady's Head w/Applied Lavender Flowers	$85
3259	6 3/4" Lady's Head w/Gloved Hand & Feathered Hat	$65
3276	6" Lady's Head w/Necklace and Gloved Hand	$65
3278	6" Lady w/Gloved Hands and Long Lashes	$55
3514	5 1/2" Lady's Head w/Lashes, Design by Marika	$60
3515	Head Vase w/Lashes, Green Hat w/White Bow	$60
3517	Head Vase w/Tiara and Red Stones	$85
4228	6" Lady w/Gloved Hands, Hat and Long Lashes	$95
4310	7" Lady's Head w/Pearl Necklace and Earrings	$85
4556	5 1/2" Lady's Head w/Scarf	$55
4596	5 1/2" Lady's Head w/Dangle Pearl Earrings	$75
4796	6" Blonde Girl w/Braids and Blue Bow	$68
5562	6" Lady's Head w/Blonde Hair & Hat w/Yellow Daisies	$50
5920	5 3/4" Blonde Lady w/Hood Head Covering	$65
6525	5 3/4" Lady's Head w/Necklace, Earrings & Ruffled Hat	$55
6638	6" Lady's Head w/Necklace and Earrings	$60
7499	6 1/4" Girls w/Basket Hats by Marika, Set of 3	$60
13438	6" Lady w/Matching Hat and Dress	$80
50414	6" Young Girl in Yellow Hat	$55
50416	6 1/2" Girl Head w/Pigtails and Large Bow - 1956	$55
50506	6" Lady w/Hat and Gloved Hand, Black, Gold, White	$65
50507	6 1/2" Lady w/Hat & Gloved Hand, Black, Gold, White	$65
70565	5 1/2" Lady's Head	$90

HISTORIC WILLIAMSBURG COLLECTION

11050	Kings Arms Taverns	$50
11051	Brunton Parish Church	$55
11052	The Governors Palace	$75
11053	George Wythe House	$25
11054	The Capitol	$75
11703	Prentis Store	$50

11704	Courthouse	$70
11705	Christiana Campbell's Tavern	$55
11706	Phaethon Coach	$29
11707	Mother w/Two Daughters	$9
11708	Pillory	$8
11709	Statesman on Horse	$9
11710	Two Soldiers w/Cannon	$15
11711	Colonial Williamsburg Band	$15

JARS

456	Jam - Strawberry	$22
623	Jam - Fruits of Italy	$24
710	Jam - Moss Rose	$18
1038	Potpourri - 8" White Bisque w/Applied Flowers	$65
1298	Jam - Celery Line	$40
1414	Jam - White Blossom w/Butterfly Handle	$25
1416	Jam - w/Strawberry on Lid	$28
1418	4" Barrel w/Strawberry on Lid	$32
1451	Jam - Cuddles	$35
1481	6" Relish w/Onion Head Lid/Spoon	$65
1482	5 1/4" Mustard w/Hamburger Head Lid/Spoon	$65
1484	5 1/2" Ketchup w/Tomato Head Lid/Spoon	$65
1485	5 1/2" Jam and Jelly, Apple Head	$80
1508	Jam - Garden Daisy	$18
1697	Jam - Thumbelina	$65
1958	Jam - Della Robbia	$18
2121	5" Instant Coffee w/Spoon, Brown Bat	$18
2128	Jam - Cabbage Cutie	$45
2526	Jam - Golden Laurel	$22
2553	Jam - Pig	$28
2661	Jam - Fruit (Many Assorted)	$28
2697	Jam - Dutch Girl	$85
2757	Jam - Floral Design	$25
2827	Jam - Whiteware	$18
2844	Jam - Grape	$45
02952	Ginger - Goldfinch	$22
02953	Ginger - Red Cardinal	$22
02954	Ginger - Daisies	$20
02957	Ginger - Bird on Branch	$22
3021	Jam - Pineapple	$18
3023	Jam - Grape	$35
3031	Jam - Vineyard	$18
3039	Jam - Blue Rose	$30
3063	Jam - Heavenly Rose	$55
3133	Jam - Fruit Delight	$18
3231	Jam - Apple Shape w/Floral Design	$22
3263	4 3/4" Stacked French Rose, Set	$32
3290	Jam - Mr. Toodles	$55
3358	Jam - Daisy Time	$22
3468	Jam - Fruit Top	$15
3804	Jar, Clock Instant Coffee Holder	$20
4116	Rustic Daisy w/Handle	$18
4127	Jam - Pear N Apple	$28
4255	Jam - Pear N Apple	$28
4407	Jam - Rose	$18
4605	Jam - Rooster	$18
4614	Jam - Blue Country Charm	$20
4615	Jam - Rooster	$18
4630	Jam - Turkey	$22
4668	Jam - Rose Design	$20
4804	JAVA, Brown Oriental Figurine	$28
4956	Jam - Pear N Apple	$28
4983	Instant Coffee, Lt Blue w/Tile Design and Apple Handle	$22
5033	Jam - Pink Daisy w/Spoon	$15
5283	Jam - Fiesta	$15
5405	Jam - Hot Poppy	$15
5704	Jam - Grape, ESD Mark	$30
5723	Jam - 50th Anniversary	$12
6318	Jam - Floral Design	$28
6358	Jam - Mushroom Forest	$32
6363	Jam - Mushroom	$28
6509	Jam - Bossie the Cow	$30

6572	Jam - Lavender Rose	$18
6727	Jam - Fruit Fantasia	$28
6748	Jam - Paisley Fantasia	$45
7151	Condiment w/Attached Tray, Floral Design	$18
7157	Jam - Floral Design	$25
07402	Ginger - Black w/Rose Pattern	$25
7541	Jam n' Jelly - ESD Holt Howard Like, ESD Mark	$45
7598	Marmalade - ESD Holt Howard Like, ESD Mark	$45
7599	Relish -ESD Holt Howard Like, ESD Mark	$45
7858	Cocktail Cherries - Holt Howard Type w/Spoon Lid, ESD Mark	$48
7859	Cocktail Olives - Holt Howard Type w/Spoon Lid, ESD Mark	$48
7860	Instant Coffee - Holt Howard Type, ESD Mark	$45
7995	Jam-Green Basketweave w/Purple Flowered Lid	$23
08051	Ginger-Bird on Branch	$22
08053	Ginger-Bird on Branch	$18
22074	Jam - ESD Dutch Girl	$48

KEWPIES

130	4 1/2" Kewpie of the Month, Each	$40
143	4 3/4" Kewpie	$46
145	6 3/4" Kewpie Bank	$50
00164	3" Box, Heart Shaped Bed w/Two Kewpies	$15
228	4 1/2" Bisque Kewpie, 3 Different Poses, Each	$33
229	4" Kewpie on Scroll w/Applied Roses	$55
338	7 3/4" Kewpie on Pillow Holding Lily Flower, Vase	$65
400	4 1/4" Kewpie on Base w/Doll - 1963	$45
400	4 1/4" Kewpie on Base w/Dog - 1963	$45
913	3" Kewpie, 6 in set, Each	$20
1233	3" Kewpie Graduate in Cap and Gown, Pair by Marika	$40
1795	3" Kewpie Playing Football, by Marika	$35
1795	3" Kewpie Playing Golf, by Marika	$35
1795	3" Kewpie Playing Baseball, by Marika	$35
1796	3" Kewpie Cowboy, by Marika	$35
1796	3" Kewpie Policeman, by Marika	$35
1796	3" Kewpie Fireman, by Marika	$35
1796	3" Kewpie Doctor, by Marika	$35
1796	3" Kewpie Nurse, by Marika	$35
1796	3" Kewpie Teacher, by Marika	$35
02132	3" Kewpie, Each	$32
2175	Girl Kewpie Holding Heart, Each	$25
2182	3 1/2" Sitting Kewpie	$32
02448	3" Kewpie in Flower	$18
2718	7" Kewpie Planter	$42
2992	Thumb Sucking Kewpie Sitting On Leaves w/Flowers	$45
2992	Frowning Kewpie Laying on Leaves w/Flowers	$45
02997	Kewpie w/White Helmet and Football	$20
3239	3 1/2" Kewpies w/Bows, Pair	$69
03268	2 1/2" Kewpie Couple	$60
3531	7" Kewpie Planter by Marika	$32
3631	7" Kewpie Planter	$38
3642	5" Double Kewpies	$38
3823	4" Kewpie Planter	$32
3841	5" Kewpie Wearing Shoes and Socks	$45
05171	3" Birthday Kewpies Years 1-6, by Marika	$300
05172	2 1/2" Kneeling Kewpie w/Heart Bib - 1985	$35
05173	2 1/3" Sitting Kewpie w/Heart Bib - 1985	$35
05174	2 1/2" Kewpie w/Bib and Booties - 1985	$35
05176	3" Kewpie Doctor - 1985	$38
05181	2 1/2" Kewpie on Leaf - 1985	$35
05182	4" Kewpie Riding A Unicorn - 1985	$50
05183	3" Clown Kewpie - 1985	$18
05187	5 3/4" Kewpie on Unicorn, "Toyland", Marika's Original - 1985	$38
05314	2 1/2" Sitting Kewpie w/Bib - 1985	$28
5718	6 1/2" Kewpie Lamp by Marika	$50

KITCHEN ITEMS

384	Egg Plate w/Floral Center	$18
00645	Teapot Teabag Holder, Shamrocks - 1992	$10
815	Tea Caddy w/Roses and Violets	$28
900	4 3/4" x 6 1/4" China Cutting Board w/Knife Slot	$32
1018	10" Two Compartment Relish Tray, Symphony in Fruit	$28

KITCHEN ITEMS (cont'd)

1295	13" Egg Plate, Celery Line	$32
1457	5" Napkin Holder, Poppy, Wheat and Corn	$20
1560	Double Spoon Rest, Man and Woman	$32
1611	7" Rooster w/Holes for Hors D'oeuvre Toothpicks	$48
1665	Fruit Covered Deviled Egg Dish	$45
1863	3 Compartment Relish Tray w/Knife Holder, Mouse Design	$35
1865	3 Compartment Jam Tray w/Knife Holder, Mouse Design	$28
1895	Napkin Rings, Set of 6	$36
1905	Bagels and Lox Serving Tray	$35
2125	Spoon Rest, Cabbage Cutie	$40
2354	Applied Grape Tea Strainer	$38
2897	Toothpick Holder, White Daisy	$22
02898	Toothpick Holder, Floral Pattern	$12
03317	Teapot Teabag Holder, Floral	$12
3655	4 1/2" "Breadsticks" Holder	$15
3731	14" x 12" Four Compartment Serving Tray, Green Orchard	$45
4003	Dove Place Card Holder	$8
4128	14" x 12" Four Compartment Serving Tray, Pear N Apple	$45
4129	12" Two Compartment Serving Tray, Pear N Apple	$38
4215	5" Square Tile Trivet w/Scalloped Edge, Daisy Pattern	$18
4273	13" x 9 1/2" Corn on the Cob Platter w/Drainer	$45
4515	14 1/2" Four Compartment Serving Tray, Bagels and Lox	$45
04679	Teapot Teabag Holder, Floral - 1984	$15
4920	Three Compartment Tray w/Handle, Gold Pear N Apple	$28
4977	12" Egg Plate w/Salt and Pepper, Pear N Apple	$40
4978	12" Egg Plate w/Salt and Pepper, Green Orchard	$32
4979	12" Egg Plate w/Salt and Pepper, Rooster	$35
05122	Egg Plate with Chick Salt and Pepper Shakers - 1985	$22
5161	Chip and Dip Server, Pink Daisy	$48
5409	Egg Tray, Fiesta	$36
5843	Napkin Holder, Hot Poppy	$28
5848	Napkin Holder, Fiesta	$35
6500	Egg Tray, Blue Aster	$35
6240	Three Compartment Dish, Chrysanthemum	$35
6243	Napkin Holder, Country Garden	$24
6324	12" Egg Plate, Mushroom Forest - 1970	$36
6360	Napkin Holder, Mushroom Forest - 1970	$22
6436	4 1/4" Toothpick Holder, Petite Fleurs	$12
6459	6" Potato Sour Cream Holder w/Spoon	$18
6465	Gravy Boat w/Platter, Mushroom Forest	$26
6474	Hors D'oeuvre Tray, Mushroom Forest	$40
6511	Spoon Holder, Bossie the Cow	$22
6523	Egg Tray, Green w/Blue & White Flowers - 1970	$35
6672	Teapot Teabag Holder	$9
6728	Napkin Holder, Fruit Fantasia	$24
6953	10" Porcelain Handled Crumb Collector, Victorian Couple	$48
7253	Napkin Rings, Pink Floral w/Blue Ribbons, Set of 6	$30
7976	Napkin Holder, Harvest Pansy	$16
8078	Pansy Ring, Pansy and Rose Floral, Glazed	$125
8282	Teabag Holder, Floral	$10
21657	9" French Dressing, Holt Howard Style, ESD Mark	$55
21658	9" Russian Dressing, Holt Howard Style, ESD Mark	$55
21659	9" Italian Dressing, Holt Howard Style, ESD Mark	$55

LAMPS

378	6" Praying Girl or Boy Musical Night Light "Brahms Lullaby"	$38
531	6 1/2" Bisque Night Light, Angel w/Flowers	$60
00846	4" Guardian Night Light	$8
931	14" Oil Lamp, Rose Pattern w/Gold Accents	$95
932	8 3/4" Hobnail Milk Glass	$36
01899	7 1/2" Night Light, Clown	$45
2059	5 3/4" Girl or Boy Musical Night Light, "Love Is A Many..."	$35
02076	5" Sleeping Dog on Basket	$45
4208	7 3/4" Oil w/Flowers	$35
04912	5 1/2" Night Light, Poodle w/Dog House - 1985	$15
04969	5" Night Light, Swans - 1985	$28
05669	6" Guardian Angel Night Light	$27
6143	6 1/4" Night Light, Bluebird	$45
6625	6 1/2" Night Light, Girl or Boy	$35
6644	6" Night Light, Poodle by Marika	$32

7090	6" Night Light, Raggedy Andy	$45
07225	8" Night Light, Boy Clown	$45
7919	6" Night Light, Boy or Girl w/Balloons by Marika	$42
7920	6" Night Light Mouse w/Mushroom	$28
10096	6" Night Light, Praying Angel	$22
10097	6 1/4" Night Light	$25
10098	6 1/4" Night Light, Angels	$25
10690	6" Night Light, Guardian Angel	$33
11891	Girl Angel Praying	$38
11892	Boy Angel Praying	$38

LAVABOES

3262	White Ware, 3 Pieces	$75
4160	Della Robbia, 2 Pieces	$65
6608	Applied Flowers, 2 Pieces	$70
8131	11" Spring Bouquet, 2 Pieces	$95
11952	White Ware, 2 Pieces	$75

LIGHTHOUSE COLLECTION/LIGHTHOUSES

01187	6" Sandy Hook, New Jersey - 1993	$38
01188	6 1/2" Cape Hatteras, North Carolina - 1993	$30
01189	6 1/4" Cape Lookout, North Carolina - 1993	$30
01190	6" Cape Henry - 1993	$162
01192	6" Assateague, Virginia - 1993	$30
01195	6" Boston Harbor, Massachusetts - 1993	$45
01201	6" Tybee Island, Georgia - 1993	$30
01203	Cana Island, Wisconsin - 1993	$25
01410	5 1/4" New London Ledge, Connecticut - 1994	$30
01419	6" Fire Island, New York - 1994	$25
08607	Limited Edition Boston Harbor, Massachusetts - 1995	$180
08649	Limited Edition Alcatraz, California - 1997	$100
08657	Limited Edition Morris Island, North Carolina - 1998	$65
10971	6" Point Isabel, Texas - 1996	$25
10975	6" Los Angeles Harbor, California - 1997	$25
11517	6" Holland Harbor, Michigan - 1997	$25
11519	6" Currituck Beach, North Carolina - 1997	$25
12116	4" Fort Niagara, New York - 1998	$23
12185	6 1/2" Cape Hatteras, North Carolina - 1998	$23
12186	5" Cape May, New Jersey - 1998	$23
12188	6" Currituck Beach, North Carolina - 1998	$23
12190	6" St. Augustine, Florida - 1998	$23
12192	6" Barnegat, New Jersey - 1998	$23
12212	3" Holland Harbor, Michigan - 1998	$23
12230	4 1/2" Fort Niagara, New York - 1998	$23
12231	6" Cape Cod, Massachusetts - 1998	$23
12232	6" Assateague, Virginia - 1999	$25
12234	3" Point Betsie, Michigan - 1998	$23
12236	4" Chicago Harbor, Illinois - 1998	$23
12237	4" Old Mackinac Point, Michigan - 1998	$23
12238	6" Fire Island, New York - 1998	$23
12248	4" New London Harbor, Connecticut - 1998	$23
12249	5" New Presque Isle - 1998	$20
12258	5 1/2" Pemiquid Point, Maine - 1999	$20
12259	5" Concord Point, Maryland - 1999	$20
12260	5 1/2" Destruction Island, Washington - 1999	$20
12261	6" Whitefish Point, Michigan - 1999	$20
12282	6" Alcatraz, California - 1999	$20
12283	6" Cape Canaveral, Florida - 1999	$20
12284	4 1/2" Hecceta Head, Oregon - 1999	$20
12285	5 1/2" Pigeon Point, California - 1999	$20
12288	4 1/2" Point Wilson, Washington - 1999	$20
12297	5 1/2" Tybee Island, Georgia - 1999	$20
12411	5 3/4" Jupiter Inlet, Florida - 1998	$20
12412	5" Marblehead, Ohio - 1999	$20
12413	6" Morris Island, South Carolina - 1999	$20
12414	6" Point Arena, California - 1999	$20
12416	4" New London Ledge, Connecticut - 1999	$20
12417	6" St. Simons, Georgia - 1999	$20
12418	5" White Shoal, Michigan - 1998	$20
12419	6" Boston Harbor, Massachusetts - 1988	$20
12420	6" Biloxi, Mississippi - 1999	$20

12421	6" Point Bolivar, Texas - 1998	$20
12428	4" Round Island, Michigan - 1998	$20
12429	5" West Quoddy Head, Maine - 1999	$20
12430	5" Harbor Town, South Carolina - 1998	$20
12431	6" Big Sable Point, Michigan - 1998	$20
12432	6" Ocracoke, North Carolina - 1999	$20
12434	6" Ft. Gratiot, Michigan - 1999	$20
12435	5 1/2" Grays Harbor, Washington - 1999	$20
12844	6" Absecon Light, New Jersey - 1999	$20
12845	4" Mukilteo Light, Washington - 1999	$20
12846	5" Bald Head, North Carolina - 1999	$20
12847	6" Aransas Pass, Texas - 1999	$20
12888	5 1/2" Amelia Island, Florida - 1999	$20
12889	5" Diamond Head, Hawaii - 1999	$20
12890	3 1/2" Grand Haven, Michigan - 1999	$20
12891	3 1/2" Hereford Inlet, Ohio - 1999	$20
12892	5" Cape Elizabeth, Maine - 1999	$20
12893	6" Fond du Lac, Wisconsin - 1999	$20
12894	5" East Quoddy Head, Canada - 1999	$20
12896	5" Minots Ledge, Massachusetts - 1999	$20

LIGHTHOUSE COLLECTION/ILLUMINATED LIGHTHOUSES

00131	9" Sandy Hook, New York	$45
00132	9" Sandy Hook, New Jersey	$45
00133	10" Cape Hatteras, North Carolina	$45
00136	8 1/2" West Quoddy Head, Maine	$45
00137	10" Assateague, Virginia	$45
00878	10" White Shoal, Michigan	$45
00881	10" Boston Harbor, Massachusetts	$45
00882	10" Cape Cod, Massachusetts	$45
01010	9" Chicago Harbor Light, Illinois	$45
01015	11" St. Augustine, Florida	$45
01119	9" New London Ledge, Connecticut	$45
01120	8" Yerba Buena, California	$45
01122	10" Heceta Head, Oregon	$45
01124	10" Ocracoke, North Carolina	$45
01332	10" Ponce De Leon Inlet, Florida	$45
04411	9" Limited Edition, Old Mackinac Point, Michigan	$45
10074	11" Port Isabel, Texas	$45
10075	11" Key West, Florida	$45
10104	9 1/2 Holland Harbor, Michigan	$45
10109	10" Los Angeles Harbor, California	$45
10834	13" Currituck Beach, North Carolina	$45
10969	9" Round Island, Michigan	$45
11522	11" Biloxi, Mississippi	$45
11525	9" Pemaquid Point, Maine	$45
11526	11" Alcatraz Island, California	$60
11537	11" Cape Florida, Florida	$45
12717	13" Boon Island, Maine	$45
13522	Absecon, New Jersey	$45
13523	11" Amelia Island, Florida	$45
13527	12" Hillsboro Inlet, Florida	$45

LIGHTHOUSE COLLECTION/LAMPS

12405	14" Cape Hatteras, North Carolina	$50
12406	14" Currituck, North Carolina	$50
12407	14" White Shoal, Michigan	$50
12408	14" Point Arena, California	$50
12409	14" St. Augustine, Florida	$50
12410	14" Thomas Point, Maryland	$50
12702	14" Montauk, New York	$50
12704	13 1/2" Alcatraz, California	$50
12705	13 1/4" Southeast, Rhode Island	$50
12706	13 3/4" Ponce de Leon, Florida	$50
12709	13 1/2" Holland Harbor, Michigan	$50
12869	13 1/4" Cape Canaveral, Florida	$50

LIGHTHOUSE COLLECTION/MAGNETS

| 10141 | Big Sable Point, Michigan - 1995 | $5 |
| 10142 | Chicago Harbor Light, Illinois - 1995 | $5 |

10144	Cana Island, Wisconsin - 1995	$5
10145	Portland Head, Maine - 1995	$5
10150	Ponce De Leone, Florida - 1995	$5
10151	Sandy Hook, New Jersey - 1995	$5
10153	Port Wilson, Washington - 1995	$5
10155	Old Point Loma, California - 1995	$5
10156	Bodie Island, North Carolina - 1995	$5
10158	Yerba Buena, California - 1995	$5
10161	Toledo Harbor, Ohio - 1995	$5
10163	Fire Island, New York - 1995	$5
10168	Cape Neddick, Maine - 1995	$5
10169	Point Isabel, Texas - 1995	$5

LIGHTHOUSE COLLECTION/MUSIC BOXES

10627	7" Chicago Harbor, Illinois "EBB Tide" - 1995	$50
10628	5 1/2" New London Ledge, Connecticut "EBB Tide" - 1995	$50
10630	7" Barnegat, New Jersey "EBB Tide" - 1995	$50
10976	5 1/2" Marblehead, Ohio "Sailing" - 1996	$50
10977	5 1/2" Old Point Loma, California "Somewhere Out There"-1996	$50
10978	5 1/2" Cape Florida, Florida "Over the Waves" - 1996	$50

LIGHTHOUSE COLLECTION/ORNAMENTS

01430	3 3/4" Cape Lookout, North Carolina - 1994	$10
01433	3 3/4" Assateague, Virginia - 1994	$10
01435	3 3/4" Cape Cod, Massachusetts - 1994	$10
01436	3 3/4" Montauk Point, New York - 1994	$10
01437	3 3/4" St. Simons, Georgia - 1994	$10
01438	3 3/4" Cape May Point, New Jersey - 1994	$10
01439	3 1/2" St. Augustine, Florida - 1994	$10
10722	3 1/4" Point Wilson, Washington - 1995	$10
10726	3 1/2" New London Ledge, Connecticut - 1995	$10
10727	3 3/4" Portland Head, Maine - 1995	$10
10984	4" White Shoal, Michigan - 1996	$9
10985	3" Big Sable Point, Michigan - 1996	$9
10986	3 3/5" Ft. Gratiot, Michigan - 1996	$9
10989	3 3/4" Bodie Island, Rhode Island - 1996	$9
11506	2 3/4" Thomas Point, Maryland - 1997	$9
11507	2 3/4" Block Island, Rhode Island - 1997	$8
11510	3 3/4" Point Isabel, Texas - 1997	$8
11513	3 3/4" Key West, Florida - 1997	$8
11514	3 3/4" Ponce de Leon, Florida - 1997	$8
11515	3 3/4" Currituck Beach, North Carolina - 1997	$8
12115	3" Holland Harbor, Michigan - 1998	$8
12116	3 3/4" Fort Niagara, New Jersey - 1998	$8
12117	3 3/4" Wind Point, Wisconsin - 1998	$8
12118	3 3/4" Point Bolivar, Texas - 1998	$8
12119	3 3/4" Point Arena, California - 1998	$8
12120	3 3/4" Biloxi, Mississippi - 1998	$8
12121	3" Alcatraz, California - 1998	$8

LIGHTHOUSE COLLECTION/PAPERWEIGHTS

10923	Cape Hatteras, North Carolina - 1998	$24
10924	St. Augustine, Florida - 1998	$24
10925	Cape May, New Jersey - 1998	$24
10926	Montauk, New York - 1998	$24
10927	Cape Cod, Massachusetts - 1998	$24
10928	Cape Lookout, North Carolina - 1998	$25
11372	Thomas Point, Maryland - 1998	$24
11373	Block Island, Rhode Island - 1998	$24
11374	Barnegat, New Jersey - 1998	$24
11375	Cape Florida, Florida - 1998	$24
11376	Split Rock, Minnesota - 1998	$24
11377	Ocracoke, North Carolina - 1998	$24

LIGHTHOUSE COLLECTION/PLATES

04778	Cape Hatteras, North Carolina	$20
08611	Portland Head, Maine	$20
08615	Fire Island, New York	$20

LIGHTHOUSE COLLECTION/PLATES (cont'd)

08618	St. Simons, Georgia	$20
08629	Pigeon Point, California	$20
08630	Admiralty Head, Washington	$20
08631	Split Rock, Minnesota	$20
08632	West Quoddy, Maine	$20
08635	Cape Neddick, Maine	$20

LIGHTHOUSE COLLECTION/TEAPOTS

11778	Split Rock, Minnesota - 1998	$35
11780	Round Island, Michigan - 1998	$35
11781	Old Point Loma, California - 1998	$35
11782	Ft. Niagara, New York - 1998	$35

LIGHTHOUSE COLLECTION/WATERBALL MUSICALS

10789	Cape Florida, Florida "La Mer" - 1998	$26
10790	Cape Hatteras, North Carolina "Now Is The Hour" - 1998	$26
10791	St. Augustine, Florida "Sailing" - 1998	$26
10792	Cape May, New Jersey "Over the Waves" - 1998	$26
10793	Assateague, Virginia "Somewhere Out There" - 1998	$26
10794	Montauk Point, New York "Ebb Tide" - 1998	$26
10879	New London Ledge, Connecticut "Somewhere Out There"	$26
10903	St. Simons, Georgia "Somewhere Out There" - 1998	$26
10904	Marble Head, Ohio "Sailing" - 1998	$26
10905	Old Point Loma, California "Now Is The Hour" - 1998	$26
11202	Bodie Island, North Carolina "Somewhere Out There" - 1998	$26
11203	Ocracoke, North Carolina "Ebb Tide" - 1998	$26
11204	Jupiter Inlet, Florida "Now Is The Hour" - 1998	$26
11205	Key West, Florida "Sailing" - 1998	$26
11206	Thomas Point, Maryland "La Mer" - 1998	$26
11207	Sandy Hook, New Jersey "Over The Waves" - 1998	$26
11449	Currituck Beach, North Carolina "Over The Waves" - 1998	$26

LILAC CHINTZ

129	4 1/2" Teabag Holder	$15
130	Compote	$28
131	5" Footed Candy Dish	$50
202	Jam Jar w/Spoon and Tray	$40
208	Sugar and Creamer w/Tray	$55
669	6 1/2" Bone Dish	$15
692	Nested Ashtrays, Round	$28
693	Teapot	$175
694	Sugar and Creamer	$42
695	Cup and Saucer	$28
696	Demitasse Cup and Saucer	$25
697	Snack Set	$28
698	Egg Cup	$18
700	Salt and Pepper	$18
701	7 1/4" Plate	$18
702	9 1/4" Plate	$30
1004	3 1/2" Shell Shaped Dish	$15
1005	5 1/4" Ashtray, Leaf Shaped w/Holder Attached	$22
1279	Two Tiered Tidbit Tray	$65
1344	Cigarette Set, Cigar Urn w/Two Trays	$25

MANGER/NATIVITY SETS

00309	3" Nativity Figurine	$19
00310	2 1/2" Mary, Joseph and Baby in Manger Figurine	$8
00831	4 1/2" Nativity Scene Musical Figurine "Silent Night"	$29
00832	3" Nativity Set Figurine	$25
00899	Nativity Set, "Spirit of Bethlehem" 10 Pieces - 1985	$115
01270	Nativity Set, 12 Piece Set	$100
01271	Nativity Set, 7 Piece Set	$45
01272	Nativity Set, 12 Piece Set	$80
04020	Nativity Set, 4 Piece Set	$30
5122	Nativity in Blue Glaze, 3 Pieces	$32
06580	Nativity Angels, 2 Assorted, Each	$15
07813	Nativity Set, 10 Piece Set by Sevilla - 1990	$175

10050	Nativity Set, 10 Piece Set	$35
10051	Nativity Set, 10 Piece Set	$35
10658	Nativity Set, 3 Piece Set	$12
10806	Shamrock Nativity Set, 3 Piece Set	$40
10876	Nativity Set, 12 Piece Set	$100
11084	Shamrock Nativity Set, 9 Piece Set	$60
11089	Nativity Set, 9 Piece Set, Each	$29
11093	Shamrock Nativity Set, 9 Piece Set	$40

MISCELLANEOUS

395	5" Angel Fish Figurine, White	$45
1072	4" Fish Figurine	$55
1097	8" Round Plain White Flower Arranger	$30
01375	6" Clock w/Roses - 1994	$36
02042	4 1/2" Angel Fish Figurine	$55
2052	Lefton Collectibles Display Sign	$28
3779	Lefton Display Sign	$20
3834	Moss Rose Tape Dispenser	$28
05190	Wedding Cake Topper, Heart Shaped w/Doves - 1985	$25
05629	6" Pot Pourri Warmer, 2 Pieces - 1986	$18
06290	Wedding Cake Topper, Heart Shaped w/Doves - 1987	$25

MISS PRISS

1502	Cookie Jar	$185
1503	4" Mug	$75
1504	Milk Pitcher	$155
1505	Cheese w/Cover	$275
1506	Teabag Holder	$55
1507	Two Compartment Dish	$185
1508	Sugar and Creamer	$65
1509	Wall Pocket	$150
1510	Egg Cup	$65
1511	Salt and Pepper	$39
1515	Jam Jar	$110
1516	Teapot	$160
1524	6" Ashtray	$60
1525	Spoon Rest w/Salt Shaker	$225
3553	Mug	$75
4916	Bank	$300
8168	Three Compartment Dish, ESD Mark	$350
8170	5 1/2" Wall Pocket, ESD Mark	$110
8172	Covered Candy Dish, ESD Mark	$295
8175	Teapot Teabag Holder, ESD Mark	$55
8176	Milk Pitcher, ESD Mark	$95
8177	Two Compartment Dish, ESD Mark	$95

MISTY ROSE

3166	Coffee Pot	$65
5517	Nappy Dish, 3 Assorted, Each	$28
5518	Salt and Pepper	$18
5519	7 1/4" Plate	$15
5520	9" Plate	$30
5521	Jam Jar w/Tray and Spoon	$30
5536	Coffee Pot	$150
5537	Sugar and Creamer	$50
5538	4 1/4" Candy Box	$50
5539	Cup and Saucer	$45
5690	Snack Set	$22
5691	Teapot	$145
5692	7" Pitcher	$125
5693	9 1/4" Cake Plate	$45
5694	6 1/4" Pitcher w/Bowl	$65
5695	5 1/2" Bud Vase, 3 Assorted, Each	$22
5696	5" Compote	$28
5697	8" Tumbleup	$125
5700	Soap Dish and Tumbler	$35
5724	6 1/2" Lemon Plate	$32
5725	5" Pitcher & Bowl	$32
5759	7 3/4" Nappy	$23

MUGS

171	Cowboy w/Pistol Handle	$38
00211	Goose Mug	$18
264	7 1/2" Barbershop Quarter w/Pole Handle	$38
674	Floral Design	$8
1059	Prairie Flower	$15
1110	Washington	$45
1112	Jackson	$45
1113	Lincoln	$45
1138	2 1/4" Pink Roses - 1993	$8
1216	3 1/2" Dad	$6
1217	3 1/2" Mother	$6
1613	Mug for Aunt	$8
1837	Fish	$12
2191	Roosevelt	$45
2326	5 1/2" Washington	$40
2352	5 1/2" Jackson	$40
2364	5 1/2" Lincoln	$50
2365	Robert E. Lee	$45
2525	Ben Franklin	$45
2681	Fish	$15
02682	Shamrocks	$9
02684	Shamrocks	$10
2985	4" Baby w/Whistle Handle	$25
03031	Holly	$7
03314	5" w/Shamrocks "Love Me I'm Irish"	$10
3533	Pink Dogwood	$10
3672	Mr. Toodles	$18
3746	3 1/4" Gold Pear N Apple	$9
3747	3 1/4" Green Pear N Apple	$9
3758	3 1/2" Grandpa	$7
3918	Hand Painted Floral or Fruit	$10
4098	Violet Floral Mug, Chintz Like	$9
04100	3 1/2" NANA w/Floral Design - 1984	$8
04113	3 1/2" SECRETARY w/Heart and Floral Design - 1984	$8
04121	3 1/4" TEACHER - 1984	$8
04128	Multi Colored Floral Design	$7
4241	5 1/2" Blue w/Ropelike Handle and Base	$10
04434	Cow	$12
04445	3 1/2" Dog	$8
4468	Rustic Daisy	$8
4500	Mustache Mug w/Horse Racing Motif	$15
4500	Mustache Mug w/Fireman's Motif	$15
4656	50th Anniversary	$6
4657	25th Anniversary	$6
04953	"Irish Coffee" Mug w/Shamrocks	$8
5349	Fiesta	$10
5685	3 1/2" Rooster	$12
6356	Mushroom Forest	$12
6496	Blue Aster	$8
6513	Bossie the Cow	$15
6730	Fruit Fantasia	$9
06775	Harvest Time - 1988	$8
7057	Yellow Tulip	$12
7124	4 1/2" Footed, Yellow Tulip	$12
7434	8 1/4" Stein	$25
07928	Lefton's 50th Anniversary Mug, 1941-1991	$15
08108	Pink Flamingo Mug, Florida - 1989	$8
8210	Heather Girl	$8
10585	25th Anniversary	$8
10596	50th Anniversary	$8

MUSICALS

00183	6" Girl Bunny, "I'm Late"	$28
00366	6 1/2" Irish Couple "My Wild Irish Rose"	$35
00378	6 1/2" Girl Saying Her Prayers "Lullaby and Good Night"	$25
00579	Water Globe, Angel w/Baby, "Brahm's Lullaby" - 1992	$38
00639	Little Drummer Boy w/Lambs "Drummer Boy"	$18
01021	6 1/2" Mary Quite Contrary "Thank Heaven For..." - 1993	$15
01022	6 1/2" Humpty Dumpty "Humpty Dumpty" - 1993	$15
01023	6 1/4" Little Jack Horner "Whistle a Happy Tune," 1993	$42
01025	Little Miss Muffet "It's A Small World" - 1993	$42
1351	8 1/4" Old Couple Walking in Rain "Those Were the Days"	$50
1438	Girl Blowing Out Candles "Happy Birthday"	$23
01444	5" Orca Whales "Over the Waves"	$23
01445	5 1/2" Penguins "Born Free"	$23
01512	Country Highjinks, Dog w/Ducks "Playmates" - 1993	$19
01514	Country Highjinks, Bathing the Dog "Doggie in the Window"	$19
01516	Country Highjinks, Goat w/Chickens "That's What Friends..."	$19
01517	Country Highjinks, Pig "Take me Home Country Roads" - 1994	$27
01577	Irish Cottage "I Will Take You Home Kathleen"	$30
01578	6" Blarney Castle Musical "When Irish Eyes Are Smiling"	$30
01589	7 1/2" Irish Girl Musical "When Irish Eyes are Smiling"	$34
1666	5 1/2" Girl at Piano Playing Chopin	$32
02354	6" Cardinal "Up, Up and Away"	$48
02504	6 1/2" Girl and Boy "Silent Night"	$50
02794	5" Mother and Baby in Cradle "Brahm's Lullaby"	$35
03000	Boy Serenading Girl "You Light Up My Life"	$27
03247	6" Victorian Doll "Fascination"	$40
03247	7 1/2" Clown "Send in the Clowns"	$45
03504	6" Goldfinches "Bye Bye Blackbird"	$32
3711	5" Angel "Happy Birthday"	$35
03900	Musical Clown Planter "Lullaby and Good Night"	$35
03912	Girl of the Month "Happy Birthday" - 1983	$25
03971	Sitting Girl Clown "Send in the Clowns" - 1998	$28
4037E	5 1/2" Clown Musical "Be a Clown"	$25
4037F	5 1/4" Clown Musical "Whistle a Happy Tune"	$25
04084	Honey Bears in Bed, "Love is a Many Splendid Thing" - 1983	$28
04394A	5" Baby Toys Musical "Pop Goes the Weasel"	$20
04394B	5" Baby Toys Musical "My Favorite Things"	$20
04454	Bride Figurine "The Wedding March"	$28
4495	6 1/2" Angel "Ave Maria	$50
05102	Ballerina "The Ballerina" - 1985	$25
5199	5 1/2" Girl w/Baby "Lullaby"	$28
05318	Doll Talking on Phone, Lollipop Music Melodies Series - 1985	$28
05322	5" Clown Musical "Toyland"	$20
05492	Kewpies w/Heart Guitar "Love Me Tender" - 1986	$45
6649	9" Old Couple "Love is a Many Splendid Thing"	$35
06709	Irish Dancing Couple "My Wild Irish Rose" - 1988	$25
06884A	Clown w/Hot Air Balloon "Love Makes the World..." - 1988	$35
06884B	Clown w/Elephant, "Send in the Clowns" - 1988	$35
06884D	Clown on Horse, "Be a Clown" - 1998	$35
7177	6" Angel of the Month "Happy Birthday"	$30
7302	Bride and Groom "Wedding March" - 1989	$18
7535	Dancing Bears "I Could Have Danced All Night," 1990	$18
7661	Little Girl Kneeling "Ave Maria" - 1990	$22
8259A	6" Boy Serenading Girl "Bessme Mucho"	$30
8259B	6" Boy and Girl "Sunrise, Sunset"	$30
8259C	6" Boy Kissing Girl "Theme from Love Story"	$30
8259D	6" Boy and Girl Holding Hands "If You Loved Me"	$30
10088	5 1/4" Clown Playing Drum "Send in the Clowns" - 1998	$17
10088	5 1/4" Clown with Umbrella "Be A Clown" - 1998	$17
10088	5 1/4" Clown with Balloon "Whistle a Happy Tune" - 1998	$17
10088	5 1/4" Clown Playing Accordion "Make Someone Happy"	$17
10602	Girl w/Gramaphone "I'd Like To Teach The World To Sing"	$17
10606	Copycat Cheerleader "What's New Pussycat" - 1995	$17
10607	Copycat Girl on Bench "Talk To The Animals" - 1995	$17
10608	Copycat Ballerina Sugarplum Fairies" - 1995	$17
10609	Copycat Girl "I'd Like To Teach The World To Sing" - 1995	$17
10610	Flapper Girl w/Banjo "Sweet Georgia Brown" - 1995	$17
10611	Flower Girl "Where Have All The World's Gone" - 1995	$17
10612	50's Girl "I'd Like To Teach The World To Sing" - 1995	$17
10613	Girl Playing Dress Up "Hello Dolly" - 1995	$17
10773	First Communion Girls w/Veils "Jesus Loves Me" - 1998	$20
10777A	Country Bear - "Mamas Don't Let Your Babies..." - 1996	$15
10777B	Country Pig - "I Believe In Music" - 1996	$15
10777C	Country Cow - "You Are My Sunshine" - 1996	$15
10777D	Country Dog - "Hound Dog" - 1996	$15
10788	Girl w/Shamrocks - "When Irish Eyes Are Smiling" - 1996	$38
10831	Houlahan's Cottage - "It's A Long Way To Tipperary" - 1998	$30
10832	Kitty Flinn's Cottage - "My Wild Irish Rose" - 1998	$30
10848	Nurse Holding Baby "You've Got A Friend" - 1996	$35

MUSICALS (cont'd)

10849	6" Two Friends "That's What Friends Are For" Yamada - 1996	$30
10850	6 1/2" Tea Party, "Tea for Two" Yamada Original - 1998	$36
10851	6" Mother w/Baby, "Thank Heavens for Little Girls" Yamada	$33
10852	7" Doll "Hello Dolly" Yamada Original - 1998	$35
10862	7 1/2" Ballerina "Sugar Plum Fairy" Yamada Original - 1996	$29
10862	7 1/2" Ballerina "Swan Lake" Yamada Original - 1996	$29
10862	7 1/2" Ballerina "Waltz of the Flowers" Yamada Original - 1996	$29
10895	5 1/2" Ballerina, "Music Box Dancer" Yamada Original - 1996	$33
10943	Goose and Goslings "Younger than Springtime" - 1996	$12
10944	Hen and Chicks "Oh What a Beautiful Morning - 1996	$12
11011	7 1/2" House, 2 Assorted "Born Free" Yamada - 1996	$28
11012	3 1/2" Grand Piano "Till the End of Time" Yamada - 1996	$26
11013	6" Girl at Piano "Fascination" Yamada Original - 1996	$27
11014	7" Boy and Girl "Younger Than Springtime" Yamada - 1996	$30
11015	7" Boy and Girl "Love Story" Yamada Original - 1996	$30
11016	5 1/4" Boy and Girl "Tea for Two" Yamada Original - 1996	$30
11017	7 1/2" Bride & Groom "I Could Have Danced All Night" Yamada	$35
11019	6" Clown "Send in the Clowns" Yamada Original - 1996	$26
11019	6" Clown "Entertainer" Yamada Original - 1996	$26
11020	5 1/2" Clown w/Dogs "Put on a Happy Face" Yamada - 1996	$26
11020	5 1/2" Clown w/ Dogs "Be a Clown" Yamada Original - 1996	$26
11021	Bird in Gazebo "Born Free" Yamada Original - 1996	$28
11063	Pink and White Ballerinas, 2 Assorted "Swan Lake" - 1997	$23
11065	White and Gold Cat on Ottoman "Memories" - 1997	$30
11065	White and Gold Cat "Can't Take My Eyes Off of You" - 1997	$20
11066	White and Gold Rocking Horse "Toyland" - 1997	$20
11067	White and Gold Carousel Horse "Carousel Waltz" - 1997	$24
11074	Hummingbirds on Flower "Waltz of the Flower" - 1997	$27
11226	5" Heart "Unchained Melody" - 1997	$22
11235	Mother and Child "Thru the Eyes of Love" Yamada - 1997	$32
11236	Girl Embroidering "My Favorite Things" Yamada - 1997	$35
11237	Girl Playing Piano "Beethoven's 9th Symphony" Yamada - 1997	$37
11238	Girl on Sofa "Somewhere Out There" Yamada Original - 1997	$28
11239	Mother with Baby "You Light Up My Life" - 1997	$33
11240	Angel "Wind Beneath My Wings" Yamada Original - 1997	$39
11241	Angel "You Light Up My Life" Yamada Original - 1997	$39
11242	Angel "Amazing Grace" Yamada Original - 1997	$39
11243	Mother Hugging Girl "Thank Heaven For..." Yamada - 1997	$37
11244	Teddy Bear "Let Me Be Your Teddy Bear" Yamada - 1997	$23
11245	Rabbit on Mat "Born Free" Yamada Original - 1997	$23
11246	Cat on Mat "Memory" Yamada Original - 1997	$23
11247	6 1/2" Irish Girl Musical "Peg O'My Heart"	$33
11248	3 3/4" Irish Dancing Couple "I'll Take You Home Irene"	$33
11250	6 1/2" Irish Leprechaun "When Irish Eyes Are Smiling"	$33
11319	Hummingbirds on Flower "Waltz of the Flower" - 1997	$30
11412	Old Woman In A Shoe "It's A Small World" - 1998	$33
11413	Owl and Pussycat "True Love" - 1998	$33
11414	Noah's Ark "Talk To The Animals" - 1998	$33
11415	Jack and Jill "Jack and Jill" - 1998	$33
11416	Kitty Soirre "Memory" - 1998	$33
11417	Frog Band "Moon River" - 1998	$33
11544	Kissing Irish Boy and Girl "When Irish Eyes Are Smiling"	$31
11545	5 3/4" Irish Couple Musical "With a Little Luck"	$31
11622	Boy, Girl and Angel "When You Wish Upon A Star" - 1998	$29
11623	Boy with Teddy Bear in Bed "Hush Little Baby" - 1998	$29
11624	Girl w/Teddy Bear in Bed "A Dream is a Wish..." - 1998	$29
11702	Angel Musical Waterball "Adeste Fideles"	$27
11715	6" Ballerina Musical "Moonlight Sonata"	$33
11716	8" Ballerina Musical "Mozart's Minuet"	$33
11717	5 1/4" Clown w/Mandolin Musical "Happy Widower"	$27
11718	6 1/2" Clown Musical "Send In The Clowns"	$29
11719	Angel Musical Waterball "Hark the Herald Angels"	$27
11720	Angel Musical Waterball "Angels We Have Heard..."	$27
11723A	9 1/2' Ballerina Musical "Emperor's Waltz"	$12
11723B	9 1/2' Ballerina Musical "Music Box Dancer"	$12
11828	Double Dove Musical Waterball "Romeo and Juliet"	$27
11829	Double Dolphin Musical Waterball "Für Elise"	$27
12197	6" Irish Girl Playing Piano "When Irish Eyes Are Smiling"	$27
12197	3" Grand Piano w/Shamrocks "My Wild Irish Rose"	$27

12199	7" Story Time Musical "My Favorite Things"	$33
12200	5 1/2" Piano Lesson Musical "Blue Danube Waltz"	$33
12201	6 1/4" Mother with Baby "Brahms Lullaby"	$33
12202	6" Father and Son w/Kite "Up, Up and Away"	$30
12203	6" Grandfather Reading to Granddaughter "Memories"	$33
12204	7 1/4" Couple w/Umbrella "Singing in the Rain"	$33
12205	6 3/4" Mother and Children Musical "Funiculi Funiculi"	$33
12206	8" Children w/Birdhouse "Everything is Beautiful"	$33
12275	StoryTime "Brahms Lullaby" - 1999	$50
12277	Kissing Couple "I Love You Truly" - 1999	$45
12834	Girl w/Basket "Edelweiss" Yamada Original - 1999	$50
12851	Girl Holding Flowers "Memory" Yamada Original - 1999	$50

PIN CUSHIONS

542	3 3/4" Mouse in Dress	$12
543	3 1/2" Small Girl	$12
993	4 1/2" Magnetic Bobby Pin Holder	$45
2042	3 1/2" Turtle w/Thimble	$25
2326	3 1/2" Mouse w/Thimble	$15
03074	3" Frog, Turtle and Owl	$10
4194	Pink Dog w/Tape Measurer and Scissor Holder	$32
04419	4 1/2" Girl w/Pin Cushion and Thimble Holder	$25

PINK CLOVER

2483	Plate	$22
2484	Cup and Saucer	$18
2485	Teapot	$90
2486	Sugar and Creamer	$50
2487	5 1/2" Pitcher	$22
2488	4 1/2" Jam Jar w/Spoon and Tray	$35
2489	7" Butter Dish w/Cover	$18
2490	6 1/2" Cheese Dish w/Cover	$45
2491	Two Compartment Dish	$30
2492	Three Compartment Dish	$38
2493	3 1/2" Egg Cup	$15
2494	14" Platter	$65
2495	10 1/4" Plate	$22
2496	6 1/2" Bread and Butter Plate	$8
2497	Salt Box	$50
2498	Cookie Jar	$90
2499	5" Candy Box	$35
2500	Divided Bowl	$50
2501	Covered Vegetable or Casserole Bowl	$80
2502	7 1/2" Plate	$12
2503	6 1/4" Bowl	$10
2504	7 1/4" Soup Dish	$12
2505	8 1/2" Gravy Boat	$28
2506	Two Tiered Tidbit Tray	$45
2507	9 1/4" Plate w/Plastic Handle	$45
2601	10 1/2" Salad Bowl	$65
2603	Snack Set	$18
2604	Mug	$7
2605	12 1/4" Chop Plate	$42
2606	8" Oil and Vinegar Bottles	$45

PITCHERS AND BOWLS

275	3 1/2" Floral Design	$32
320	3 3/4" Floral Design	$28
322	3 1/2" Violet Design	$38
323	5 1/2" Floral Design	$45
324	Pink Floral Design	$35
325	5 1/2" Pitcher with Violets	$32
696	Floral Design with Butterfly	$26
734	Hand Painted Floral Design	$20
1286	5 1/2" Hand Painted Flower Design	$32
1386	5 1/2" Pansy	$45
1406	Floral Design	$25
1521	6" Pansy	$38
1914	Floral Design with Red, Gold and Blue Daisies	$28

1937	3 1/2" Rose Heirloom	$45
1967	3 1/4" Violet	$15
2008	4" w/Tiny Pink Roses and Green Leaves	$25
2027	Miniature Pink Roses w/Pink Trim	$18
2124	Dutch Girl Pitcher	$55
2187	3 1/2" Shamrock	$16
2565	4" Pitcher, White w/Violets	$35
2565	4" Pitcher, White w/Elegant Rose	$35
2591	Cardinal on Flowering Tree Branch	$29
02871	White Floral	$20
03084	3 1/4" w/Clovers	$20
3221	4" Pitcher w/6 1/2" Bowl, Floral Bisque	$40
3383	3 1/2" French Rose	$25
3406	5 1/4" Daisytime	$28
3566	5" Renaissance	$20
3568	4 1/2" Renaissance	$15
3570	3 1/4" Pitcher Renaissance Line	$22
3684	8 1/2" Pitcher Renaissance Line	$28
4189	5 1/4" Pitcher & 7 1/4 Bowl, Blue Forget-Me-Nots	$40
4190	6 1/4" Forget-Me-Not	$65
4260	6 1/2" Pitcher, White, Pear N Apple	$75
04311	5" Pink Floral - 1984	$22
4333	6 1/2" Pitcher Pear N Apple	$20
4334	9" Pear N Apple, Gold	$35
4459	8 1/2" Pitcher, Pear N Apple, Green	$55
4584	6" Spring Bouquet	$15
4585	Spring Bouquet	$18
04602	3 1/2" "You'll Never Know How Much It Means..."	$15
4672	3" Floral	$17
4685	5 1/4" Spring Bouquet	$38
4929	25th Anniversary	$12
5245	6 1/4" Green or Floral Design	$55
5522	3 1/2" Heirloom Elegance	$30
5523	Heirloom Elegance	$48
5684	8 1/2" Chicken Pitcher	$38
5777	4 1/4" Green Daisy	$20
5910	Fiesta	$18
5991	5 1/4" 50th Anniversary	$32
6281	Fruit Pattern	$25
6326	6 1/2" Floral Design	$45
6328	Pink and Yellow Roses	$23
6452	6 3/4" Green w/Blue and White Flowers	$28
6453	Pitcher, Ewer, Romance	$25
6466	7" Mushroom Forest	$30
6467	Mushroom Forest	$21
6469	5 1/2" Mushroom Forest - 1970	$25
6515	6 1/2" Bossie The Cow - 1970	$35
6516	8" Bossie the Cow - 1970	$65
6548	25th Anniversary	$18
6549	50th Anniversary	$18
6585	6" Water Pitcher, Lavender Rose	$65
6627	6" Rose Garden	$58
6626	5 1/2" Floral Design	$35
6628	5 1/2" Lavender Rose	$36
6666	6 1/2" Renaissance	$25
6668	3" Renaissance	$23
6806	3 1/2" Paisley Fantasia	$35
6807	Paisley Fantasia	$50
6843	3" w/Floral Bouquet	$15
7114	Happy Anniversary	$12
7254	3 1/2" Floral Bouquet	$17
7255	7 1'4" Floral Design	$55
7544	Celery and Carrots	$20
7643	6" Floral Design	$55
7977	Harvest Pansy	$28
8038	Multi Floral, Chintz Like	$22
8040	3 1/2" Multi Floral, Chintz Like	$22
8136	6 1/2" Spring Bouquet	$80
8203	Shamrock Girl	$20
8208	3 1/2" Floral Design	$18
8212	Heather Girl	$15
8244	4 1/2" Antique Ivory Bisque w/Applied Flowers	$35

8279	6 3/4" Pitcher, Hot Poppy	$32
13019	7" Pitcher, Irish Lace - 1999	$18

PLANTERS

008	3 Legged Elegant White w/Applied Rose & Gold Accents	$18
016	5 1/2" Three Baseball Players	$36
046	White Planter and Dog	$38
047	Telephone, Elegant White w/Rose	$30
056	5 1/2" Girl w/Basket	$75
056	5 1/2" Girl w/Ball	$75
065	7" Humpty Dumpty	$75
071	3 1/2" Wheelbarrow, Matte Elegant White	$15
075	6" Green Football Playing Frog, by Marika	$19
076	Green Grass w/Butterfly on Tree Branch	$18
076	Green Grass w/Lady Bug on Tree Branch	$18
076	Green Grass w/Bird on Tree Branch	$20
079	White Basket Weave Planter	$20
084	Puppy w/Pink Bow and Heart	$18
087	Bird Bath w/Three Birds	$45
088	5" Urn on Stand, Elegant Rose w/Applied Flowers	$42
092	Dog	$18
00101	4 1/2" Baby Roller Skate	$15
147	3 1/2" Baby King w/Bottle	$30
153	Ruffled Edge, Lilac w/Rhinestones	$42
154	Pitcher, w/Boy or Girl and Applied Flowers	$32
156	Lilacs and Rhinestones	$55
164	8 1/2" Lady w/Hat and Parasol, Teal w/Pink Flowers	$48
165	Angel w/Stars, Each	$40
166	5 1/2" Christmas Girl w/Muffler and Hat	$32
167	6" Poodle Puppy w/Bow and Flower	$15
178	Baby Shoe w/Baby and Chick, Pearl Luster	$22
192	9" Cherub on Fish Holding Urn, Antiqued Bisque	$48
193	9" Cherub Holding Urn, Antiqued Bisque	$48
194	8 1/2" Renaissance Whiteware	$28
224	6" Little Girl w/Pony Tail	$25
230	Rooster, White Matte w/Gold Accents	$15
242	Planter w/Coral Colored Applied Roses	$38
246	6" Little Girl or Boy w/Wide Brimmed Hat	$30
249	5 1/4" Sprinkling Can w/Applied Flowers	$32
251	5 3/4" Cat with Flowered Bonnet	$30
260	5" Two Cats in Tub	$18
269	4 1/4" Raggedy Ann and Raggedy Andy	$35
275	Pink or Blue, w/Kewpie	$50
277	6" Lady in Blue or Brown Dress, Each	$35
282	Fan Shaped w/Hand	$60
283	Watering Can w/Blue Flowers	$18
290	9" Lady in Strapless Gown w/Bow - Each	$45
350	5" Pair of Owls w/Rhinestone Eyes	$28
381	4 1/2" Footed, Blue and White Oriental Design	$18
384	6" Matte Antiqued Ivory	$30
408	Bible Planter, Ten Commandments w/Lilacs and Rhinestones	$18
410	Lord's Prayer w/ Lilacs and Rhinestones	$18
413	4" Reticulated Pot, Only A Rose	$45
414	4 1/2" Bucket, Only A Rose	$50
415	4" 3 Legged Pot, Only A Rose	$38
423	6 1/2" Lady, White w/Green Dress	$45
424	4 1/2" Girl Dressed as Bunny	$12
425	6" Garden, Black Velvet	$30
428	6 1/4" Lady in Ruffled Dress	$58
429	6 1/2" Girl w/Baskets of Flowers	$75
462	5" Pot w/Daisies	$12
482	6 1/2" Lady w/Hat and Flower Basket	$60
500	8" Lady w Hat and Parasol	$55
504	4" Square w/Pink Flowers and Gold Accents	$23
519	Hat w/Tennis Racquet and Ball	$28
523	4 1/2" w/White Teddy Bear on Blue Background	$12
529	12" Cherub Urn	$38
535	8" Lady	$68
538	Poodle w/Polka Dot Bow	$28
553	4" Pink or White w/Flowers, Glazed	$20
554	5 1/2" Modern Shape, White w/Pink Flowers	$22

PLANTERS (cont'd)

555	3 1/2" Pink or White Watering Can w/Applied White Flowers	$28
558	7" Bicycle Built For Two w/Couple - Pre 1954	$60
569	3 1/2" Mug Planter w/Cherub	$12
570	7" Cardinal, Matte Finish	$28
571	8" Robin, Matte Finish	$25
572	7" Horned Lark, Matte Finish	$25
573	7" Blue Jay, Matte Finish	$25
577	7" Goldfinch	$25
578	8" Rooster	$28
580	7" Ruffled Grouse	$25
587	Girl w/Flower Basket and Umbrella	$32
593	Poodle w/Cart	$38
623	Collie Head, Glazed	$25
662	6 1/2" Dutchgirl or Dutchboy	$28
667	Basket, Elegant White w/Gold Rose	$25
722	5" Egg Shaped, Antiqued Bisque	$20
723	3 1/2" Egg Shaped, Antiqued Bisque	$14
729	Cream Color w/White Applied Roses & Gold Accents	$14
763	4 1/2" Robin	$39
775	5" Luster w/Applied Flowers	$16
780	7" White Poodle	$25
790	4" Man's Hat w/Bowling Ball and Pins	$28
798	4 1/2" Humpty Dumpty	$30
802	9" Gold and White Planter w/Greek Motif	$28
808	4 1/4" Bamboo Bucket w/Leaves	$15
811	5" w/Cherubs and Rams Heads, Gold Accents	$48
815	6" Angel in Blue or Pink Dress, Each	$15
816	6 1/2" Leprechaun	$25
817	6 1/2" Wishing Well	$15
821	Pastel Pony	$12
823	4" Flower, Milk China	$38
824	Harvest Pansy	$16
826	3 1/2" w/Applied Roses	$35
827	4" White Bisque w/Applied Flowers	$30
0831	6" White Hippopotamus	$12
851	6" Boy and Girl on Swing, Planter by Marika	$25
852	6 1/2" Boy or Girl on Swing, Planter by Marika, Each	$25
852	6 1/2" Doe w/Fawn	$20
867	5 3/4" Baby, Pink	$18
875	Urn, 25th Anniversary	$10
881	4 3/4" Pixie on Log	$16
888	6 1/2" Pheasant	$30
889	6 7/8" Mallard Duck	$35
890	Golden Pheasant	$35
892	6 1/2" Peacock	$32
904	5 1/2" Pheasant Planter	$40
905	5 1/2" Duck Planter	$40
928	4 1/2" Baby Shoe w/Flowers	$18
933	4 1/2" Milkglass, Chain Link Pattern w/Shell	$22
936	7 1/4" Round, Lilac	$48
964	Heart w/Love Birds	$28
966	4" Pot, White Blouse w/Pink Bow	$15
982	4 1/5" Angel w/Flowers	$20
983	4 1/2" Baby King on Scale	$25
984	4 1/2" Baby King	$20
997	7" w/Lady on Bicycle	$30
1030	4" Rippled Top Pot, Pink w/Applied Flowers	$35
1034	4" Pink or White Bisque w/Four Legs	$42
1036	Pink Bisque w/Applied Roses and Forget-Me-Nots	$65
1042	4 1/2" w/Flowers	$30
1043	12 Sided White Bisque w/Applied Flowers	$42
1044	6" Pedestal w/Applied Flowers	$45
1046	6" Bisque Pedestal w/Applied Flowers	$45
1081	3" Cat or Dog w/Applied Flowers	$15
1092	4" Golf Planter	$18
1099	4 1/2" Bird	$18
1157	6" Lady in Blue w/Flower Basket	$42
1159	4 1/2" Round Shape, Colonial Figurine Design	$25
1165	4" White w/Flower and Butterflies	$15
1171	4 1/2" White w/Painted Flowers	$15
1172	12" Boat Shaped Planter, White w/Gold	$32

1179	6 1/4" Baby Blocks w/Duck	$15
1182	4" Ice Pink Bisque w/Applied Flowers	$35
1183	3 1/2" Ice Pink Bisque	$32
1190	4" Milk Glass w/Applied Flowers	$45
1198	4" White Bisque, w/Applied Flowers	$28
1199	5" Sprinkling Can, White Bisque	$25
1202	Six Sided, Bisque w/Applied Flowers	$35
1220	6" Rocking Chair w/Pipe on Side	$20
1221	4" Tall Man's Hat w/Pipe	$32
1222	8 1/2" Curly Haired Schnauzer	$18
1223	6 3/4" Curly Haired Cocker Spaniel	$18
1264	4" Kissing Angels on Bench	$20
1271	7 1/2" Angel Fish	$32
1324	White w/Collie Dog	$18
1337	Beautiful Lady in Fancy Green Dress and Gloves	$55
1380	Turkey, Matte Finish	$22
1466	Rooster	$15
1421	5 1/2" Kitten Holding Baby Bottle	$12
1422	Large Eyed Poodle	$18
1449	8 1/4" Girl Wearing A Flowered Blue Dress and Hat	$55
1465	5 1/2" Plymouth Rock Rooster	$35
1466	Rooster	$30
1473	7" Bluebird	$28
1511	8 1/2" Garden Daisy	$15
1555	4 1/4" Lady, Pink	$22
1558	5 3/4" w/Humpty Dumpty	$38
1561	4 1/2" Planter, Garden Daisy	$18
1568	6 1/2" Tennis Bag	$15
1571	8" Dog	$19
1598	8" Golfers Hat Planter - 1963	$38
1629	7" Spaghetti Dog w/Cart	$40
1680	5" Bowling Ball w/Pins	$23
1683	Elf on Violin w/Applied Flowers, Pearl Luster	$42
1684	8" Lady w/Flower Basket	$45
1685	3 Ladies - Priscella, Olive and Matilda	$45
1686	5" Girl In Pink Dress and Hat	$35
1710	6" Old Fashion Car	$20
1713	Fishing Hat	$25
1714	7" Angel Praying	$22
1716	Planter w/Rifle and Amo Belt	$25
1718	Man's Hat w/Skis	$38
1723	3 1/2" Chinese Pulling Cart	$25
1734	7 1/4" Planter, Violin	$23
1750	5 3/4" Golf Trophy Planter w/Clubs and Balls	$15
1761	2" Shoe	$8
1766	5 1/2" White Bisque	$50
1775	6" Pink Bisque w/Flowers	$50
1777	8" Pink Bisque w/Flowers	$75
1780	7" Curly Haired Poodle - 1963	$28
1789	5" Stork w/Baby	$18
1809	White Urn w/Two Handles	$18
1811	4" White or Pink Baby Shoe w/Pink Roses	$30
1814	5 1/2" Pink Swan w/Applied Flowers	$28
1854	6" Lady in Yellow w/Flower Basket	$42
1855	6" Lady in Green Holding Flowers	$42
1856	6 1/2" Lady w/Pink Dress and Hat	$65
1857	6" Lady w/Blue Dress and White Dots	$65
1869	7 3/4" Lady w/Shawl	$52
1870	7 3/4" Lady w/ Shawl and Umbrella	$52
1874	7 3/4" Lady w/Umbrella	$60
1888	Pheasant	$28
1953	6" Horse Head	$30
2021	5" Fruit	$25
2123	5 1/2" Blue Elephant Planter	$12
2124	4 1/2" Turtle Planter, by Marika	$12
2124	5" Owl Planter, by Marika	$12
2128	4" Baby ABC Block	$12
02129	Blue Pottie	$12
2171	6" Horse w/Colt	$30
2174	6 1/4" Girl	$22
2179	4" Blue Bisque w/Applied White Flowers	$28
2180	3 Legged Blue Bisque w/Applied White Flowers	$38
2189	3 3/4" White Bisque w/Applied Pale Blue Grapes	$32

2221	11" White Rabbit	$23		3810	3 3/4" Crib	$10
2312	6" Whiteware w/Child	$30		03855	4" Baby Diaper w/Pins	$12
2313	8" Whiteware w/Cherubs Holding Bowl	$45		03858	5" Baby Bassinet Planter in Pink or Blue, by Marika	$12
2348	6" Lady w/Multicolored Dress	$30		3866	8" Lady w/Hat, 3 Colors	$30
2350	6" w/Teenage Girl and Juke Box	$40		3867	8" Hobo w/Red Lamp	$55
2352	5" Baby w/Safety Pin, Blue	$22		3886	6" Sleeping Baby	$13
2365	8" Long Old Fashioned Car	$35		3888	6" Clown	$26
2524	3" Purse w/Floral Design	$12		3895	Man's Hat w/Bowling Ball and Pins	$28
2559	3 1/4" Donkey and Cart	$15		4020	8" Old Fashion Car	$35
2560	4 1/2" Donkey and Cart, Pear N Apple Design	$18		4033	7 1/4" w/Painted Flowers	$22
2587	8 1/4" Lady w/Flower	$30		4067	4 1/2" Praying Hands	$18
2631	Mr. Toodles	$95		04131	3 1/2" ABC Block w/Sleeping Teddybear - 1984	$12
02678	GAL Planter w/Kitten	$15		04132	4 1/2" GAL planter w/ Teddy Bear - 1984	$12
02679	5" Lion Planter, by Marika	$12		04133	Baby Shoes - 1984	$12
02680	6" Pink Frog	$15		4172	Bay Horse Head Planter	$36
02681	Musical BOY Planter "Rock A Bye Baby"	$28		4197	White Bisque Urn w/Ruffled Edge & Applied Flowers	$38
2703	4 1/2" White Luster w/Girl Laying on Side w/Flowers	$18		4226	6" Lady w/Basket of Flowers & Flowing Dress, Each	$35
2707	4 1/2" Matte, Elegant White	$20		4292	Nurse	$23
2731	Lily of the Valley and Butterfly	$35		4304	6" Girl or Boy, Glazed	$20
2770	4 1/2" White Porcelain Swan w/Applied Flowers	$35		4306	6" Cat w/Glass Eyes	$14
2772	6" Boy and Girl w/Hearts	$28		4308	5 1/2" Rabbit w/Glass Eyes	$15
2773	Heart w/Little Boy or Boy and Girl Kissing, Each	$18		4309	5 1/2" Orange and Yellow Baby Duck	$12
2785	8" Lady w/Flowers and Pearl Luster Dress	$45		4311	5 1/2" Dog	$12
2790	10" Girl, 2 Colors, Each	$75		4317	4 3/4" Pedestal Planter	$15
2796	5" Footed Planter w/Two Cherubs & Applied Flowers	$35		4318	4" Green Planter	$12
2804	7 1/2" x 4" Green w/Gold Accents	$15		4323	4 1/4" Baby Shoe, Pink	$15
2908	8" Lady in Brown and Tan Dress	$35		04326	Baby Buggy w/Bear "Our Little Treasure" - 1984	$12
2921	6 1/2" Raggedy Ann	$32		04326	Block w/Bear "Our Little Treasure" - 1984	$12
2925	5 3/4" Chicken Standing in Grass	$28		04326	Pot w/Bear "Our Little Treasure" - 1984	$12
2944	3 3/4" Luscious Lilac	$40		4330	Pear N Apple	$28
2945	Luscious Lilac w/Wavy Top and Applied Flowers	$32		04332	5 1/2" Hat w/Pipe - 1984	$15
2952	5 1/2" Stork w/Diaper	$28		04336	5 1/2" Owl - 1984	$12
2953	6 1/2" Cat	$35		4337	7 1/2" Lady, 2 Shapes, 3 Colors, Each	$35
2958	6" Heart w/Small Couple	$25		04338	5" Mother Duck w/Babies	$14
2962	6 1/2" Bunny	$18		4338	9" Lady, 2 Shapes, 3 Colors, Each	$55
2964	3 1/4" Luscious Lilac Pitcher w/Applied Flowers	$28		4339	8" Lady, 3 Colors	$55
2970	4 1/2" w/Guns, Duck, Pheasant and Hunters Cap	$23		4425	8" Lady w/Hat and Umbrella	$45
2978	8 1/2" Lady, Collette	$30		4470	6" Owl	$18
2986	6" Horse Head	$28		4496	6" Pitcher w/Applied Flowers	$42
3000	6" Lady w/Basket and Shawl	$30		4497	6 3/4" Girl	$32
3002	3 3/4" Pine Cone	$30		4498	4" Clown Head	$55
3075	7" Colonial Man	$35		4525	Lady in White w/Hat, Gloves and Umbrella	$45
3076	Girl and Duck in Pond, Bisque	$30		4550	6 1/2" Green Porcelain	$20
3078	5 1/2" Cherub on Branch w/Acorn Bowl	$65		4551	5" Green Porcelain w/Pedestal	$18
3099	3" X 4" Whiteware bowl Held up w/Cherubs	$15		4557	5" Pearlized Pixie	$36
3138	Young Girl w/Full skirt and Wide Brimmed Hat, Each	$40		4560	4" Pear N Apple	$25
3164	8" Renaissance Whiteware	$30		4597	4 1/4" Hat in Shiny Green	$15
3165	9 1/2" Urn w/Two Angels, Renaissance	$65		4598	6 1/2" Lady in Blue w/Flower Basket	$48
3174	7 1/2" Angelfish	$42		4598	7 1/2" Half Moon w/Pixie, ESD Mark	$50
3241	7 1/2" Rabbit	$28		4609	5 3/4" Cat	$28
3318	6 1/2" Dutch Girl	$35		4625	7" Cat or Dog w/Glass eyes	$33
3321	5 1/2" Planter w/Blue Polka Dots and Bow & Pink Teddy Bear	$15		4642	7" Baby Girl w/Bottle and Milk Pail	$35
3517	3 3/4" Renaissance	$18		4731	5" Sprinkling Can w/Applied Flowers	$18
3554	9" Lady in Mauve Dress	$45		4748	4" Fairy on Shell	$14
3561	5 3/4" Cherub Renaissance	$22		4864	7 1/2" Ruffled Grouse, Glazed	$35
3562	6 1/2" Renaissance	$20		04868	5" Long Train	$18
3563	4 14" Cherub or Angel, Renaissance	$18		04868	5" Baby Shoe - 1985	$15
3565	4" Renaissance Whiteware	$25		04869	5" GAL Planter - 1985	$18
3572	5" Renaissance Whiteware	$28		04870	3 1/2" Baby Booties - 1985	$15
3575	10" Renaissance Whiteware	$40		4906	5 1/2" Cat or Dog	$20
3578	7" Cherub Renaissance	$35		4907	Donkey Pulling Cart	$15
3605	6" Canary	$32		04947	3" Cat w/Basket Planter	$12
3622	6 1/4" Oriole	$25		4955	5 1/2" Purse, Bisque w/Flowers	$28
3625	6" Waxwing	$28		4965	7" Green Pedestal w/Cherubs and Flowers	$22
3628	Baby Girl or Boy	$32		4999	Green Rocking Chair	$15
3631	7" Baby	$30		5004	6 1/2" Cart, Daisy	$18
3632	4 3/4" Renaissance	$13		5006	6 1/2" Rustic Daisy	$23
3638	Cradle w/Baby	$21		5029	Pink Daisy Cart W/Handle and Wheels	$32
3706	4 1/2" Pennsylvania Dutch	$18		5030	6" Pink Daisy Pot	$12
03716	Baby Planter w/Flowers and Butterflies	$10		5114	6" Owl	$15
3782	5" Swan, Bisque w/Applied Flowers	$22		5116	7" Old Stove, Mustard	$22
3806	7 1/2" Renaissance	$35		5129	9 1/2" Trout	$18
3807	Bowl Shaped, Renaissance	$32		05151	4 3/4" Turtle	$15

PLANTERS (cont'd)

5260	5" Dutch Shoe w/Boy or Girl, Each	$65
5293	5" Bucket w/Egyptian Motif	$18
5356	Lord's Prayer w/Forget-Me-Not	$15
5443	5" Urn w/Applied Flowers	$28
05557	4" Round w/Lamb on Body	$12
5571	Clown Popping Out of a Box	$25
5575	4" Planter w/Goose and Golden Egg	$32
05598	4 3/4" Cradle	$15
05599	6" Cart w/Teddy Bear - 1986	$15
05600	4" Pink Planter w/Duck and Bear w/Balloons - 1986	$15
5668	3 3/4" Milkwhite w/Grape Pattern	$25
5697	6 1/2" Lady, White w/Green Dress	$50
5741	7" White Elephant w/Pink Bib	$20
5741	7" White Kitten w/Polka Dot Tie	$20
5766	6 1/2" Squirrel or Teddy Bear	$18
5772	6" Green Daisy w/Tree Root Pedestal	$18
5832	6" Wheelbarrow w/Fruit, Pink	$35
5839	7" Girl w/Large Flowers on Dress	$42
5881	5" Humpty Dumpty in Plaid	$70
5882	4" Humpty Dumpty	$30
5897	5 1/2" Calico Donkey	$25
5901	6" Elephant	$15
5937	8" Black w/Gold Handles and Accents	$30
5959	Hat and Pipe	$18
5960	Hat w/Golf Ball and Club	$18
5973	7" Little Girl w/Hat in Hand, Each	$22
6094	6 3/4" Girl w/White Dress & Hat, Yellow or Blue Flowers	$22
6162	4 1/2" Work Boots	$18
6170	6" Mouse, Duck or Elephant	$15
6189	7" White Lamb	$20
6191	5 1/2" Heart Planter w/Cupid and Valentines	$25
6207	4" Goose - 1987	$10
6208	6" Goose - 1987	$12
6365	6" Baby Planter	$15
6388	7" Pedestal Planter, Ornate Antique Bisque	$30
6397	6" Train	$20
6467	Watering Can, Mushroom Forest - 1970	$25
6470	4" Cart, Mushroom Forest - 1970	$25
6471	Mushroom Forest - 1970	$23
6584	6" Crib	$32
06589	5" Long Train	$20
06207	4" Goose	$16
6636	Baby Carriage, Musical	$23
6639	7" Girl in White dress w/ Yellow Hair	$30
6640	7 1/2" Girl in White Dress w/Yellow Flowers and Bow	$35
6742	5" Yellow Tulip	$15
6744	6" Celery Line	$15
6745	6 3/4" Yellow Tulip	$18
6746	6 3/4" Celery Line w/Pedestal	$18
6818	4 1/2" Blue Puppy w/Flowers and Bow	$12
6834	6" Baby Chick	$15
6863	4" Watering Can w/Flower Design	$15
6921	Raggedy Ann or Andy Head	$25
6950	White Bisque Cart w/Applied Flowers	$38
6962	4 1/2" Lord's Prayer w/Applied Flowers	$15
6968	6" Sprinkling Can, Floral Bisque Bouquet	$28
6974	6" Large Eyed Cat or Dog	$28
7011	Old Fashion Telephone	$18
7065	4 1/2" Wicker Basket	$14
7075	5 3/4" Chicken	$16
7116	7" Kitten Planter	$28
07141	Girl Bunny Pushing Cart - 1989	$14
7147	7 1/2" x 4" White w/Detailing in the China	$48
7194	4 1/2" Rabbit	$20
7210	4 1/2" Square Bisque, Basketweave w/Applied Flowers	$28
7327	6" Elephant	$30
7341	7" Baby Angel in Blue Praying	$28
07354	3" Birds and Flowers - 1989	$15
7430	4 1/2" Snail	$20
7432	4 1/2" Milkglass w/Daisy Pattern	$18
7436	4" Turtle, Owl, or Snail	$20

7530	6 3/4" Basketweave w/Flowers	$18
7627	6" Dog w/Puppy	$20
07678	4 1/2" C A T Planter w/Cat	$18
07690	Teddy Bear on Roller Skate	$14
7744	6" Bulldog w/Top Hat	$23
7859	8" Poodle	$40
7862	8 1/4" Wishing Well Planter, by Marika	$27
7878	5" Pheasant	$23
7879	5 1/2" Duck	$26
7882	6 1/2" Spinningwheel Planter	$20
7882	7 1/2" Brown Lantern	$20
7882	6" Coffee Grinder	$20
7885	6" Falling Leaves Planter	$18
8023	2 1/2" Bisque Boot w/Applied Flowers	$20
8085	5 1/2" Baseball and Glove	$22
8144	4 3/4" Pot w/Raised Flowers	$15
8184	4 1/2" Scalloped Edge Pot w/Floral Design	$18
8202	4" "Our Irish Collection"	$15
8225	4" Sprinkler w/Floral Design	$15
8466	Football Planter	$15
8507	5" Victorian Shoe	$35
8573	3" Renaissance w/Cherubs	$18
8823	4" White Hobnail w/Applied Roses	$42
9175	Blue Bisque w/Applied White Flowers, Wavy Top	$32
11229	Musical Block Planter "Brahm's Lullaby"	$15
11230	Party Bear Planter, 2 Assorted	$8
11231	Baby Bootie Planter, 2 Assorted	$8
11232	Cradle Planter, 2 Assorted	$7
11233	Blocks Planter w/Clown, 2 Assorted	$9
11234	Musical Blocks Planter w/Elephant, "Rock-A-Bye-Baby"	$13
11927	8" Tulip Planter	$20
11928	7" Tulip Planter	$28
11929	6 1/4" Tulip Planter	$20
11930	7 1/2" Tulip Planter	$24
12322	7" Tulip Jardiniere	$22
12323	9" Tulip Jardiniere	$30
12324	6" Tulip Planter	$17
13324	6 1/2" Lady w/Black Gloves and Pink Dress	$60
40037	4 1/2" w/Pink Roses and Bows	$60
40205	White Poodle	$25
46974	5 3/4" Siamese Cat	$8
50252	5" Chicken	$20
50253	5" Pink Well Bucket w/Applied Flowers w/Stones	$45
50261	5" Birdhouse, Pink, "Home Tweet Home"	$45
50265	5 3/4" Girl	$45
50430	3 1/2" Shoe w/Stones, Mardi Gras	$35
50432	6 1/2" Bag Shaped, Pink w/Gold Flowers	$50
50433	4 1/2" Kettle Shaped, Pink w/Gold Flowers	$45
50434	5" Bucket, Pink w/Gold Flowers	$50
50440	6 1/2" Bag Shaped, Mardi Gras	$60
50441	4 3/4" Mardi Gras	$45
50442	4" Pot, Mardi Gras	$40
50455	The Lord's Prayer	$22
50456	The Lord's Prayer	$18
50467	Girl in Pink Dress and Hat	$42
50478	6 1/2" Shoe w/Elf and Flowers	$28
50480	Pixie w/Bunny, Pearl Luster	$25
50482	8 1/2' French Lady, Each	$60
50515	Ponytail Girl Holding Dog	$30
50517	8" Bicycle w/Boy and Girl	$75
50555	5" Spaghetti Poodle Pulling Cart	$38
50584	5 1/2" Girl Pushing Cart, Pink	$38
50585	6 12" Little Girl Holding a Basket	$35
70260	Pink w/Flowers and Stones, 2 Handled	$50

PLATES

104	9 1/4" Eastern Star	$18
105	8" Eastern Star	$13
00237	10 3/4" Octagonal Cake Plate, Roses w/Pedestal Stand	$35
278	9 1/2" 50th Anniversary in Gold	$15
285	9 1/4" 25th Anniversary	$15
321	8 1/2" Woodpeckers Eating Grapes	$32

497	7 1/2" Daisy Line	$12
514	7 1/2" Pale Green Plate w/Pink and Red Roses	$18
642	8" Grape Cake	$18
674	7 1/2" Crimson Rose	$27
675	9" Violets	$32
694	9" Spring Bouquet	$28
711	Reticulated Edge w/Painted Fruit or Flowers	$35
00734	6 1/2" Pink Rose - 1993	$18
911	9 1/2" Grape Pattern	$28
1020	Cake Plate w/Knife, Symphony in Fruit	$30
1058	8" Prairie Flower	$22
1071	10 1/4" Cake w/Metal Handle	$42
1079	10 1/2" 1st Anniversary Plate	$18
1080	7 1/2" Cosmos	$20
1130	10 1/4" 25th Anniversary	$14
1133	9" 25th Anniversary	$12
1139	25th Anniversary	$10
01142	9" 50th Anniversary	$15
1189	14" Plate 50th Anniversary	$19
01208	10 1/2" Cake Plate w/Server, Rose Pattern - 1993	$45
01209	10 1/2" Cake Plate w/Server, Violet Pattern - 1993	$45
01220	9" Plate w/Guardian Angel	$30
01247	10 1/2" Cake Plate, Floral Design	$28
01356	9" Decorative Plate w/Guardian Angel	$28
1381	7 1/2" Violet Heirloom	$22
01447	9" Decorative Plate w/Flowers and White Cats - 1994	$28
1821	10" Rose Heirloom	$35
1822	9" Rose Heirloom	$32
1893	9" Cake w/Handle, Fruit Basket	$45
1905	12 1/2" Scalloped Platter, Garden Bouquet	$48
1974	9 1/4" Dinner, Country Squire	$24
2107	Cake Plate w/Metal Handle, Pink Floral w/Brown Stems	$28
2163	9" Silver Wheat	$18
2281	7" Square w/Rounded Corners, Hand Painted Couple	$18
2378	25th Anniversary Pedestal Cake Plate	$18
2521	9" Magnolia	$25
2522	7 1/2" Magnolia	$18
2565	10" w/Hand Painted Roses	$32
2592	9" Gold Laurel	$22
2910	9" Violets	$35
2998	8" Scalloped w/Violet Design	$28
3017	8 1/2" Apples	$16
3188	8" Cotillion	$22
3195	7" Pink	$12
3371	9 1/4" Vineyard Line	$20
3452	7 1/2" French Rose	$12
3455	9" French Rose	$23
03537	9" Pink Floral	$18
3650	8 1/2" Reticulated w/Fruit, Each	$18
3696	9 1/4" 50th Anniversary	$20
3698	25th Anniversary Dinner Plate	$14
3753	8 1/4" Two Handled Rose Plate w/Gold Accents	$38
4023	3 3/4" Round Plate w/Gold Rose	$10
04128	Cake Plate, Multi Colored Floral	$18
4132	7 1/4" Pear N Apple, Gold	$15
4181	9" Blue Forget-Me-Not	$20
04360	7 1/4" "Tis a Blessing to be Irish"	$15
04470	50th Anniversary - 1983	$18
4589	7 1/4" Spring Bouquet	$10
4590	9" Spring Bouquet	$15
04692	40th Anniversary - 1983	$18
04706	40th Anniversary, by Michio Suzuki - 1983	$25
04777	9 1/4" "On Your Wedding Day" - 1983	$13
4868	50th Anniversary Cake Plate	$15
4931	7" Plate, 25th Anniversary	$10
4932	9 1/4" Plate, 25th Anniversary	$12
4937	6" Plate, 50th Anniversary	$18
5509	10" Plate, Happy Anniversary	$20
5882	8 1/2" Decorative Plate w/Birds, Each	$22
6220	6 1/2" Heart Shaped "To Mother with Love" - 1987	$22
6284	9" Handled Fruit Plate	$28
6329	9 1/4" Pink and Yellow Rose with Gold Accents	$18
6329	9" Moss Rose	$22

6341	8" Reticulated w/Eastern Star Emblem	$16
6347	8" Reticulated w/Lord's Prayer, Elegant Rose	$18
6348	8" Reticulated w/Lord's Prayer, Violets	$18
6350	8" Reticulated w/Fruit	$22
6361	9" Mushroom Forest	$28
6575	9" Rose Garden	$28
6674	10 1/2" Plate w/Handle, 45th Anniversary	$23
6674	10 1/2" Plate, Twentieth Anniversary	$20
6803	7 1/2" Paisley Fantasia	$25
6805	Paisley Fantasia Cake Plate	$32
6850	8 1/4" Milk Glass Reticulated w/Fruit	$20
6932	4" Fruit or Flower	$14
07022	9 1/2" "Happy Anniversary with Love" - 1988	$18
7043	9" Yellow Tulip Cake Plate	$38
07112	9" 50th Anniversary Plate - 1988	$14
07248	7 1/4" Pink Dogwood - 1989	$18
07384	8" Floral w/Black Background - 1989	$25
07404	60th Anniversary Plate - 1989	$18
8129	8" w/Hand Painted Roses w/Gold Overlay	$25
8130	8" w/Hand Painted Birds w/Gold Edging	$23
8307	10" Plate, 30th Anniversary	$18
08626	8 1/4" Plate, Madonna with Child, Limited Edition	$30
10562	8 1/4" Plate, 25th Anniversary	$19
10563	8 1/4" Plate, 50th Anniversary	$19
10564	8 1/4" Plate, 1st Anniversary	$19
10565	8 1/4" Plate, 5th Anniversary	$19
10566	8 1/4" Plate, 10th Anniversary	$19
10567	8 1/4" Plate, 15th Anniversary	$19
10568	8 1/4" Plate, 30th Anniversary	$22
10569	8 1/4" Plate, 35th Anniversary	$24
10570	8 1/4" Plate, 45th Anniversary	$19
10571	8 1/4" Plate, 60th Anniversary	$19
10572	8 1/4" Plate, 40th Anniversary	$26
10573	8 1/4" Plate, Happy Anniversary	$19
10574	8 1/4" Plate, Happy Anniversary With Love	$19
10575	8 1/4" Plate, Happy 25th Anniversary	$19
10576	8 1/4" Plate, Happy 50th Anniversary	$19
11824	8 1/2" Plate w/Hummingbird and Hibiscus	$35
11825	8 1/2" Plate w/Hummingbird and Magnolia	$35
11826	8 1/2" Plate w/Hummingbird and Lily	$35
11827	8 1/2" Plate w/Hummingbird and Trumpet Flower	$35
13014	7 1/4" Irish Lace - 1999	$10
13015	8 1/2" x 6 Irish Lace - 1999	$15
20230	8" Golden Wheat	$22
20602	9 1/2" Golden Wheat	$25
60588	8" Reticulated w/Fruit, Gold Edge, Each	$38
60593	8 1/2" Reticulated w/Floral or Fruit	$22

PLATTERS

767	15" Fish, Small Mouth Bass	$65
4919	19" w/Turkey	$55
5615	17 1/2" Fish	$48
05758	19" w/Turkey	$45
6474	Mushroom Forest Serving Platter	$35
06812	19 1/2" Oval Platter, Blue and White	$60

RELIGIOUS

004	Set of Nuns	$45
006	Priest and Two Alter Boys, 3 Piece Set	$45
044	Choir Boy	$28
122	Infant of Prague Planter	$28
223	5 3/4" Infant of Prague	$25
225	6" Infant of Prague	$45
00238	Bible w/Verse, Bisque w/Cross and Applied Rose - 1991	$23
241	Madonna and Child Planter	$32
243	6 1/4" Madonna and Child	$32
245	8" Infant of Prague, Planter	$45
252	4 1/2" Infant of Prague	$80
337	8" Madonna	$30
339	7" Madonna w/Baby	$42
349	8" Madonna Head	$38

RELIGIOUS (cont'd)

440	4 1/2" Nun w/Glasses	$22
432	3" Sleeping & Awake Cherubs, Pastel Pink and Blue, Pair	$80
433	9 1/4" Madonna, Pastel w/Gold Trimmed Halo	$80
00482	Prayer Scroll w/Applied Roses - 1992	$15
491	10 1/2" St. Francis w/Bowl	$50
543	8 1/2" Madonna w/Child	$60
578	8" Madonna and Baby Wall Hanging	$55
609	8" St. Francis, Planter	$32
619	5 1/2" Praying Madonna	$65
00698	7" Holy Family	$24
00708	7" Holy Family Musical "Silent Night"	$18
718	8 1/4" Infant of Prague	$95
944	5" Choir Boys, 3 Piece Set	$45
1057	8 1/2" Madonna of the Flowers	$85
01101	8 3/4" Celtic Cross	$16
1135	7" Virgin Mary Water Font	$60
1158	10" Madonna, Blue	$55
1179	5" Madonna w/Glass Vase or Candle Holder	$45
01270	9" Madonna - 1985	$22
1328	8" Joseph and Jesus	$45
1330	8" Sacred Heart of Maria	$38
1331	8 1/4" Madonna Holding Jesus	$25
1403	6 1/4" Madonna, Water Font, Pale Purple	$60
1404	7 3/4" Monk Water Font w/Doves	$60
1416	7" Madonna and Child Jesus	$80
1419	8 1/2" Sacred Heart of Jesus	$60
1426	5 1/2" Infant of Prague	$45
1428	5" Nuns Playing Baseball, 3 Piece Set	$95
1431	5" Choir Boys, 3 Piece Set	$75
1462	7 3/4" Madonna Bust	$40
1463	7" Madonna w/Applied Flowers	$38
1486	5" Infant of Prague	$32
1549	6 3/4" Madonna, Planter	$27
1550	7" Madonna and Child Planter	$30
1571	8" Theresa	$40
1617	5" Madonna, Planter	$25
1618	5" Infant of Prague, Planter	$20
1645	8" Madonna and Child Jesus	$55
1695	Madonna and Child Jesus	$28
1719	6" Planter, Praying Madonna	$18
1720	8" Madonna Bust, Planter	$40
1750	8" Sacred Heart of Jesus, Planter	$35
1763	6" Madonna Planter	$32
1910	Madonna and Child Jesus	$45
1912	8" Madonna	$38
1938	7 1/2" Madonna Kissing Jesus, Planter	$40
2027	5" Praying Nun w/Cross, Planter	$20
2488	3" Angels w/Baby Jesus	$20
2583	6 1/2" Madonna w/Child	$42
2610	7 1/2" Madonna Bust	$38
2641	12 1/4" Infant of Prague, Planter	$65
3043	6" Madonna w/Ceramic Lace Head Cover	$55
3054	8" Madonna and Baby	$45
3055	5 1/2" Madonna, Font	$45
3106	10" White Glazed Madonna	$25
3207	4 1/2" Madonna Bust, Glazed	$20
3208	5" Madonna, Planter	$18
3645	10 1/4" Madonna, Planter	$45
3646	10" Madonna w/Baby Jesus, Planter	$45
3647	10" Open Armed Madonna, Planter	$38
3648	10 1/4" Joseph Holding Jesus, Planter	$45
3649	10" St. Francis w/Doves	$38
3712	10" St. Jude, Planter	$35
3713	10" Infant of Prague, Planter	$45
3904	Mary and Baby Jesus	$15
3961	9 1/2" Madonna	$38
4646	10" Mary w/Jesus	$35
05071	7 1/4" Cross with Little Boy or Girl Praying	$12
05682	7 1/4" Cross with Little Boy or Girl Kneeling	$12
5792	8 1/2" White Glazed Madonna	$28
6196	Madonna	$32

06321	7 1/2" Cross, Angel w/Children	$12
6417	4 1/2" Angel Wall Plaques, Pair	$80
6418	Madonna w/Child, Pair	$45
6429	6" Madonna Holy Water Font	$32
6563	10" Madonna	$22
06854	6" Madonna - 1988	$18
7188	5" Infant of Prague	$65
07200	8" Madonna	$8
07356	10 1/2" Madonna w/Baby	$16
8619	5 3/4" Madonna	$28
8695	6" Sacred Heart of Joseph	$55
8695	6" Sacred Heart of Mary	$50
8762	8" St. Anthony w/Child	$50
10165	5 1/2" Child of Prague w/Rhinestones - 1956	$45
10167	Madonna w/Applied Roses	$45
10272	8 1/2" Lady of Grace	$11
10299	7" Virgin Mary "Ave Maria"	$65
10768	6 3/4" Madonna w/Baby	$22
10769	5 1/2" Madonna Praying	$12
10770	6 1/2" Madonna Praying	$14
10772	8 1/2" Lady of Grace	$22
10801	8" Madonna	$15
10802	8" Praying Madonna Musical "Jewels of the Madonna"	$25
10804	Madonna	$20
10805	Irish Cross Water Font	$10
10896	Madonna w/Baby "Ave Maria"	$25
10897	8 1/2" Madonna w/Halo	$22
10898	8" Madonna	$20
10929	6 1/2" Guardian Angel Font	$22
10930	6 1/2" Madonna Font	$15
10931	6" Madonna Font	$17
10932	Madonna w/Baby "Ave Maria"	$20
11874	Maria Musical "Ave Maria"	$25
11877	9" St. Francis Musical "Amazing Grace"	$27
11878	Jesus w/Children Musical "Jesus Loves Little Children"	$27
11989	7" Our Lady of Knock w/Shamrock	$24
11990	4 1/2" Maria w/Baby Musical "Ave Maria"	$24
12225	6 3/4" Praying Madonna	$35
50270	6" Madonna Planter	$38
50278	5 1/2" Madonna Planter	$35
60594	Plate, The Last Supper	$38
90030	6" Holy Water Font	$50

ROADSIDE U.S.A.

01174	Diners, The Empire Diner - 1993	$38
01175	Diners, Commuter Diner - 1993	$38
01177	Diners, Tip Top Diner - 1993	$38
01178	Diners, The Patriot Diner - 1993	$38
01179	Diners, The Market Diner - 1993	$38
01181	Diners, White Tower Diner - 1993	$38
01601	Billboard, Miller High Life Beer - 1994	$15
01602	Billboard, Dorsey's Kew-Bee Bread - 1994	$15
01603	Billboard, Campbell's Soups, Campbell's Kids - 1994	$15
01604	Billboard, Smokey Bear, Prevent Forest Fires - 1994	$18
01605	Billboard, "Pepsi-Cola Hits the Spot" - 1994	$15
01606	Billboard, Ford Coupe $520 - 1994	$18
01607	Billboard, Campbell's Soup "Eat Soup and Eat Well" - 1994	$15
01608	Billboard, "Work for Victory" - 1994	$15
01609	Billboard, Pepsi "More Bounce to the Ounce"- 1994	$15
01610	Billboard, Ford Motor Company - 1994	$15
01611	Billboard, Smokey Bear, Don't Play with Matches - 1994	$15
01612	Billboard, U. S. Employment Service - 1994	$15
01613	Roadside Delights, Kone Inn - 1994	$48
01614	Roadside Delights, Airplane Café - 1994	$45
01615	Roadside Delights, The Coffee Pot - 1994	$42
01616	Roadside Delight, Mother Good Pantry - 1994	$48
01617	Roadside Delights, Zep Diner - 1994	$48
01618	Roadside Delights, The Flamingo Inn - 1994	$45
01619	Roadside Delight, The Dog House - 1994	$42
01620	Roadside Delights, The Dairy Café - 1994	$40
01621	Roadside Delights, The Tepee - 1994	$38
01622	Roadside Delights, The Toed Inn - 1994	$40

01623	Great Halls of Fire, Truck #47, Chicago, IL - 1994	$40
01624	Great Halls of Fire, Fire Station #6, Seattle, WA - 1994	$40
01625	Great Halls of Fire, Engine House #26, Buffalo, NY - 1994	$40
01626	Great Halls of Fire, Alpine House #2, Georgetown, CO - 1994	$40
01627	Great Halls of Fire, Narragansett No. #3, Warren, RI - 1994	$40
01628	Great Halls of Fire, Relief Engine Co., Mt. Holly, NJ - 1994	$40
01629	Railroad Depot, Ottawa Junction - 1994	$55
01639	Railroad Depot, Perris Station - 1994	$60
01631	Railroad Depot, Fond du Lac - 1994	$55
01632	Railroad Depot, Gettysburg Station - 1994	$75
01633	Railroad Depot, New Albany - 1994	$65
01634	Railroad Depot, De Long Station - 1994	$69
01635	Trolly, Payne Avenue - 1994	$25
01636	Trolly, Market Street - 1994	$25
01637	Trolly, Wilkins Avenue - 1994	$25
01638	Trolly, City Hall 6 - 1994	$25
01639	Trolly, Sioux City - 1994	$25
01640	Trolly, North Chicago - 1994	$25
08608	Gas Station, Deep Rock Gasoline, Limited Edition - 1995	$95
08609	Gas Station, Butch's Old Gold, Limited Edition - 1995	$95
10120	Gas Station, Bobby's Quick Service - 1995	$50
10121	Gas Station, Texaco No.2, Circa 1930's - 1995	$50
10122	Gas Station, Acme Gas, Circa 1940's - 1995	$50
10123	Gas Station, Texaco No.1 - 1995	$50
10124	Gas Station, Gas-O-Mat, Circa 1920's - 1995	$50
10125	Gas Station, Texaco No.3, Circa 1940's - 1995	$50
10512	Billboard, Ringling Bros. Barnum & Bailey w/Tigers - 1996	$15
10513	Billboard, Ringling Bros. Barnum & Bailey w/Rider - 1996	$15
10514	Billboard, Ringling Bros. Barnum & Bailey w/Trapeze - 1996	$15
10515	Billboard, Ringling Bros. Barnum & Bailey w/Clowns - 1996	$15
10516	Billboard, Ringling Bros. Barnum & Bailey w/Bears - 1996	$15
10517	Billboard, Ringling Bros. Barnum & Bailey w/Chariots - 1996	$15
10518	Billboard, Ringling Bros. Barnum & Bailey w/Lions - 1996	$15
10519	Billboard, Ringling Bros. Barnum & Bailey w/Clown - 1996	$15
10520	Billboard, Ringling Bros. Barnum & Bailey w/Elephants - 1996	$15
10521	Billboard, Ringling Bros. Barnum & Bailey w/Balkani - 1996	$15
10522	Billboard, Ringling Bros. Barnum & Bailey w/Clown - 1996	$15
10523	Billboard, Ringling Bros. Barnum & Bailey w/Gorilla - 1996	$15
10526	Classic Cinema - King Kong "Born Free" - 1995	$20
10527	Classic Cinema - Singing in the Rain "Singing in Rain" - 1995	$20
10528	Classic Cinema - Ben Hur "Chariots of Fire" - 1995	$20
10529	Classic Cinema - Dr. Zhivago "Lara's Theme" - 1995	$20
10530	Victorian Queens - Katherine	$30
10531	Victorian Queens - Heather	$30
10532	Victorian Queens - Gwen	$30
10533	Victorian Queens - Elizabeth	$30
10534	Victorian Queens - Diana	$30
10535	Victorian Queens - Cynthia	$30
10536	Victorian Queens - Miranda	$30
10537	Victorian Queens - Penelope	$30
10538	Victorian Queens - Nancy	$30
10539	Victorian Queens - Alison	$30
10540	Victorian Queens - Rachel	$30
10541	Victorian Queens - Sarah	$30
10542	Victorian Queens - York Dry Goods	$30
10543	Victorian Queens - The Mercantile Bank	$30
10544	Victorian Queens - McGill's	$30
10545	Victorian Queens - The Gazette	$30
10546	Victorian Queens - Hall's Chemists	$30
10547	Victorian Queens - Ritz Hotel	$30
10548	Victorian Queens - St. Mary's	$30
10549	Victorian Queens - Grace Church	$30
10742	Kentucky Fried Chicken - 1995	$20
10743	Kentucky Fried Chicken	$20
10745	Howard Johnson's	$20
10746	Bob's - Home of the Big Boy	$35

ROSE CHINTZ

564	Tea Strainer	$100
566	Pin Box	$15
627	8" Bone Dish	$18
637	Snack Set	$35

649	Two Tier Tidbit Tray	$85
650	Compote	$55
651	One Tier Tidbit Tray	$35
656	Cup and Saucer	$18
658	7" Plate	$28
659	9" Plate	$40
660	Coffee Pot	$185
661	Sugar and Creamer	$75
662	Cup and Saucer	$30
663	Sugar and Creamer	$45
664	Egg Cup	$55
665	Salt and Pepper	$28
671	Tidbit Tray	$28
679	6 1/4" Bud Vase	$32
686	5 3/4" Lamp	$55
793	6 1/4" Bone Dish	$22
794	Sugar and Creamer, Small	$38
911	Teapot, Swirl China w/White Spout	$195
911	Teapot, Smooth China w/Floral Spout	$155
912	Sugar and Creamer	$65
1239	2" 3 Footed Round Pin Dish	$20
1424	Demi Cup and Saucer	$26
1512	Demi Cup and Saucer	$18
1793	Teabag Holder	$35
1979	Demi Cup and Saucer	$18
2044	Sugar and Creamer on Tray	$55
2107	10" Cake Plate w/Handle	$45
2282	10 1/4" Chip and Dip	$65
2283	13" Dish, Two Compartment w/Metal Stand, Set	$48
2356	Cup and Saucer, Jumbo	$55
2425	Happy Anniversary Cup and Saucer	$20
2537	6 1/2" Heart Shaped Dish	$35
2537	Scalloped Edge Nappy Dish	$35
3064	Jam Jar	$48
3185	Miniature Tea Pot	$60
05617	Musical Cup and Saucer	$45

ROYAL EGG COLLECTION

10453	Pink and Purple Roses "Michelle" - 1995	$29
10454	Yellow Daffodils "Gigi" - 1995	$29
10455	Pink Floral "Lara's Theme" - 1995	$29
10456	Lily of the Valley "Hello Dolly" - 1995	$29
10457	Pink and Yellow Floral "Hi Lilly Hi Lo" - 1995	$29
10456	Black Eyed Susans "Für Elise" - 1995	$29
11427	Saint Nick "Silver Bells" -1995	$29
11429	Wedding Couple "Wedding March - 1995	$29
11430	Angels "The Wind Beneath My Wings" - 1995	$29
11431	Love Birds "I Love You Truly" - 1995	$29
11432	Nativity Scene "Joy To The World" - 1995	$29
11434	Yellow Tulips "Waltz of the Flowers" - 1995	$29
11435	Pink Tulips "Waltz of the Flowers" - 1995	$29

RUSTIC DAISY

3855	Teapot	$55
3856	Sugar and Cream	$28
3858	Jam Jar	$22
3859	Cookie Jar	$60
4115	Canister Set	$80
4117	Cup and Saucer	$18
4121	11 1/4" x 6" Relish Tray	$20
4122	13" x 7" Two Compartment Dish	$42
4123	7 1/2" Spoon Rest	$12
4126	6 1/4" Pitcher and Bowl	$26
4360	8" Wall Hanging, Ladies Hat	$25
4466	7 3/4" Butter Dish	$22
4467	Wall Hanging, Pitcher and Bowl	$40
4468	Mug	$8
4607	5" Handled Basket	$14
5004	6 3/4" Wheelbarrow Planter	$28
5005	Compote	$16
5006	Planter w/Pedestal	$20

RUSTIC DAISY (cont'd)

5008	Vase w/Pedestal	$20
5182	12" Egg Plate w/Salt and Pepper	$40
5196	Soup Tureen w/Ladle and Tray	$70
5402	7" Match Box	$25
5403	Napkin Holder	$18
5408	6" Candleholder	$14
5565	6" Pitcher and Bowl	$28
5841	7" Handled Basket	$16
6189	Poodle Planter w/Rustic Daisies	$28
7995	Jam Jar w/Green Basket Base	$17

SALT AND PEPPER SETS

004	Cow and Bull	$18
005	White Cats w/Pink Bows	$20
006	White Puppies w/Bows	$20
085	Owl w/Stones, Black and Brown	$25
103	Eastern Star	$15
216	Ducks w/Bonnets	$12
260	Mouse and Cheese	$22
351	Pine Cone w/Colored Stones	$22
654	Mushrooms	$18
676	Violets	$25
676	Elegant Rose	$22
749	Green Orchard	$12
901	Cheese and Mouse	$23
922	Moss Rose	$22
1023	Roosters, Pair	$25
1131	25th Anniversary	$8
1141	50th Anniversary	$10
1227	Hand Painted Violets	$18
1241	Gold and White Matte Turkey's	$29
1450	Cuddles	$20
1455	Wheat Poppy	$14
1608	Country Squire	$18
1670	Turkey, Pair	$15
1711	Thumbelina	$35
1723	5" w/Matching Trivet	$28
1926	White Dogs w/Pink Bows	$15
1955	50th Anniversary	$7
1957	25th Anniversary	$7
2009	Lambs	$16
2011	3" Angels Playing Instruments	$38
2126	Cabbage Cutie	$45
2197	White Rabbits	$20
2234	7" Marigolds	$27
2333	Pheasant	$22
2367	Dutch Boy and Girl	$38
2777	Comical Ducks	$18
2823	Donkeys or Kangaroos, Each Pair	$15
3032	Vineyard Line	$18
3053	Pineapple	$30
3235	Mr. Toodles	$38
3362	Daisytime	$18
03669	Shamrocks	$14
3748	Pear N Apple, Gold	$12
3749	Pear N Apple, Green	$12
3788	Eastern Star	$10
3805	Bag Shaped	$15
3968	Elf Head	$35
4142	Rustic Daisy	$25
4168	White Rose Bud w/Gold Leaves	$14
4184	Forget-Me-Not	$25
04191	Teddy Bears	$12
4233	Della Robbia	$32
4474	Flower Basket w/Blue Flower	$13
4474	Flower Basket w/ Purple Flower	$13
4586	Spring Bouquet	$9
4631	Turkey	$18
5163	Pink Daisy	$15
5218	Fiesta	$25

5269	Coffee Grinder and Coffee Pot	$18
5269	Bread Basket and Cheese Wedge	$18
5281	Fiesta	$25
5311	Lettuce	$15
5311	Beets	$15
5400	Hot Poppy	$18
6087	Chipmunks	$18
6196	Ducks w/Bows - 1987	$12
6225	7" Apple and Grape w/Flowered Top	$18
6234	6 3/4" Chrysanthemums	$24
6293	Happy Anniversary	$12
6355	Mushroom Forest	$21
06396	Pigs - 1987	$12
6433	Rose Heirloom	$25
6510	Bossie the Cow	$25
6542	Mushroom w/Yellow Tops	$15
6741	Yellow Tulip	$18
6754	Fruit Fantasia	$18
6836	Owls w/Rhinestone Eyes	$10
06983	Squirrel on Tree Stump	$15
7129	Tisket A Tasket	$25
10580	25th Anniversary	$14
10591	50th Anniversary	$14
21174	Cutie Pie and Kid - Holt Howard Like	$38
30119	Golden Wheat	$10
30132	Dark Green Heritage	$28
30145	Owls w/Rhinestone Eyes	$20
30232	3 3/4" Coffee Pot w/Rooster and Rose	$18
30285	Man and Woman Chefs	$28
30404	Dogs or Mice w/Rhinestone Eyes	$22

SMOKEY THE BEAR

10678	5 1/4" Smokey with Deer - 1998	$20
10679	5 1/2" Smokey Reading a Letter - 1998	$20
10680	4 1/2" Smokey On A Rocking Chair - 1998	$20
10681	5" Smokey in Bed Musical "Brahms Lullaby" - 1998	$29
10682	5 1/2" Smokey By The Waterfall - 1998	$31
10683	6" Smokey w/Jeep Musical "Take Me Home Country..." - 1998	$30
10684	5" Smokey Backpacking - 1998	$22
10685	5 1/4" Smokey Teaching - 1998	$30
10686	6 1/4" Smokey Planting A Tree - 1998	$20
10687	5 1/2" Smokey With Poster - 1998	$22
11436	Smokey Water Globe "Oh What A Beautiful Morning" - 1998	$31
11437	Smokey Reading Water Globe Musical, "Side By Side" - 1998	$31
11438	Smokey w/Poster Water Globe Musical "Stand By Me" - 1998	$31

SMOKING ITEMS

027	Leaf Shaped w/Cigarette Holder, Fleur de Lis	$28
091	4" Ashtray, Hand Painted Couple Fishing	$10
114	Cigarette Holder and Ashtrays, Single Pink Rose	$30
121	Ashtray, Pink Swan w/Pansies	$18
131	3 1/2" Ashtray, Hand Painted Rose	$28
132	Ashtray w/Hand Painted Flowers and White Trim	$16
136	Ashtray w/Lilacs and Rhinestones	$28
139	3 1/2" White Swan w/Violets	$22
139	3 1/2" Pink Swan w/Lily of the Valley	$22
140	5" White Swan w/Violets	$28
140	5" White Swan w/Roses	$28
140	5" Pink Swan w/Lily of the Valley	$28
154	8" Double Ashtray w/Lilacs and Rhinestones	$38
161	5" Poodle Cigarette Holder, Lilac - 1957	$35
194	Ashtrays with Lilacs in one Corner, 4 Piece Set	$36
203	4" Four Ashtrays w/Lighter, Set	$55
204	6 Sided Cigarette Holder w/Oval Ashtray, Set	$28
213	Ashtray, Antiqued Bisque	$18
216	Ashtray, Antiqued Bisque	$18
219	Ashtray, Antiqued Bisque	$15
226	Stacking Ashtrays w/Nest, Silver Wheat	$18
227	Cigarette Holder and Two Ashtrays, Silver Wheat	$14
242	Box w/Lid & 2 Ashtrays, Lily of the Valley, 4 Piece Set	$60
265	Cigarette Holder and Ashtrays, Woodland Rose	$32

277	2" Cigarette Holder, Striped	$10
286	3 1/2" Cigarette Holder w/Lily of the Valley, Scalloped Edge	$35
287	Ashtray, Leaf w/Lily of the Valley	$24
346	Fish in Basket	$25
358	Box w/Lid and 2 Ashtrays, White Roses, 4 Piece Set	$55
359	6" Square Box w/Lid, Applied White Flowers	$30
361	Ashtray w/Applied Rose	$18
387	Ashtray, Only A Rose	$22
402	Ashtray w/Baseball Glove and Ball	$28
515	5" Round, Rose Design	$20
559	6 3/4" Ashtray, Eastern Star	$20
584	25th Anniversary, 4 Nested	$12
654	Footed Cigarette Holder and Two Oval Ashtrays	$30
633	5 1/2" Ashtray w/Gold Feather	$18
666	4 Round or Square in Holder, Set	$26
681	Stacking Leaf Shaped, 3 Piece Set	$50
792	4" w/Card Suits, Rose and Violets	$45
809	Ashtray, w/White Poodle Figurine	$32
815	4 3/4" Cigarette Lighter w/Applied Rose	$38
837	Bisque Cigarette Box w/Applied Flowers	$22
844	3 1/2" Ashtray, Milk China w/Roses	$13
877	3 1/2" Ashtray w/Applied Roses, Glazed	$13
902	Cigarette Lighter and Ashtray, Rose Design	$38
910	Pink Oval Ashtray w/Applied Forget-Me-Nots, Glazed	$22
928	5" White w/Ruffled Edge and Flower, Gold Trim	$18
934	3 Stacked Leaf shaped, Set	$42
954	4 1/2" Ashtray, Swan, White w/Pink Roses	$40
1028	Cigarette Holder and Ashtray, Fleur de Leis	$15
1196	4" Cigarette Holder and Ashtrays w/Applied Flowers	$28
1237	Ashtray, Leaf Shaped w/Butterfly	$30
1240	Ashtray, Leaf Shaped w/Parakeet	$35
1441	Rose or Violet Heirloom, 7 Piece Set	$45
1500	Cigarette Holder and Two Oval Ashtrays w/Applied Flowers	$38
1631	25th Anniversary, Cigarette Box w/Two Ashtrays, Set	$15
1642	Cigarette Holder, Greek Key Design	$15
1663	Happy Anniversary, Stacking Ashtrays w/Holder	$15
1760	Ashtray, Majestic Gold	$15
1764	Cigarette Holder and Ashtrays, w/Scalloped Edge & Flowers	$38
1790	Stacking Ashtrays w/Nest, Antiqued Bisque	$18
1795	Urn w/2 Ashtrays, Rose or Violet Heirloom, 3 Piece Set	$30
2124	Fleur de Lis, 5 Piece Stacking Ashtray Set	$22
2224	Ashtray Shaped Like Artists Pallet	$15
2226	Ashtray, Blue Oval w/Applied White Flowers	$20
2301	Cigarette Box and Ashtrays, Kewpie on Top	$65
2308	Lighter, Cigarette Holder and Ashtrays, Floral, 4 Piece Set	$45
2325	4" Swan	$15
2409	Cigarette Box and Ashtrays, Golden Laurel	$30
2410	Cigarette Holder and Ashtrays, Golden Laurel w/Seed Pearls	$38
2458	Cigarette Holder w/Oval Ashtrays, Applied Blue Grapes	$32
2642	5 1/4" Cigarette Holder, French Rose	$15
2656	4" Ashtray, French Rose	$12
2756	4 1/2" Round Ashtray w/Flowers and Gold Leaf, 4 Piece Set	$23
2817	Ashtray, Red Floral Design	$20
2831	Ashtray, Gold Leaf w/Gold Filigree	$18
2955	Ashtray, Oval Luscious Lilac w/Applied Flowers	$13
2956	Ashtray, w/Pink, Black & Gold Swirl Design - 1955	$22
2958	Ashtray and Cigar Holder, Luscious Lilac	$28
2962	Ashtray, Round, Luscious Lilac	$15
3357	Ashtray, Green w/Gold Accents	$18
3600	Cigarette Holder, Forget-Me-Not (Applied)	$35
3894	Ashtray, Green Hat w/Pipe	$15
3895	Ashtray, Hat w/Bowling Ball and Pins	$18
3934	Leaf Shaped, Violets, 3 Piece Set	$45
4123	Ashtray, Pink Glazed w/Applied Roses	$12
4150	5" Box w/Lid and 2 Ashtrays, White w/Pink Roses, Set	$45
4246	Holder w/Ashtrays, Violets or French Rose	$35
4340	4 1/2" Eastern Star	$11
4345	4" Ashtray, Masonic Emblem	$20
4557	Cigarette Holder and 2 Ashtrays, Violets	$70
4700	3 1/2" Cigarette Urn w/2 Ashtrays, Pink, 3 Piece Set	$80
4744	Swan Ashtray	$23
4995	Square Shaped w/Roses in Holder	$30
4995	Heart Shaped w/Violets in Holder	$30

5252	Ashtray, Yellow w/Pink and Green Design	$14
5830	2 1/2" Square Ashtray w/Applied Flowers	$8
6553	Nested Ashtrays in Holder, 50th Anniversary	$15
6681	Ashtray, Hat w/Bowling Ball and Pins	$18
6964	6" Ashtray w/Flowers, Set of 3	$36
6965	Ashtray, Bisque High Heel Shoe w/Applied Flowers	
40111	3" Cigarette Lighter, Gold Wheat	$35
40124	Nested Ashtrays in Holder, Golden Wheat, Set	$15
40133	Holder w/Two Ashtrays, Bird w/Flower, 3 Piece Set	$28
40417	5 1/2" Leaf w/Bird Figurine	$25
40423	Ashtray, Ripple Edge in Pink w/Gold Flowers	$32
40452	Ashtray, Hand w/Roses	$35
40539	Ashtray w/Pink, Blue and Purple Applied Flowers	$28
48543	3 1/2" Ashtray, Mardi Gras	$30
50564	Ashtray, Black and White w/Bow Tie	$12

SNACK SETS

108	Eastern Star	$15
169	Rose Design	$18
202	Spring Time	$12
224	Silver Wheat	$15
261	Summertime	$30
262	Grapes	$22
517	Wild Columbine	$18
668	Rose Design	$20
690	Spring Bouquet	$21
884	Cherry Blossom	$26
907	Eastern Star	$22
1074	Rose Heirloom	$28
1074	Violet Heirloom	$32
1082	Cosmos	$32
1376	Rose Heirloom	$32
1493	Moss Rose	$18
1801	Fleur de Lis	$15
1933	Black Chintz	$32
2108	Rose Design, Cup's Interior Matches Color of Rose	$18
2122	Modern Abstract in Blue and Green	$18
2124	White and Purple Violets	$30
2265	White, Lt Blue Cups w/White Interior	$18
2415	White Plate w/Colored Cups	$15
2599	Magnolia	$25
2759	Yellow w/Yellow Roses	$18
2759	Pastel Green w/Moss Rose Pattern	$18
2768	Golden Wheat	$12
2769	Golden Wheat	$13
3144	Rose Design	$18
3171	Moss Rose	$22
3234	White w/Gold Boarder	$12
4035	French Rose	$14
4179	Forget-Me-Not	$16
4263	White Pear N Apple	$18
6580	Golden Flower or Stars	$20
7214	ESD Summertime	$22
20054	Violets	$32
20402	Bird on Tree	$22

SOUP TUREENS

085	Tray & Ladle, Daisy & Marigold	$115
599	Citrus Basket w/Oranges & Lemons	$55
770	Fish, Small Mouth Bass	$55
960	Tray & Ladle, Country Daisy, Yellow Background	$110
1503	Tray & Ladle, Garden Daisy	$85
6223	Tray & Ladle, Country Garden	$145
6464	Tray & Ladle, Mushroom Forest	$85
6487	Tray & Ladle, White Ware	$75
6560	Tray & Ladle, Mushrooms	$75
6915	Tray & Ladle, Fruit Fantasia	$125
7016	Tray & Ladle, White Ware	$100
7123	Tray & Ladle, Yellow Tulip	$130
7134	Tray & Ladle, Tisket a Tasket	$120
7282	Tray & Ladle, Dancing Leaves	$125

SPOON RESTS

001	Early American Rooster	$18
1162	Mammy, Colored Nodder	$225
1649	Chef	$20
5235	Rose Design	$15
6301	Country Garden	$12
7126	Yellow Tulip	$18
90413	Chef, Colored Nodder	$135

SUGAR AND CREAMERS

058	Stacked Violets	$95
058	Stacked Elegant Rose	$80
102	Eastern Star	$25
149	Cuddles	$55
192	Rose Pattern, Mini	$35
202	Spring Time	$25
215	Antiqued Bisque w/Cherubs	$15
225	Golden Wheat Swirl	$28
238	Golden Flower or Stars	$35
247	Striped	$28
273	Roses	$23
274	50th Anniversary	$15
280	25th Anniversary	$18
292	White w/Floral Design	$55
355	Pine Cone	$30
371	Golden Leaf	$25
456	Strawberry	$18
596	Bee Hive	$30
678	Miniature Violets	$28
686	Flower Bouquet w/Butterfly	$26
702	Violets	$35
1022	Brown Wicker Basket w/Black Rim	$28
1075	Rose Heirloom	$65
1075	Violet Heirloom	$65
1078	Cosmos	$60
1144	25th Anniversary	$18
1297	Celery Line	$39
1425	Sweet Lil'	$40
1449	Cuddles	$32
1454	Wheat Poppy	$22
1607	Country Squire	$40
1708	Thumbelina	$32
1800	Fleur de Lis	$38
1934	Black Chintz	$80
1937	Rose Heirloom	$30
1938	Rose Heirloom	$25
2154	Silver Wheat	$25
2276	Elegant Rose, Ribbed	$65
2364	Stacking, Elegant Rose	$55
2427	Golden Laurel	$18
2520	Magnolia	$60
2526	Golden Laurel	$45
2584	Violets	$60
2664	Grapes	$28
2698	Dutch Girl	$70
2759	Floral	$32
2789	Eastern Star, Mini	$24
2909	Fleur de Lis	$28
3029	Vineyard	$30
3167	Moss Rose	$30
3187	Pink Cotillion	$35
3192	Blue Cotillion	$35
3292	Mr. Toodles	$55
3359	Daisytime	$32
3365	Gold Flowers w/Gold trim	$28
3391	French Rose	$18
3449	French Rose, Ribbed	$22
3611	Pennsylvania Dutch	$60
03630	Pigs Eating Corn	$22
3743	Pear N Apple, Gold	$22
3744	Pear N Apple, Green	$22

3967	Bloomer Girl	$75
3970	Elf Head	$75
3977	Pink Elephant	$23
4071	French Rose, Mini	$22
4135	Della Robbia	$20
4175	Blue Forget-Me-Not	$35
4185	Blue Forget-Me-Not	$35
4445	Orange and White	$23
4581	Spring Bouquet	$35
4829	Spring Bouquet, Ribbed	$40
4829	Elegant Rose, Ribbed	$45
4934	50th Anniversary	$14
5065	Rose Design w/Tray	$55
5436	White w/Gold Trim	$20
5585	Yellow and Red Floral	$20
5884	Happy Anniversary	$18
6512	Bossie the Cow	$45
6734	Paisley Fantasia	$65
6736	Yellow Tulip	$25
6842	Small Pink and Violet Floral, Mini	$18
7051	Small Pink and Violet Floral	$18
7121	Tisket A Tasket	$18
7237	Rose and Violet Chintz	$48
7245	Miniature Rose and Violet Chintz	$38
7286	Falling Leaves	$28
8279	Hot Poppy	$40
8626	Sweet Lil' Sug' & Lil' Cream Jug - Holt Howard Type	$40
10578	25th Anniversary	$30
10589	50th Anniversary	$15
11985	Mini Ivory Color - 1998	$15
12172	Nautical - 1998	$18
13016	Irish Lace	$18
20120	Golden Wheat	$18
20595	Golden Wheat	$28

SWEET VIOLETS

1305	Pitcher and Bowl	$46
2838	10 1/4" Plate	$28
2839	6 1/2" Bread and Butter Plate	$12
2840	7 1/4" Salad Plate	$15
2841	11" Dish, Two Compartment	$40
2842	7 1/4" Coffee Pot	$85
2843	Sugar and Creamer	$35
2844	Salt and Pepper Shakers	$20
2845	Jam Jar w/Spoon	$45
2846	8 1/2" Gravy Boat	$60
2847	10" Dish, Two Compartment	$32
2848	Dish, Three Compartment	$32
2849	9 1/4" Tidbit Tray	$22
2850	Two Tiered Tidbit Tray	$55
2851	Egg Cup	$18
2852	5 1/2" Pitcher	$40
2853	7 1/2" Cookie Jar	$75
2854	7" Butter Dish	$35
2855	3 3/4" Mug	$10
2864	6 1/2" Plate	$28
2865	Cup and Saucer	$22
2866	7 1/4" Soup Dish	$15
2867	12" Platter	$60
2868	14" Platter	$70
2869	8 1/2" Covered Vegetable Dish	$110
2870	10" Bowl, Salad	$60
2872	10" Spoon and Fork, Salad	$30
2873	12 1/4" Cake Plate w/Server	$55
2874	8 1/2" Snack Set	$20
2875	Canister Set	$110
2876	5" Spice Jar	$22
2877	Oil and Vinegar Set	$45
2878	5 1/2" Candy Box	$38
2879	6" Candleholder, Pair	$45
2880	8" Two Compartment Dish	$30
2881	Demi Cup and Saucer	$28

2882	6" Bowl, Salad	$10
2890	4 1/4" Pot w/Underplate, Planter	$18
2891	6 1/2" Pitcher	$50
2892	6 1/2" Covered Cheese Dish	$45
2893	7 1/4" Spoon Rest	$22
2894	6 1/2" Wall Pocket	$25

SWITCH PLATES

077	3 1/2" Single w/Flowers and Stones	$35
197	5" Single w/Violets or Roses	$18
200	5 1/4" Double, Roses or Violets	$28
2377	5" Single, Gold Design	$18
2685	5 1/4" Single, w/Stones	$28
2686	Double w/Flowers and Stones	$35
3006	Single, French Rose	$25
3690	Single White and Gold	$18
4560	5 1/4" Single w/Children Praying	$12
8058	Double w/Gold Butterflies	$25

TASHA TUDOR COLLECTION

12262	4 3/4" Laura in the Snow - 1999	$20
12263	4 1/4" Love Comforts - 1999	$20
12264	4 3/4" At the Water Pump - 1999	$30
12265	5" Secret Garden Mary - 1999	$30
12266	4 1/4" Secret Garden Dickon - 1999	$23
12267	3 1/2" Take Joy - 1999	$30
12268	4" Tea Party - 1999	$30
12269	5 1/2" "Mothers Joy - 1999	$35
12270	5" Madonna w/Baby and Children "Ava Maria" - 1999	$35
12271	5" Silent Night "Silent Night" - 1999	$35
12272	3 3/4" Away in the Manger "Away in the Manger" - 1999	$35
12273	4 3/4" Wedding Day "Wedding March" - 1999	$35
12274	5" Mother's Love "Brahm's Lullaby - 1999	$35
12275	5" Story Time "Brahm's Lullaby" - 1999	$35
12276	3 3/4" Birthday Girl "Happy Birthday" - 1999	$35
12277	5" Kissing Couple "I Love You Truly" - 1999	$35
12278	4 1/2" April Showers Musical Waterball "Music Box Dancer"	$39
12279	4 1/2" Summertime Musical Waterball "Summertime"	$39
12280	4 1/2" Autumn Leaves Musical Waterball "Autumn Leaves"	$39
12281	4 1/2" Christmas Night Musical Waterball "Joy to the World"	$39

TEAPOTS

092	White w/Violets or Roses	$68
202	Spring Time	$65
239	Golden Flower or Stars	$65
273	50th Anniversary	$35
279	25th Anniversary	$45
353	Pine Cone	$45
369	Gold Leaf	$35
523	Daisytime	$45
698	Violets	$45
700	Elegant Rose	$85
885	Stacking, Violets	$135
985	Stacking, Dresden Style w/Creamer and Sugar, Rose or Violet	$135
1075	Rose Heirloom	$185
1075	Violet Heirloom	$185
1136	25th Anniversary	$30
1137	Musical, 25th Anniversary	$35
1296	Celery	$75
1448	Cuddles	$95
1606	Country Squire	$85
1695	Thumbelina	$195
1799	Fleur de Lis	$65
2123	Cabbage Cutie	$95
2156	Silver Wheat	$45
2275	Elegant Rose, Ribbed	$125
2275	Violets, Ribbed	$135
2299	Elegant White	$48
2327	Stacked w/Creamer and Sugar, Rose	$215
2426	Golden Laurel	$65

2439	Violets	$200
2519	Magnolia	$105
2663	Grape	$65
2699	Dutch Girl	$225
2725	Eastern Star	$60
03080	Shamrocks	$45
3149	Tomato	$95
03290	Shamrocks, Musical "My Wild Irish Rose"	$60
3291	Mr. Toodles	$145
3360	Daisytime	$65
3448	French Rose	$50
3529	Stacked w/Creamer and Sugar, Pansies	$38
3610	Pennsylvania Dutch	$110
3741	Pear N Apple	$38
3855	Rustic Daisy	$55
3973	Elf Head	$225
4063	French Rose	$25
4136	Della Robbia	$70
4258	Pear N Apple	$105
4583	Spring Bouquet	$85
4829	Elegant Rose, Ribbed	$55
05060	Musical, 25th Anniversary	$32
5191	Pink Daisy	$42
5885	Happy Anniversary	$30
6195	Country Garden	$48
6316	Lavender Rose	$55
06443	Poinsettia - 1987	$32
6712	Miniature Rose Garden	$40
6735	Yellow Tulip	$95
6755	Fruit Fantasia	$65
6797	Miniature, Paisley Fantasia	$45
6841	Miniature, w/Small Pink and Violet Flowers	$32
7236	Musical, Rose and Violet Chintz	$95
08030	Musical, Pink and Purple Roses, "The Rose" - 1993	$65
10419	Holly w/Berries and Gold Trim	$65
10577	7 1/2" 25th Anniversary	$32
10581	6 1/2" Musical 25th Anniversary "Anniversary Waltz"	$40
10588	7 1/2" 50th Anniversary	$32
10592	6 1/2" Musical 50th Anniversary "Anniversary Waltz"	$40
12174	Nautical w/Anchor and Rope Handle - 1998	$55
13018	Irish Lace - 1999	$35
13042	Stacking Teapot and Cup w/Pink Handle and Spout - 1999	$28
13416	Rose Bouquet, Musical "Tea for Two" - 1999	$55
20182	Golden Wheat	$40
20202	Masonic	$60
20610	Violets	$85

TEA SETS, MINIATURE

00125	3 3/4" Shamrocks with Round Tray - 10 Piece Set	$11
00215	Shamrock with Rectangular Tray - 10 Piece Set	$11
00617	Violets with Rectangular Tray - 10 Piece Set	$11
00618	Cardinal with Rectangular Tray - 10 Piece Set	$11
00960	Rose with Rectangular Tray - 10 Piece Set	$11
01102	Hearts with Rectangular Tray - 10 Piece Set	$11
10645	Lilac Daisy with Rectangular Tray - 10 Piece Set	$11
10646	Lily of the Valley with Rectangular Tray - 10 Piece Set	$11
10647	Paisley with Rectangular Tray - 10 Piece Set	$11
10648	Yellow Pansy with Rectangular Tray - 10 Piece Set	$11
10649	Rose with Rectangular Tray - 10 Piece Set	$11
10650	Lilac Daisy with Round Tray - 10 Piece Set	$11
10651	Lily of the Valley with Round Tray - 10 Piece Set	$11
10652	Paisley with Round Tray - 10 Piece Set	$11
10653	Yellow Pansy with Round Tray - 10 Piece Set	$11
10654	Rose with Round Tray - 10 Piece Set	$11
10655	Shamrock with Round Tray - 10 Piece Set	$11
10654	Floral Pattern - 10 Piece Set	$11
10784	Holly with Rectangular Tray - 10 Piece Set	$11
10785	Holly with Round Tray - 10 Piece Set	$11
11090	Shamrocks Mini Tea Set - 7 Piece Set	$30
11110	Rose Mini Tea Set - 6 Piece Set	$30
11111	Rose Mini Tea Pot	$7
11112	Violet Mini Tea Set - 6 Piece Set	$30

TEA SETS, MINIATURE (cont'd)

11113	Violet Mini Tea Set	$7
12823	White w/Gold Trim - 8 Piece Set	$14

TIDBIT TRAYS

00438	Pink and Blue Floral w/Blue Rim - 1992	$14
651	Crimson Rose	$18
671	French Rose or Violets	$18
672	Two Tier Tidbit, Rose Design	$55
911	Grape Design	$18
2090	Two Tiered, Della Robbia	$20
2351	Three Compartment, Violets	$28
2442	Two Tier, Golden Laurel	$38
2918	Two Tier Tidbit, Fleur de Lis	$30
2993	Roses	$35
4182	Two Tier Tidbit, Forget-Me-Not	$65
6729	Fruit Fantasia	$60
6799	Two Tier Tidbit, Paisley Fantasia	$45
7241	Two Tier Tidbit, w/Pink Roses and Lavender Flowers	$40
20129	Two Tier Tidbit, Dk. Green Background w/Fruit Design	$35
20231	Golden Wheat	$25

TIGER TAILS COLLECTION

11642	4 1/2" Tiger Tales "Play It As It Lies"	$25
11643	4 1/2" Tiger Tales "Gold is a Good Walk Spoiled" - 1997	$25
11644	4 1/2" Tiger Tales "Never Up Never In" - 1997	$25
11645	4 1/2" Tiger Tales "Start of a Purrfect Day" - 1997	$25
11646	4 1/2" Tiger Tales "Expect the Unexpected" - 1997	$25
11647	4 1/2" Tiger Tales "You're Great" - 1997	$25

TO A WILD ROSE

2561	Teapot	$165
2562	Water Pitcher	$125
2563	Creamer and Sugar	$50
2564	Coffee Pot	$125
2566	Cup and Saucer	$32
2567	Demi Cup and Saucer	$35
2573	7 1/2" Plate	$18
2578	9 1/4" Plate	$32
2579	Jam Jar	$45
2580	Snack Set	$25
2582	Tumbleup	$70
2584	Salt and Pepper	$25
2592	Two Tiered Tidbit Tray	$65
2597	Plate, Cake	$42
2598	6 1/2" Bone Dish	$12
2602	7 1/4" Dish, Nappy, 3 Assorted, Each	$20
2603	5" Dish, Nappy	$12
2639	Salt and Pepper	$21
2803	Shell Shaped Dish	$14
4173	5 1/2" Pitcher and Bowl	$50

TRAYS

1664	13 1/2" Fish, Green	$40
1961	13" Square 5 Compartment, Della Robbia	$75
1966	9 1/4" Violets	$20
2665	10" Grape	$22
6499	12" Navy & Lt Blue Floral, 3 Compartment	$42

TUMBLEUPS

4188	White w/Blue Floral Design	$65
6580	White w/Pink Roses	$65

VALENTINE ITEMS

033	4" Valentine Girl	$20
00150	Valentine Girl w/Heart and Gift	$14
00164	Valentine Cat in Dress and Hat - 1991	$16
179	3 1/2" Box, Heart Shaped w/Floral Design	$15
376	4" Girl w/Heart, Set of 3 - Each	$18
471	4" Figurine, Little Red Riding Hood w/Hearts, Each	$25
967	4" Planter, Heart Shaped w/Boy and Girl Angels	$15
1379	4" Mug w/Red Hearts	$8
1583	4 1/2" Figurine, Valentine Girl	$18
1609	2 1/2" Planter, Heart Shaped w/Girl	$10
1636	Cup and Saucer w/Large Heart "To My Sweetheart"	$15
02475	Heart Shaped Box w/Valentine Mouse	$10
02647	3 1/2" Heart Handled Bell w/Hearts and Red Ribbon	$12
02652	Mug, Hearts and Ribbons w/Heart Handle	$12
02733	3 1/2" Girl in Heart Dress Holding Gift	$18
2772	6" Planter, Valentine Boy and Girl	$28
2773	4 3/4" Valentine w/Little Boy and Girl Kissing	$20
2818	5" Box, Heart Shaped w/Cupid	$22
2828	4" Box, Heart Shaped w/Angel Holding Hearts	$20
2958	Heart Shaped, w/Boy and Girl Angels Kissing	$28
2995	4" Planter, Heart Shaped w/Cupid	$22
03087	Heart Shaped Box w/Hearts, "I Love You"	$18
03681	Vase w/Hearts, Valentines	$10
03730	Vase, White Bagged Shape w/Red Hearts	$8
3837	Angel Heart, Musical, "My Sweet Little Valentine"	$32
04279	Pitcher and Bowl w/Valentines - 1984	$18
04280	Pitcher and Bowl w/Valentines - 1984	$20
04386	6 1/2" Bud Vase w/Hearts and Bows	$14
4544	4 3/4" Valentine Baby, Pair	$18
4986	6" Vase, Valentine Girl w/Large Hat	$32
05562	4 1/2" Basket, Heart Shaped w/Hearts - 1985	$12
5597	4 3/4" Box, Heart Shaped w/Doves	$28
05971	Heart Shaped Box w/Hearts "Love" - 1987	$11
6013	3" Valentine Girl Holding Heart	$15
6191	5 1/2" Heart Shape w/Angel on Front	$18
6747	4 1/2" Heart Shape w/Little Girl on Front	$18
7173	4" Figurine, Valentine Girl Holding Two Hearts	$15
7697	4" Heart Shaped Box w/Kewpie and Valentine	$25
7699	4 1/2" Angel w/Hearts	$24
7701	5 1/4" Ballerina Holding Heart, Heart Planter	$15
8104	6 1/4" Vase w/Girl and Heart Design	$12
8105	Heart Shaped Box w/Girl, Heart and Feb. 14th Calendar	$15
8107	3 1/2" Pitcher and Bowl w/Girl & Heart Design	$18
8335	4" Bell, Valentine Girl	$28

VASES

008	6" Bud, Eastern Elegance	$22
089	5 1/2" 3 Legged, Rope Style Handles & Applied Roses	$65
103	7" Hands, White w/Flowers	$40
00108	6 1/2" w/Rose Pattern - 1991	$10
124	2 3/4" Miniature w/Stippled Gold & Applied Flowers	$32
137	7" w/Lilacs and Rhinestones	$55
138	6" w/Lilacs and Rhinestones	$45
152	6" w/Lilacs and Rhinestones	$45
156	7" Ewer w/Colonial Boy and Girl, Pair	$40
178	Mini Vase, Lily of the Valley	$23
191	6 1/4" White w/Pink Flowers or Pink w/White Flowers, Each	$21
218	6 1/2" Antiqued Bisque Bud Vase	$18
254	8" Bud, Woodland Rose	$23
270	6" Pink w/Forget-Me-Nots	$55
277	6" Lilac w/Floral Design	$32
277	Pitcher/Vase, Mint Green w/Yellow, Pink & Blue Flowers	$24
383	6 1/2" Only A Rose	$85
393	Three Sided Lilacs and Rhinestones	$49
420	6" Only A Rose	$55
421	6" Only A Rose	$55
424	8" Only A Rose	$65
427	Bisque w/Hand Painted Roses, Each	$15
475	6" Pitcher Vase w/Floral Design	$15
502	7" Vase w/Blue, Pink and Lavender Applied Flowers, Glazed	$24
543	7" Antique Ivory w/Applied Flowers	$32
644	7" Antique Ivory w/Applied Flowers	$32
645	5 1/2" Antique Ivory w/Applied Flowers	$28
730	8 1/2" White Rose on White	$30

00731	6 1/4" Lavender Rose on White - 1993	$25
733	10" White on White	$35
777	6 1/4" Antique Ivory Bisque	$28
795	6 3/4" Pitcher Vase, Black and White w/Cherubs	$28
813	6 1/4" Pitcher Vase w/Hand Painted Violets	$38
825	6" White w/Three Handles & Applied Flowers, Glazed	$55
828	6 1/2" White or Pink Bisque w/Applied Roses	$45
829	6" Pitcher Vase w/Applied Flowers	$30
830	6 1/4" White Porcelain Hobnail w/Applied Flowers	$30
832	8" Milk Glass w/Applied Flowers	$80
839	6" Fluted Milk China w/Applied Flowers	$55
840	6 1/4" Fan Shaped, Milk China w/Applied Roses	$80
859	6" Tulip Vase	$22
893	5" Hands w/Applied Flowers	$45
905	4" Antique Ivory Basketweave w/Applied Flowers	$18
929	5" Hand w/Rose, Holding Urn	$75
1031	7 1/2" Pink Pitcher, Applied Flowers	$40
1032	6 1/2" Ice Pink Bisque	$45
1040	7 " Bud, Pink w/Wavy Top and Applied Flowers	$32
1040	7 1/4" Pitcher w/Applied Flowers	$35
1043	5 1/2" Vase w/Applied Flowers	$50
1102	50th Anniversary	$15
1184	6 1/2" Bud Vase w/Applied Flowers	$52
1185	6" Ice Pink Bisque w/Applied Flowers	$42
1186	Pitcher/Ewer, Ice Pink Bisque w/Applied Flowers	$45
1195	Bisque w/Applied Flowers	$23
1200	6" Vase w/Applied Flowers	$32
1214	9" Pitcher w/Applied Flowers	$36
01367	7" Bud, White Daisies	$12
1403	6 1/2" White w/Mixed Florals	$18
1482	Egg Shaped w/Floral and Wheat Design	$12
1484	5 1/2" Egg w/Floral and Wheat Design	$18
1543	7 3/4" Vase w/Long Tailed Rooster	$90
1544	7 3/4" Vase w/Macaw	$90
1546	7 1/2" Crane	$90
1548	5 1/2" Flower Shaped	$18
1558	6 1/2" Bud w/Roses	$22
1597	6 1/4" Brown Bisque w/Cherubs	$12
1620	6 1/4" White or Pink w/Applied Flowers	$18
1630	5 1/2" Mermaid	$60
1770	6" Bisque w/Applied Flowers	$43
1771	6" Bisque w/Applied Flowers	$45
1772	10" Ewer Shaped, Bisque w/Applied Flowers	$60
1773	10" Ewer Shaped Bisque w/Applied Flowers	$58
1787	5 1/2" Hands w/Applied Flowers	$38
1791	7" Double Hand w/Applied Flowers	$45
1794	Pink Double Hand Vase w/Applied Flowers	$55
1809	6" White w/Two Handles	$22
1817	3" Heart, Antiqued Bisque w/Cherubs	$10
1847	4" Bud Vase w/Applied Flowers	$17
01909	6 1/2" w/Floral Bouquets	$15
1962	6 1/2" Bud, Violets	$13
1984	6 1/2" For Mother - 1984	$12
2144	8 1/2" Two Handled Urn Type w/Rose Design	$55
2181	6 1/4" Two Handled, Applied Blue Grapes	$35
02186	6 3/4" Bud Vase, Shamrocks	$18
2186	7 1/4" Pitcher, Applied Blue Grapes	$28
2187	6" Pitcher, Applied Blue Grapes	$30
2188	4 1/2" Pitcher, Applied Blue Grapes	$25
2193	5 1/4" Blue Bisque	$28
2282	10" Two Handled Vase, 50th Anniversary	$18
2283	8" 25th Anniversary	$15
2331	6" Bud, White Bisque	$22
2381	6" Ballerina Foot Vase w/Gold Accents, Pair	$38
2447	7" Pitcher w/Flower Garland	$33
2456	7" Bud Vase w/Red Roses	$16
2460	6 1/4" Applied Pine Cone	$27
2461	6" Pitcher Vase, Applied Pine Cone	$32
2471	7" Bud w/Leaves and Branches	$16
2479	5" Vase, Pine Cone	$15
2494	4 1/2" w/Applied Flowers	$15
02495	7" White Basket Weave w/Applied Flowers	$32
2499	4 1/2" Morning Glory	$24

02533	Egg w/Basket Weave and Applied Flowers	$18
2585	5" Pitcher w/Hand Painted Flowers	$23
2591	4" Bisque w/Applied Roses	$22
02612	6 1/2" Bud, Shamrocks	$15
2634	3 3/4" French Rose	$15
2651	6 1/4" Bud, French Rose	$15
02692	6 1/2" Bud, w/Grandmother Verse	$12
2736	Bisque Swan Vase w/Applied Flowers	$32
2780	Bud Vase, Dogwood	$18
2831	7" w/Hand Painted Daisy Flowers	$15
2832	6 1/2" w/Floral Bouquets	$12
2834	6 1/2" Bird on Branch w/Berries	$18
02870	6 1/4" Bud, White Dogwood	$18
2942	6 1/2" Luscious Lilac	$35
2943	6" Luscious Lilac Ewer	$38
2946	6" Luscious Lilac	$40
2950	4" Miniature, Luscious Lilac	$30
02971	6 1/2" Bud, Rose w/Blue Ribbon	$18
03161	6 1/2" White Vase w/Painted Violets	$18
3203	Modern Style w/Hand Painted Flowers	$23
03543	6 1/2" White Vase w/Painted Flowers	$18
3593	8 1/2" Renaissance w/Hexagonal Scalloped Top	$18
3629	8" Renaissance w/Cherub	$20
03658	6 1/2" Bud Vase w/Lily of the Valley	$18
03730	White Bag Shape w/Red Hearts	$8
03733	White Bag Shape w/Violets	$8
4075	6 1/2" Bud w/Rose Design	$18
4195	7" White Bisque w/Applied Flowers	$24
4198	5 1/2" Hands w/Applied Flowers	$28
4209	7" Pitcher w/Applied Flowers	$24
04293	6 1/2" Wild Violets, Each - 1984	$18
4331	Pear N Apple	$15
4342	4 1/2" Egg Shaped w/Applied Flowers	$15
4540	6 1/4" Pitcher w/Applied Flowers	$18
4654	6" Bud, 25th Anniversary	$7
4655	8" Bud, 50th Anniversary	$9
4732	4 1/4" Bag Vase w/Applied Flowers	$28
4740	6" French Shoe, Floral Bisque Bouquet	$40
5008	8" Rustic Daisy	$23
5032	8" Pink Daisy	$18
05130	6 1/4" White w/Basket Weave on Bottom -1985	$25
05163	4" White w/Basket Weave and Pink Dogwoods - 1985	$16
5203	7 1/4" Vase, Hand Painted Flowers	$20
5272	9" Pitcher w/Eagle	$28
5442	3 1/2" Egg Urn, Floral Bisque	$18
06004	8 3/4" Floral Bud	$28
06005	8 1/2" White w/Goldfinch on Rosebud	$28
06218	7" Violets - 1987	$18
6291	7" Happy Anniversary Vase	$12
6321	5 3/4" Pitcher Bud Vase w/Pink Roses	$15
6374	9" Whiteware	$32
6472	6 1/2" Urn, Mushroom Forest	$16
06474	4 1/2" Vase, Bisque w/Purple Roses	$15
6509	Blue Bisque Ewer w/Applied White Flowers	$32
6810	6 1/4" Bud, Paisley Fantasia	$20
6811	5 1/2" Paisley Fantasia	$10
06971	11" Japanese Style Urn Floral Vase	$45
7053	7" Bud, Petite Fleurs	$12
07072	Happy Anniversary - 1988	$12
07103	6 1/2" Fiftieth Anniversary - 1988	$10
7160	7 1/4" w/Painted Flowers	$14
7201	8" Pitcher, Antiqued Bisque w/Cherub	$28
7217	6 1/2" Ornate Floral Bisque	$32
7234	7 1/2" w/Two Handles, Lavender Rose	$30
7283	5" Pineapple	$70
7290	Bag, Pink w/Forget-Me-Nots	$38
7292	6" Pink w/Forget-Me-Nots & Stippled Gold Sand Border	$85
7295	7" w/Forget-Me-Nots and Gold Trim	$90
7363	7 1/2" Pitcher w/Applied Fruit	$50
07386	10 1/2" Urn Vase, Multicolored w/Roses - 1989	$55
07391	Round Vase, Black Background w/Pink Roses - 1989	$20
07393	6" Bud, Black Background w/Pink Roses - 1989	$20
07394	4 1/2" Black Background w/Pink Roses - 1989	$23

VASES (cont'd)

7904	6 1/2" Ewer w/2 Handles, Blue Floral	$18
8204	7" Bud, Green w/Shamrock Girl "Our Irish Colleen"	$12
8021	Bud, Urn w/Two Handles & Applied Flowers	$32
8029	7" Pitcher w/Applied Poinsettias	$25
8049	7" Bud, 25th Anniversary	$9
8050	6" Bud, 50th Anniversary	$14
8051	4" Yellow Bird on Flowering Tree w/Bamboo	$18
8052	6" Ginger Jar Vase w/Bird on Flowering Branch	$22
8080	4 1/4" White Bisque w/Applied Poinsettias	$30
8181	6 1/4" Floral Design w/2 Handles, Each	$18
8189	3 1/2" Egg Vase w/Flowers	$15
8198	3 1/2" Egg Vase	$15
8209	6 1/4" Heather Girl	$18
8217	4" Urn, Egg Shaped w/Legs, Heather Girl	$16
10704	6 1/2" Bud Vase, 25th Anniversary	$8
10705	6 1/2" Bud Vase, 50th Anniversary	$8
11031	6 1/2" Shamrock Vase	$9
11604	Large Vase, Blue Bisque with White Roses, Baltic Rose	$20
11605	Large Vase, Blue Bisque with White Roses, Baltic Rose	$15
11931	9 3/4" Tulip Vase	$28
11938	5" White Basket Weave w/Wavy Top - 1998	$18
11939	4 1/2" Jade Porcelain Irish Vase	$13
11941	8 1/4" Jade Porcelain Irish Vase	$9
11942	6 3/4" White Basket Weave - 1998	$16
11943	6 3/4" Jade Porcelain Irish Bud Vase	$8
11944	5 1/4" White Basket Weave w/Wavy Top - 1998	$18
11945	6" Jade Porcelain Irish Vase	$11
12325	6" Tulip Vase	$12
32001	Pitcher/Vase w/Applied Flowers	$12
41998	5 1/2" Hands w/Applied Flowers	$45
50431	4 1/2" Bag, Pink w/Gold Flowers	$50
50432	6 1/2" Bag, Pink w/Gold Flowers	$55
50439	6 1/2" Bag, Mardi Gras	$75
70274	6" Flower, Turquoise w/Flowers	$45
70425	Pink Ewer w/Gold Flowers	$40
70430	7" Pink w/Gold Flowers	$20
70435	6" Pink w/Gold Flowers, Each	$35
70443	6" Ewer, Mardi Gras	$75
70444	6 3/4" Mardi Gras	$75
70448	3 1/2" Open Work Vase w/Gold Trim	$20
70457	3 1/2" Miniature w/Forget-Me-Not and Stones	$36
70459	6" Pink w/Forget-Me-Nots and Stones	$60
70464	7 1/2" Pink Cat w/Rhinestone Eyes	$38
70541	6 3/4" Bud , Pink w/Flowers and Stones	$40

VICTORIAN CATS OF THE ROYAL CASTLE

11467	"Full House" - 1996	$20
11468	"Pretty As A Picture" - 1996	$20
11469	"All Washed Up"	$20
11470	"Top Hat and Tails" 1996	$20
11471	"Playtime" - 1996	$20
11472	"Good to the Last Drop" - 1996	$20
11473	"Rock-A-Bye Kitties" - 1996	$20
11474	Uninvited Guest - 1996	$20
11475	"Full House", plays "Oh What A Beautiful Morning" - 1996	$25
11476	"Pretty As A Picture" plays "You Oughta Be In Pictures"-1996	$25
11477	"All Washed Up" plays "It's A Small World" - 1996	$25
11478	"Top Hat and Tails" plays "Top Hat and Tails" - 1996	$25
11479	"Playtime" plays "Playmate" - 1996	$25
11480	"Good to the Last Drop" plays "Memory" - 1996	$25
11481	"Rock-A-Bye Kitties" plays "Brahms Lullaby" - 1996	$25
11482	"Uninvited Guest" plays "What's New Pussycat" - 1996	$25

VIOLET CHINTZ

599	Pin Box	$25
631	8" Bone Dish	$18
638	Snack Set	$35
649	Two tiered Tidbit Tray	$80
650	Compote	$45
651	One Tiered Tidbit Tray	$35
656	Cup and Saucer	$40
658	7" Plate	$20
659	9" Plate	$35
660	Coffee Pot	$185
661	Sugar and Creamer	$80
662	Cup and Saucer	$30
663	Sugar and Creamer	$45
664	Egg Cup	$35
665	Salt and Pepper	$35
686	5 1/2" Lamp	$55
793	6 1/4" Bone Dish	$22
794	Sugar and Creamer, Mini	$55
911	Teapot	$185
912	Sugar and Creamer	$85
1423	Demi Cup and Saucer	$26
1793	Teabag Holder	$35
1979	Demi Cup and Saucer	$18
2044	Sugar and Creamer on Tray	$55
2537	4 1/2" Heart Shaped Dish	$30
2744	Butter Dish	$45
3185	Miniature Tea Pot	$60

WALL HANGINGS

010	Plaques, Diamond w/ Mill, Barn, House, Barn and Silo, Each	$28
046	6" Milkglass w/Fruit	$23
056	Pocket, 5 1/2" Girl	$75
057	Whimsical Birds, Yellow, 3 Piece Set	$95
093	8" Plate Floral Design	$30
094	8" Plate Fruit Design	$30
099	8 3/4" Dolphin Wall Plaque	$32
105	7 1/2" Violin w/Applied Flowers	$32
115	8" Oval Colonial Man or Woman, Each	$35
117	6 1/4" Plaque, Colonial Girl or Boy	$30
119	8" Scalloped Edge Plate, Fruit Pattern	$32
171	6" Plate w/Applied Bird	$10
201	9 3/4" x 3 1/2" Plaque w/Applied Flowers	$28
209	Plaque, Double Spoon "Kissin' Don't Last Good Cooking Do"	$32
00210	6 1/2" White Straw Hat w/Flowers and Pink Bow	$30
216	6 1/2" Teapot "God Bless This House"	$20
219	7" Old Fashioned Stove "Home Sweet Home"	$20
220	Dustpan "God Bless Our Home"	$20
260	5" Wall Pocket, Kittens in Basket	$38
266	8" Latticed, Rose	$21
268	8" Plate, Fruit	$18
285	9 1/2" 25th Anniversary	$20
350	8 1/2" Wall Plaque w/Applied Victorian Couple	$65
369	7" Violin	$32
370	7 1/2" Windmill w/Fruit	$32
372	7 1/2" Wall Clock w/Fruit	$28
373	7" Old Fashioned Stove w/Fruit	$23
391	Plaque w/Wine Bottle and Fruit, Pair	$36
394	Plaque w/Wine Bottle and Fruit	$16
397	7" Roosters, Pair	$35
399	8" Plaques, Fox Hunting, Pair	$40
409	4" Wall Pocket w/Violets, 10 Commandments	$15
434	Pitcher and Bowl w/Grape Design	$30
508	Heart Shaped Plate "To Mother"	$22
516	5" Square w/Fruit or Flowers, Each	$20
531	5" Plate w/Raised Rooster	$18
540	8" Picture Frame Plaque w/Fruit, Pair	$30
541	5 3/4" Plaque, Man Smoking Pipe	$32
614	8 1/4" Latticed w/Rose Design and Gold Trim	$32
622	8" Latticed w/Bird	$22
642	8" Chef's Head Wall Pocket	$38
711	8" Reticulated Plate w/Cherries	$23
817	Angel Fish w/Two Babies	$65
820	4" Plate w/Applied Roses	$15
821	Round Plate w/Applied Flowers	$20
855	Hummingbird on Branch	$45
894	7 1/4" Pheasant, 3 Piece Set	$135
899	6" White Plate w/Pink and Blue Flowers	$22

901	7" Plaques, Antique Ivory Basket Weave w/Flowers, Pair	$40
914	6 3/4" Plaque, Cat or Dog in Oval	$25
921	Diamond Shaped Plaques w/Fruit, Each	$15
983	4 1/2" Plaque, Boy and Girl Framed, Pair	$50
984	4 1/2" w/Child's Head in Relief, Fuzzy Hair	$35
1017	6 1/2" Wall Plate w/Applied Cardinal and Flowers	$32
1073	8" Scalloped Edge Plate, "God Bless Our Home"	$20
1091	5 3/4" Wall Pocket, Rearing Horse	$30
1258	6 1/2" Mother Goose	$55
1495	8" Teapot w/Spigot, Apple and Cup and Saucer	$38
1499	9" x 6" Skillet Plaque w/Fruit	$18
1512	Plaques, Old Fashioned Coffee Grinder & Oil Lamp, Pair	$42
1551	6 1/4" Two Angel Busts	$48
1634	5 1/6" Mermaid Wall Pocket	$80
1648	5" Scottie Dog Wall Pocket	$28
1829	8" Scalloped Edge Plate, "God Bless Our Home"	$20
1831	Last Supper on Rose Heirloom	$35
1890	6 1/2" Round Plaque w/ Vegetable, Pair	$24
1917	5" Angels w/Flowers, Pair	$65
1946	6 1/2" Mermaid on Shell w/Shells, 3 Piece Set	$125
2043	Scalloped Edge Plate w/Roses, Each	$23
2088	5 3/4" Peach or Pear, Each	$24
2090	6" Round Plaque w/Gold Trim and Applied Flowers	$18
2113	6 1/2" Pitcher w/Fruit	$18
2118	6 1/2" White Pitcher and Bowl	$28
2148	4" Plate w/Applied Flowers and Gold Rim	$22
2150	4 3/4" Wall Pocket, "The Lord's Prayer"	$18
2172	8 1/2" Chinese Figures, Pair	$75
2316	Pocket, Bellow Shaped w/Fruit	$16
2342	3" Angel Head and Wings w/Gold, Pair	$28
2395	8" Ballerina w/2 Girls, 3 Piece Set	$50
2419	7" Plaque, Teapot, Plate and Fruit	$28
2478	6 1/2" Plate w/Pine Cones	$18
2512	8" Kitchen Prayer	$22
2513	Hand Painted Scalloped Edge Plate, Beige w/Pink Roses	$18
2565	10" Plate, Floral Design	$20
2577	7" Plates w/Duck Figurines, Pair	$40
2580	5" Plate w/3D Bird	$35
2627	Plate w/Madonna and Child	$38
2629	8" Fish w/Bubbles	$30
2649	6" Pocket, Pitcher and Bowl w/Grapes	$25
2660	6" Plaque w/3D Orchid, Glossy	$32
2678	8" Jug Shape w/Fruit	$16
2756	7" Oval Plaque w/Applied Flowers, Pair	$30
2780	8" Diamond Shape w/Applied Flowers, 4 Piece Set	$50
2783	Plaque, w/Musical Instruments, 4 Piece Set	$50
2816	8 3/8" Plate, Pale Blue w/Pink and Yellow Roses	$28
2817	8 1/4" Plate, Red Floral "Indian Paint Brush, Wyoming"	$15
2928	8 1/4" Pink Rose	$32
2997	6" Praying Girl, Bedtime Prayer	$22
3003	Diamond Shaped Plates w/Kitchen Utensils, 4 Piece Set	$32
3020	Plaques, 5 1/2" Apples and Grapes, Pair	$30
3022	Pocket, 6" Apple	$20
3090	6" Plate w/Applied Flowers, Each	$20
3107	8" Mermaid w/2 Small Mermaids	$90
3208	8 1/4" Plate, Fruit Design	$18
3215	Girl Praying, Lord's Prayer Verse	$16
3245	6" Round Wall Plate w/Applied Grapes, Glazed	$22
3321	7" Horse Heads, Pair	$40
3331	12" Diamond Shape	$28
3352	5 1/2" Round Frame w/Applied Branch w/Roses and Leaves	$25
3462	4 1/4" Gold Pear N Apple Wall Plaques, Pair	$36
3504	8" Pinkie and Blue Boy, Pair	$80
3644	Oval Plaque w/Purple Ribbon and Applied Flowers	$28
3743	6" Plate w/Applied Flowers, Each	$32
3848	7" Pear N Apple	$20
3849	Pocket Dust Pan, Pear N Apple, Green	$18
3853	Pocket, Apple Shaped, Pear N Apple, Green	$18
3920	6" Pocket, Blue and White Keg w/Spigot	$32
4202	Roadrunner Wall Plaque	$30
4249	4" Colonial Lady or Man	$15
4268	11" Girl Holding Cat	$45
4288	Basket w/Fruit	$23

4374	6 1/2" Plaque w/Applied Flowers	$25
4381	8" Rooster, Green, Pair	$30
4424	8" Plate w/Hand Painted Bird and Flowers	$14
4510	Plaque, Donkey, Dog, Cat, Rooster "The Travelers"	$25
4690	7" Rectangular w/Fruit In Relief	$14
4691	8" x 5" Rectangular w/Fruit in Relief, Each	$16
4713	6" Sea Captain Smoking Pipe	$35
4743	6" Round w/Applied Flowers	$18
4846	8" Plate w/Basket of Flowers	$18
4900	Fighting Roosters, Pair	$40
4927	8 1/2" Four Seasons, Set	$120
5077	6" Plaque, Strawberries	$15
5145	8" Plate w/Hand Painted Floral Design	$18
5244	8" Plate w/Hand Painted Fruit Design	$18
5356	4 1/2" Pocket, The Lord's Prayer w/Forget-Me-Nots w/Stones	$22
5749	5 1/2" Pocket, Angel Sleeping on Cloud "Now I Lay Me Down…"	$23
5785	Oval Plaque w/Applied Flowers, Each	$23
5786	7 1/2" Oval Plaque w/Applied Flowers, Each	$25
5788	7" Diamond Shaped Plaque, w/Applied Flowers	$18
5789	8" Plaques, Floral	$18
5826	Colonial Couple Wall Plaques, Pair	$120
5923	Rectangular Plaque w/Applied Flowers	$23
5935	8" Plate, Fruit	$15
5936	8" Plate, Floral	$15
6347	8" Reticulated Plate, Lord's Prayer	$25
6350	8" Wall Plate w/Roses	$28
6417	Angel Bust w/Flowers, Pair	$80
6486	6" Plaque w/Cherub Playing Flute	$26
6692	6 1/2" Kettle Wall Pocket w/Metal Handle	$32
6719	Plate, Girl Praying "Now I Lay Me Down to Sleep…"	$25
6731	8 1/2" Plate "Bless This House…"	$18
6733	11" Colorful Lantern	$28
6839	4 1/2" Wall Pocket, Decorated w/Fruit	$40
6926	8" Flower Design	$18
6927	8" Scalloped Plate, Fruit or Floral	$30
6932	4" Round Plate, Each	$12
6961	4" Lord's Prayer	$18
6967	8 1/4" Oval, Colonial Boy and Girl, Pair	$55
6994	Scalloped Plate w/Fruit, Dark Back Ground	$25
7068	6 1/2" Pitcher and Bowl, Mushroom Forest, Pair	$65
7220	6 1/2" Plaques w/Cherub Figurines, Pair	$80
7338	5 1/2" Pitcher and Bowl Wall Hanging, Tisket A Tasket	$23
8219	9" Plaque, w/Flowers in Relief	$28
10888	7" Plaque, Angel of Prosperity - 1996	$32
50188	6" Cuckoo Clock	$38
50264	Pocket, 7" Little Girl in Blue Dress Holding Basket, Each	$50
50267	Birdhouse Wall Pocket "Home Tweet Home"	$38
50288	4" Girl Ballerina w/Bunny Ears Next to Egg	$32
50410	5 1/2" Pocket, Cardinal on Basket	$28
50608	5" Pocket w/Torah and Gold Scrollwork	$38
60084	Plate, Scalloped Edge, Pastel Green w/Pink Flowers	$20
60153	Two Mermaids w/Three Bubbles	$145
60328	8" "God Bless Our Home"	$22
60329	8" "My Guests Like My…"	$28
60408	8" Round w/Fruit	$27
60409	6" Round w/Fruit	$28
60528	6 1/2" Baby Face, Smiling and Weeping, Each	$55
60593	8 1/2" Latticed Plate w/Floral Design	$28

WEDDING COUPLES

00302	3 1/2" Wedding Couple	$10
536	5 1/4" Bride and Groom, Set	$50
715	5 1/4" Bride and Groom w/Attendants, Set	$125
00763	5" Bride and Groom with Arms Around Each Other	$12
914	3 1/2" Bride and Groom, Pair	$55
00963	2 3/4" Bride and Groom - 1993	$18
1147	2 3/4" Bride and Groom	$22
2198	4 1/8" Bride and Groom	$22
2199	4 1/8" Bride and Groom	$22
03567	Cowboy Bride and Groom	$26
03576	Kissing Bride and Groom	$18

WEDDING COUPLES (cont'd)

04237	Kissing Bride and Groom	$15
04398	4 3/4" Groom Carrying Bride	$12
04567	4" Bride and Groom	$12
4645	Bride and Groom on Couch	$45
4703	4 1/2" Bride and Groom	$10
04744	Bride and Groom - 1985	$17
04745	Bride and Groom in Grey Suit - 1985	$17
04940	Bride and Groom - 1985	$25
04965	5" Bride and Groom Dancing	$12
04966	5" Bride and Groom - 1985	$20
05004	Bride and Groom	$28
05509	3 1/2" Bride and Groom - 1986	$18
05510	3 1/2" Bride and Groom - 1986	$18
05695	3 1/2" Bride and Groom, Mesh Veil - 1986	$18
05908	4 3/4" Bride	$10
06159	7" Bride and Groom by Sevilla - 1987	$28
06372	5 1/2" Bride and Groom - 1987	$25
06505	5" Bride and Groom	$28
07915	7" Bride and Groom, Mesh Veil	$25
08957	Bride and Groom	$23
10487	5 3/4" Bride and Air Force Groom	$20
10488	5 3/4" Bride and Navy Groom	$20
10489	5 3/4" Bride and Marine Groom	$20
10490	5 3/4" Bride and Army Groom	$20
10633	6" Bride and Groom, Mesh Veil	$20
10634	6" Bride and Groom, Mesh Veil	$20
10637	6" Bride and Groom Dancing, Mesh Veil	$20
10638	6" Bride and Groom Dancing, Mesh Veil	$20
10641	6" Bride and Groom, Mesh Veil	$20
10855	6 1/2" Irish Bride and Groom "Irish Wedding Song"	$35
10946	4 1/2" Bride and Groom	$14
10947	4" Bride and Groom	$10
10953	4 3/4" Bride and Groom	$10
10954	4 3/4" Bride and Groom	$10
10990	4 1/2" Cake Topper Bride and Groom Dancing	$9
10991	4 1/2" Cake Topper Bride and Groom	$9
10992	4 1/2" Cake Topper Bride and Groom	$9
10993	4 1/2" Cake Topper Bride and Groom	$9
10994	4 1/2" Cake Topper Groom Carrying Bride	$9
10995	3 1/2" Cake Topper Bride and Groom Dancing	$7
10996	3 1/2" Cake Topper Bride and Groom	$7
10997	3 1/2" Cake Topper Bride and Groom	$7
10998	3 1/2" Cake Topper Bride and Groom	$7
10999	3 1/2" Cake Topper Groom Carrying Bride	$7
11000	4 1/2" Bride and Groom Dancing	$9
11001	4 1/2" Bride and Groom	$9
11002	4 1/2" Bride and Groom	$9
11003	4 1/2" Bride and Groom	$9
11004	4 1/2" Groom Carrying Bride	$9
11005	3 1/2" Bride and Groom Dancing, Mesh Veil	$7
11006	3 1/2" Bride and Groom, Mesh Veil	$7
11007	3 1/2" Bride and Groom, Mesh Veil	$7
11008	3 1/2" Bride and Groom, Mesh Veil	$7
11009	3 1/2" Groom Carrying Bride, Mesh Veil	$7
11010	4 1/2" Bride and Groom, Mesh Veil	$9
11138	5 3/4" Bride and Air Force Groom	$20
11213	5 3/4" Bride and Air Force Groom	$20
11214	5 3/4" Bride and Navy Groom	$20
11215	5 3/4" Bride and Marine Groom	$20
11216	5 3/4" Bride and Army Groom	$20
11217	5 3/4" Bride and Air Force Groom	$20
11218	6" Dancing Bride and Groom	$20
11219	6" Bride and Groom, Mesh Veil	$20
11356	3 1/2" Bride and Groom on Cake Hinged Box	$18